The Flatbed Sutra of Louie Wing
The Second Ancestor of Zen in the West

Millennial Mind Publishing
An imprint of American Book Publishing
5442 So. 900 East, #146
Salt Lake City, UT 84117-7204
www.american-book.com
Printed in the United States of America on acid-free paper.

The Flatbed Sutra of Louie Wing: The Second Ancestor of Zen in the West

Designed by Jana Rade, design@american-book.com

Publisher's Note: American Book Publishing relies on the author's integrity of research and attribution; each statement has not been investigated to determine if it has been accurately made. The author and publisher specifically disclaim any responsibility for any liability, loss, or risk, personal or otherwise, which is incurred as a consequence, directly or indirectly, of the use and application of any of the contents of this book. In such situations where medical, legal, or other professional services may apply, please seek the advice of such professionals directly.

ISBN-13: 978-1-58982-517-8
ISBN-10: 1-58982-517-9

Library of Congress Cataloging-in-Publication Data available on request:
info@american-book.com.

Special Sales

These books are available at special discounts for bulk purchases. Special editions, including personalized covers, excerpts of existing books, and corporate imprints, can be created in large quantities for special needs. For more information e-mail
info@american-book.com.

The Flatbed Sutra of Louie Wing
The Second Ancestor of Zen in the West

Ted Biringer

Dedication

To my son, Henry, the polestar that keeps my course true. And, to the memory of my daughter, Jade, the bodhisattva whose soft whisper cleanly severed the entangling vines. I love you both.

Foreword

"I have a posie of other men's flowers and nothing but the thread that binds them is my own." So penned Montaigne, and deeply ingrained in my psyche are words, thoughts, and images bound of the thread of implicit universal meaning. They are reflections that come to the 'individual in stillness' and clarity of expression.

In Ted Biringer's *The Flatbed Sutra of Louie Wing,* there is a resonance and amplitude of thoughtfulness that will remain in our retentive memory.

In his writings, Biringer uses a unique and surprising approach in conveying the wisdom of Zen. While not hailing from either the Zen Orthodoxy or the world of academia, he combines the best attributes of both and infuses them with originality and imagination in the character of Louie Wing.

Through the quasi-iconic and intimate character, there is a powerful and provocative new voice in Zen. Being the Second Ancestor of Zen in the West, Louie Wing unflinchingly confronts and meets the most difficult challenges of finding and actualizing the enlightened mind in the chaotic modern world. While using wisdom, clarity, and humor he provides the reader with practical step-by-step instructions on meditation and a detailed analysis of some of Zen's profound doctrines.

Most importantly, Biringer's *Flatbed Sutra* is written with authority, sincerity, and relevancy, providing a scope and range of mind that entices the reader to look at the world in a new light and see a new light in the world–consequently laying the foundation of new possibilities acquired of the heart–concurrently vital in the ascendancy of personal enlightenment.

—*D. M. Gugich*
Northwest poet and author of The Unwilling *and* Romantic Reaches

Preface

I first became aware of Louie Wing in 1987. At that time, he was only the shadow of a doubt in the back of my mind.

Drawn to Zen by the wisdom and humor of the classic masters, I read and re-read the records of their teachings and deeds. These records seemed to resound with the authority born of experience rather than learning. I did not understand the nature of that experience, but I trusted it, and continued to follow a regular routine of meditation and study.

A f̶ ̶ ̶ ̶ or five years I had a fair understanding of the traditional Zen doctrines. In addition, I had developed a deep faith in them. Nevertheless, I was bothered by a recurring doubt.

The doubt centered around a discrepancy on the teachings about enlightenment. The classic Zen records are brimming with references to experiences that result in deep and immediate transformations. Indeed, such sudden transforming experiences are described and attributed to *every* major figure of Zen. Yet, with few exceptions, contemporary teachers often *minimized* the importance of such experiences, and some even *denied* they occurred. I could not understand why they differed so widely.

Eventually, I accepted the fact that my doubt might never be resolved, dismissing it as a small matter in the overall status of my study and practice. What was one doubt about one aspect of Zen? I was certain it was the right path for me, confident it would provide me with competence, serenity, and wisdom in every aspect of my life.

One morning in 1993, that confidence was shattered by two little words: *"She's dead."*

The knowledge and faith I had developed offered little relief from the intensity of my anguish. It was a deeply disillusioning experience. All my study seemed trivial, worthless. I felt that all the hours I had devoted to meditation had been frivolous, a pointless waste of time.

Louie Wing transformed from a shadow of doubt in the back of my mind to a red-hot iron ball in the back of my throat. I could not swallow it; I could not spit it out.

For months, it was all I could do to force my body through the motions of living. I sought solitude. When alone, I wept until I was too tired to do anything but sit, breathe, and doubt.

Then one day everything stopped. I was simply driving home one day and the whole universe suddenly emptied. Everything was there one moment the next moment *nothing* was there. An indiscernible amount of time later I became aware of the sound of my own laughter, then of the tears streaming down my face. At that moment, all my doubts were resolved. The source of authority I had sensed in the teachings of the great Zen masters was suddenly the most obvious thing in the world.

From that moment to this, I have not experienced a single instance of depression, overwhelming doubt, or fear, nor have I ever suffered from any sense of boredom. While I continue to struggle with the usual difficulties inherent in the human condition, the experience of being alive has been transformed in a profoundly fundamental way.

In the years since that initial opening, there have been many similar experiences—some shallower, some deeper—but it was that first one that opened the door for me, and it is the one I think of when I hear of similar accounts or read of them in the records of Zen.

Louie Wing personifies the mystery, wonder, and infinite potential of the unnamable, dimensionless void that is the source of the cosmos and is nothing more, nor less, than your own true nature and mine.

Although I often lose sight of that vast unnamable source, it follows me like the full moon on a cloudless night; I need only to look and it is there.

Table of Contents

Introduction

> **Seeing your nature is Zen. Unless you see your nature, it's not Zen.**
> –Bodhidharma, Traditional founder of Zen[i]

When the Indian Prince Siddhartha discovered that everyone eventually suffered from old age, sickness, and death, he was so horrified he refused his throne and set out to liberate all beings. After trying a variety of practices, he finally sat down under a tree and meditated. After six years he suddenly realized that all beings were free from old age, sickness, and death and only delusion kept them from realizing this fact. Thus, he became known as Buddha (awakened one).

About 1000 years later this teaching was brought to China by another awakened one named Bodhidharma. Like Buddha, he claimed people had always been free from old age, sickness, and death and needed only to 'see their nature' to realize it. To see their nature people needed only 'behold their own mind'.

Observing Bodhidharma's students practicing *dhyana* (meditation), people called the teaching *Ch'an*, which is the Chinese pronunciation of *dhyana*. So began the tradition known to most westerners by its Japanese pronunciation, Zen.

For more than 1500 years the Zen masters have affirmed the teaching of awakening by pointing to the human mind.

Directly inspired by the classic records of Zen, *The Flatbed Sutra of Louie Wing* provides the reader with a clear understanding of the Zen teaching of awakening and how it is achieved. The modern sage, Louie Wing, guides contemporary readers through the classic teachings, offering them an inside view and a working knowledge of this ancient and profoundly liberating message.

The son of an Italian fugitive, Louie Wing is a six-and-a-half foot illiterate farmhand–and the unlikely sage of the modern West. His chance encounter with a woman reciting an ancient text in a marketplace triggers a profound, transforming experience. This experience eventually leads him to an orchard on Waldron Island where he meets his teacher, the First Ancestor of Zen in the West.

In contrast to the ambiguous language of some modern "Zen" books, Louie Wing speaks in a direct, straightforward manner–even when discussing the most challenging and subtlest of doctrines. Modeled in the style of the classic masters, Louie Wing lucidly describes how the doctrines of Zen meet, and resolve life's most difficult challenges.

Although *The Flatbed Sutra of Louie Wing* is firmly grounded in and inspired by the Zen tradition, its message applies to students of all traditions or of no tradition at all. Louie Wing repeatedly reminds his students that Zen is only one path among many. According to him, the wisdom of Zen is not esoteric or unique. It is the wisdom of reality, common to all beings. In one talk recorded by a student, he said:

> The truth of reality existed long before the establishment of any religion or spiritual tradition. It is simply the truth of the oneness of the essence of the vast, unnamable, fathomless void and your own mind . . . Awakening to this reality is the function and reason of all true religious practice…When you awaken to your own source, wrong notions cease to exist, ideas and concepts can no longer bind you, the tangles and snares of the various religions are transcended . . .

For Louie Wing, claims of superiority of one doctrine over another are meaningless; only direct personal experience can bring true liberation. Not acknowledging any significant differences between the great spiritual traditions, he asserts that reality cannot be contained by words and, therefore, any claim of superiority is pointless.

In harmony with the classic masters of Zen, Louie Wing proclaims that everyone is inherently enlightened. Regardless of their particular circumstances, Louie Wing insists that rich or poor, monastic or homeowner, intelligent or slow-witted, criminal or saint–everyone has the ability to realize enlightenment.

Rejecting the notion that Zen practice requires any form of isolation or retreat from normal activities, Louie Wing offers practical guidance on how to practice in our everyday lives. In one talk he says:

> You should know that anyone with genuine aspiration can awaken in whatever circumstances his or her life situation is in. In all times and places people from all lifestyles have been able to realize awakening.

The methods or practices described and recommended by Louie Wing are thoroughly grounded in the Zen tradition. Nevertheless, along with the sages of all the great traditions, he warns his listeners about the dangers of becoming attached to any method or doctrine, insisting that no practice or teaching–including his own–is right for everyone. According to Louie Wing, all doctrines, techniques, and practices are merely tools or guidelines aimed at bringing practitioners to the actual experience of enlightenment.

Louie Wing clearly explains and recommends the fundamental practice of Zen meditation, often referring to it as 'ceasing conceptualization'. He explains that this term is only a provisional name for the practice of authentic Zen meditation. Some of the common terms for this practice in the classic Zen texts are: *no-mind, nonthinking, zazen,* and *cessation meditation.* This practice–by whatever name–is the essential art of Zen practice and enlightenment; it is the keystone of Zen.

While Louie Wing urges his listeners to avoid becoming attached to verbal or written teachings, he consistently maintains that such teachings are vitally important for the ongoing process of practice and enlightenment. *Attachment* poses the danger, not the teachings themselves.

Louie Wing challenges and debunks the common misperception in the West that Zen masters regard reading and study as non-essential or even counter-productive to Zen practice. He demonstrates how this fallacy contradicts Zen's own records, which testify to a thorough knowledge of, and profound insight into, the literature, doctrines, and techniques of Buddhism as well as many of the other great traditions.

While acknowledging the fact that the authentic masters do advocate the primacy of awakening, he points out that they also affirm the necessity of acquiring *useful* knowledge and developing proficiency in *useful* practice.

Louie Wing makes it clear that the Zen insistence on awakening is not a *rejection* of knowledge or practice, but a demand to activate the faculties through which knowledge and practice become truly useful.

The Flatbed Sutra of Louie Wing sheds light on some of the most powerful doctrines of Zen. Louie Wing methodically examines the four major aspects of the enlightened mind through the classic doctrine known as the *Four Prajnas of Buddhahood.* In a clear and detailed commentary, he examines each of the four prajnas one by one, explaining exactly what they are and how they function. In a similar manner, he reveals the inner working and subtle meaning of the powerful Zen teaching known as *The Five Ranks.* He also offers in-depth explanations on the meaning and methods of *koan-introspection,* zazen, cessation and observation meditation, and a host of other classic Zen doctrines.

Perhaps the greatest contribution of *The Flatbed Sutra of Louie Wing* is the insight it offers on the *Shobogenzo* (Treasury of the True Dharma-Eye), the Zen masterpiece by the thirteenth century Japanese master, Eihei Dogen. Louie Wing's own enlightenment experience was triggered upon hearing this text recited, and he often refers to its teachings, sometimes quoting it at length.

For a number of reasons, this massive collection of writings is often treated independently of its context within the Zen Buddhist tradition. This kind of treatment has inevitably led to a great deal of misunderstanding. Reading the work of Eihei Dogen without regard to its context within the Zen tradition is like reading the works of Saint Augustine without regard to its context within the Christian tradition. Such an approach obviously lends itself to erroneous interpretations, to say the least.

Unrestricted by allegiance to institutional authority or the myopia of sectarian bias, Louie Wing discerns the *Shobogenzo* in its proper context: the traditional and authentic teaching of Buddhism. In a line-by-line analysis of the extraordinary text, *Genjokoan,* Louie Wing uses clear and convincing, systematic explanations to demonstrate some of the many subtle, and even startling, implications that the *Shobogenzo* reveals about the teachings of Zen regarding the great questions of life and death.

Louie Wing brings to light some of the most profound insights revealed in the *Shobogenzo,* including the nature of time, the implications of interdependence, the resolution of original vs. acquired enlightenment, the essence and function of Zen koans, the various meanings and implications of zazen, and others.

Part I, *The Flatbed Sutra of Louie Wing*, is modeled after *The Platform Sutra of Huineng*, one of the most revered texts by all schools of Zen. Anyone familiar with this text will immediately recognize parallels. This is especially true of the first chapter, of the *Flatbed Sutra*, "Autobiography," which reads like a kind of modernized mirror image of the *Platform Sutra* "Autobiography," and more or less follows its general outline throughout.

While the other chapters of the *Flatbed Sutra* often begin in a similar vein as chapters of the *Platform Sutra*, the parallels are less frequent, and serve as little more than a launching pad for Louie Wing's own instructions. Regardless of these differences, the *Flatbed Sutra* retains the spirit of formality and earthiness that is so endearing in *the Platform Sutra*.

Part II contains commentaries by Louie Wing on two classic Zen texts. The first, "Skeleton Key to the Treasury of the True Dharma-Eye," is a commentary on the *Genjokoan* chapter of *Shobogenzo*. This work is a detailed analysis of one of the most important and influential essays by the great Japanese master, Eihei Dogen. In his examination, Louie Wing reveals its unique and vital role as a skeleton key to the major doctrines of the entire collection of writings that make up the *Shobogenzo*, which ultimately reveal some of the subtlest implications of the profound teachings of Zen.

The second commentary, "Bodhidharma's Vast Unnamable Fathomless Void," is Louie Wing's treatment of the koan in case one of the *Blue Cliff Record*. This commentary sheds light on the essence and function of true nature by unlocking one of the most important koans in the Zen collection.

Part III is a collection of sayings and doings compiled by Louie Wing's students. These talks and incidents are briefer, and more informal than the other parts of the book. They are arranged by topic for easy reference. Although arranged by topic, there are, of course, many areas that overlap; for instance, a talk in the section on meditation might also include the topic of enlightenment.

Like most teachers, Louie Wing has his own preferences for the terms and expressions he uses. Nevertheless, he does not restrict himself to any particular terms, using whatever terms seem appropriate to the time and audience. "Enlightenment," for example, is used synonymously with awakening, realization, liberation, seeing true nature, realizing Buddhahood, etc. In addition, the meaning of particular terms used by Louie Wing varies according to the context in which the terms are employed. Hence, the term "enlightenment" can be used to indicate the ongoing process of an awakened practitioner or as a reference to a particular moment of awakening or as a term for true nature, etc.

Aware of the confusion such differences could arouse, Louie Wing often defines the intention of his words or phrases within the particular talk or writing he is presenting. Nevertheless, for those who are unfamiliar with his teaching or with Buddhist terms and ideas generally, the contents of this book are arranged to gradually introduce the reader to the Zen teachings of Louie Wing. Often, the latter sections of the book build upon teachings introduced in the earlier sections. For this reason, you may want to follow the order of the book on your first reading.

Throughout this book, Louie Wing uses a number of terms for 'true nature', often referring to it as 'the vast, unnamable, fathomless void'. This is a reference to that which is finally beyond the limitations of language to define. Some of the traditional terms for this all-inclusive reality include Tao, buddha-nature, mind, essential nature, God, Brahma, and the universe. In one instance, Louie Wing breaks down his term like this: *vast* indicates its all-inclusive nature. *Unnamable* indicates its indefinable nature. *Fathomless* indicates its inconceivable nature. *Void* indicates its self-less nature.

The word "void" may be the most prone to misunderstanding. It does not mean nothingness or nonexistence. It is called void simply because it is not a thing that is somehow apart from other things. It is not a self in that it is not a separate individual entity. It is all-things and no-things. As you read and become more familiar with this idea in a variety of contexts, it should become clear.

A glossary and a list of names, with brief biographical summaries of the historic persons mentioned in this book, are included at the back of the book.

Throughout this book, the Japanese pronunciation is used for names of Chinese masters. Where applicable, the Chinese and Japanese equivalents have been listed in the glossary and the list of names.

Japanese terms that are widely recognized in the west have been used throughout.

The sources for quoted material are noted at the back of the book. Unless otherwise noted, quoted material of historical persons and/or Zen records are my own translations, or as I learned them orally from teachers during personal training.

Part I
The Flatbed Sutra of Louie Wing

Prelude

Louie Wing said, "Do you want to know what awakening to the vast, unnamable, fathomless void is? It is the certain realization that you are, always have been, and always will be the entire universe and everything in it."
—From the collected Sayings and Doings of Louie Wing

The Second Ancestor of Zen in the West avoided fame and sought to remain in obscurity where he transmitted the lamp of wisdom to a small group of students. Nevertheless, a copy of his early commentary on the *Genjokoan,* the celebrated Zen Classic by Eihei Dogen, was widely distributed throughout the Western Zen world, alerting wise men to the presence of a modern sage.

When Louie Wing announced he would die before the end of the season, students and wise men gathered from everywhere seeking his final instructions. The assembly consisted of teachers and students, clergy and laymen, religious and secular.

The small cabin where he lived and taught was not big enough to hold the gathering, so they assembled in a nearby meadow. Louie Wing mounted a small flatbed truck parked on the eastern edge of the field, and delivered these instructions.

Chapter 1:
Autobiography

Louie Wing nearly always traveled on foot, but when he needed to get somewhere faster, he would sometimes ride his bicycle. His bicycle was old, rusty, and small, a child's bike really. When people saw him ride it, they could not help but gawk; the six-and-a-half-foot man on the child's bike was an unusual sight.

One day Louie Wing rode up to his cabin where several students were sitting on the porch chatting. One of them said, "Louie Wing, you are a giant, why do you ride such a tiny bike?"

Louie Wing said, "It only looks tiny from there. Once you get on it, it is so big that you can't see anything else."

Another student said, "If you can't see anything else, how can you find where you're going?"

Louie Wing said, "By not looking."

—From the collected Sayings and Doings of Louie Wing

Learned Audience, our own true nature is the nature of the universe, and awakening to this fundamental truth is called enlightenment. When you realize this directly, you achieve Buddhahood. You may ask me how I can make this assertion. I can only tell you about my own life, and how I came to the realization that this is the truth of all the buddhas and sages.

My father was the son of an Italian farmer. He fled his country after being accused of murder. He came to America where he met, and married my mother. They combined what little they had and managed to buy a small chicken farm in Pennsylvania. I was born a year later, and raised with love, though we suffered from poverty.

My father died when I was eight years old, leaving only me to look after my ailing mother. We lost the farm after two difficult years, then moved to the West Coast where my mother's sister and her husband owned a berry farm. We moved into a little shack on the farm. I did not go to school, but worked the farm and cared for my mother, who was not strong enough to work. When I was thirteen, my mother died. I continued to work on the farm for three more years.

One day I made a delivery of berries to the farmers market in Anacortes. After unloading the berries, I was preparing to get in the truck when I heard a woman reading aloud.

When she read the words, "That people drive the self to actualize awareness of the many things is delusion," I suddenly realized my own identity with the many things.

I asked the woman what book she was reciting, and she said that it was the *Shobogenzo*, the Treasury of the True Dharma-Eye by the thirteenth century Zen Master, Eihei Dogen. I asked her where she got it and why she was reciting it. She said that she was from Waldron Island, where she worked at an orchard that was owned by a sage. The sage was a living buddha, the First Ancestor of Zen in the West. He taught people to master the teaching of this book in practice, proclaiming that Buddhahood was achievable by anyone; they need only awaken to the truth of their own true nature.

When I returned to the farm, my friend Antelmo, a kind farmhand, said my appearance had changed and asked me what happened and I told him.

Antelmo said, "She was surely a messenger from the unseen world. You must go and meet this Buddhist sage."

I told my aunt of my intentions and stayed long enough to help her and her husband through the harvest season. Then I set out for Waldron Island to meet the First Ancestor

When I arrived, I went to the orchard where the First Ancestor made his home. I was directed to a wooden and canvas yurt where he was teaching about thirty students.

I entered, bowed to the sage, and introduced myself, saying, "Hello teacher, I learned about you from one of your students and came here to meet you."

He asked, "Where did you come from?"

"Although that place has a name, it is not distinguished," I said.

The First Ancestor thrust forth the sheet of paper he was holding and said, "Without distinguishing, what do you call this?"

I snatched the page and quickly folded it into a paper airplane and sailed it across the room.

He said, "If you are like that, what do you want by coming here?"

I said, "I am Buddha, and I am in want of nothing. To thank you and also to inquire about helping others, thus come I."

The First Ancestor said, "When Buddha is Buddha, he is not conscious of being Buddha, how could there be others that need helping?"

I said, "Buddhas do not know they are Buddha, yet buddhas go on being Buddha, and although there are no others, others do not know there are no others."

He was about to say more, but seeing the astonishment on the faces of his students, he remained silent. After a moment, he told me I could stay and help the workers in the orchard. I said, "Since hearing the words of the *Shobogenzo*, all activities of workers in the past, present, and future are manifest as the result of my efforts now. What work would you have me do?"

The First Ancestor said, "One expects clear vision from someone so tall, but why use such foul language? Perhaps your unseemly height could be put to use pruning the topmost branches. Go to the orchard and be quiet."

Eight months later, the First Ancestor saw me working alone in the orchard. He said to me, "I know you have awakened, but I have ignored you because some people might do you harm. Do you know that?"

"Yes," I said, "That is why I have not gone back to the yurt."

"Do you practice zazen?" he asked.

"I have been fortunate enough to hear the *Fukanzazengi* chanted," I said, "Discerning the intention of that teaching, I realize that sitting meditation is only one meaning of the profound teaching of zazen. In true zazen, meditation and ordinary activities are originally not two. Whether sitting, standing, walking, or lying down, nothing is apart from the still-still state. I prune the trees, the trees prune me, the trees prune the trees, I prune myself, pruning prunes pruning."

The First Ancestor said, "You really know how to practice zazen."

Shortly after this conversation, the First Ancestor said to his students, "The one great matter of life and death does not wait for you. If you ever hope to be liberated from the anguish of old age, sickness, and death you must arouse genuine aspiration and awaken to the enlightened mind. All of you should apply yourselves diligently. If you have realized truth, you will naturally be able to express wisdom. Write me a verse expressing wisdom and I will give you the certificate of transmission verifying that you have received the Treasury of the True Dharma-Eye and make you the Second Ancestor in the West. If you have awakened to the truth of the unnamable void, you will not need to deliberate. Go at once and write the verse."

After this, I overheard the students talking amongst themselves in the orchard and in the bunkhouse. Their reasoning was this: "There is no point in us writing a poem to present to the Ancestor, because the transmission will clearly go to our senior, Thaitan Mereck. He has been with the Ancestor for almost thirty years, and he holds degrees in both philosophy and physics. Surely, he is by far the wisest among us. If we try to write something, we will just be wasting our time. We will simply wait for Thaitan Mereck." Thus, none of them gave the issue any further consideration.

I also heard from Thaitan Mereck's attendant, Daniel, who often came to sit in the field and smoke with me at night, that Thaitan Mereck was troubled. He knew that the other students expected him to write a poem to present to the First Ancestor. He said to Daniel, "If I do not, how will the Ancestor be able to evaluate my attainment. Yet, if I do so only to receive the title of Second Ancestor that will indicate my attachment to prestige. If, however, I do so for the sake of the Treasury of the True Dharma-Eye, who would question my motives?"

When Thaitan Mereck had composed a poem, he attempted many times to present it to the First Ancestor, but whenever he was about to deliver it he would suffer from fear and doubt and break into a sweat. Thirteen times, he attempted to bring his poem before the Ancestor, but his courage flagged and he was tortured with doubt.

In the entryway to the yurt was a wall, which was to be painted by the artist Donna Rachelle, with pictures depicting the life of Eihei Dogen, the First Ancestor's spiritual guide, for encouragement to students. Now when Thaitan Mereck failed to overcome his fear he reasoned to himself, "I could write my poem on the wall outside the zendo where the Ancestor would see it. If he approves of it, I shall come forward and claim it; if he disapproves of it, then, since it will appear that I have wasted three decades seeking truth, I will deny that it is mine." At midnight, Thaitan Mereck went secretly to the wall and wrote the poem there. It read:

The truth of Zen is not anything special,
The myriad things are void; the true goal is no goal.
Enlightenment is realizing that there is no enlightenment.
Zazen is just sitting, allowing things to be as they are.

After writing this, he quickly scurried back to his private room. Daniel did not come to smoke with me on that night because, as he told me later, Thaitan Mereck did not sleep but restlessly paced his room. He did not need to worry about the First Ancestor seeing through him however, the sage already knew that Thaitan Mereck had not entered the gate of enlightenment.

The next morning, the First Ancestor sent for Donna Rachelle, the artist, and went with her to have the wall painted. When he saw the poem, he said, "This wall no longer need be painted, I will have you paint a different wall. I will leave this poem here, so that people may study it and recite it and master it in practice." He then burned incense, and advised his students to recite it and master it in practice so they could enter the truth. All of the students marveled over it and praised its profundity amongst themselves.

At midnight, the First Ancestor sent for Thaitan Mereck and asked him if he had written the poem. "I did write it, Master," Thaitan Mereck said, "But let me assure you that I did it in secret only from modesty. I dare not flaunt my wisdom publicly and appear to lust after the prestige of the title of Second Ancestor. I only wish to use my wisdom to save all beings."

The First Ancestor said, "Your poem shows that you have not yet entered the gate of truth, but only linger in the dark cave of no enlightenment Zen. The true wisdom of enlightenment is the marvelous working of the buddha-mind. To one that has truly awakened, all things are one's own true nature; all actions are one's own buddha-mind, freely and spontaneously adapting to the world from mind moment to mind moment. You should consider these words carefully. When you have mastered this, present another poem to me and I will certify your realization."

Thaitan Mereck was unable to control his anger, and kicked over the master's table and stomped out of the room. For several days, nobody knew where he went. Finally, he returned and appeared privately before the Ancestor, apologizing and asking forgiveness. The First Ancestor compassionately allowed him to keep his privileged position as the senior student.

I had been too busy working the orchard at this time to hear of it until a week or so later. Daniel told me of it one night as we smoked together while viewing a wonderful harvest moon. As soon as I heard the words of the poem, I knew that the writer had failed to realize enlightenment.

Daniel, Thaitan Mereck's attendant said, "Still, the poem must contain the truth or the First Ancestor would not have advised students to study it."

I said to the attendant, "Although I have been busy working in the orchard, and do not know all the circumstances, I do know that the poem you recited misses the truth."

Then I asked him to take me to the wall where it was written so I could see it for myself. The attendant took me to where it was and I asked him to read it to me, as I was illiterate at the time. After he read it, I told him I too had composed a verse and asked him to write it for me.

"Are you serious?" He asked, "You never even went to school, much less listened to the teaching of the dharma."

I said, "You should be careful not to discriminate by appearances. If you meet a five-year-old girl that can teach you, you should become that child's student."

The attendant said, "Okay, tell me the verse and I will write it for you. Remember though, if you do receive the dharma, please deliver me."

My verse read:

The truth of Zen, how marvelous, how extraordinary!
The myriad things are void; the void is the myriad things.
Enlightenment is the void's own self-awareness.
Zazen is the void's awareness within all the myriad things.

The next morning, the students saw what was written. They were astonished when the attendant identified me as the author. "How marvelous!" They said to one another, "Clearly, we should not judge someone by age and appearance alone."

When the First Ancestor heard about what happened, he used his shoe to rub off the verse, being concerned that someone would harm me out of jealousy. He then told his students that the author of this poem had clearly failed to realize the truth of Buddhism.

The next day the First Ancestor came alone to where I was working in the orchard. As I continued to pick the apples he said to me, "A true sage abandons his life for the sake of Truth. Is this not the correct path?"

I said, "Truth abandons Truth, thus Truth realizes Truth."

He said, "Are the apples ripe?"

I said, "They have long been ripe, they just need delivering."

Then he thumped the basket of apples I was holding three times with his cane and left.

Understanding his meaning, at three-o clock in the morning, I went to his cabin. Closing the blinds on the windows so that nobody would see us, he began expounding the *Shobogenzo* to me. When he came to the line reading, "That the many things actualize awareness of the self is enlightenment," I immediately achieved unsurpassed enlightenment, realizing with certainty that all things in the universe are this very mind itself.

"Who would have thought," I said to the Ancestor, "that the nature of all things is intrinsically pure, that our own true nature was never born and can never die! Who would have thought the nature of mind is all-inclusive, that the nature of all things is eternally abiding! Who would have thought that the vast, unnamable, fathomless void is the manifestation of all things!"

Knowing that I had realized unsurpassed enlightenment, the Ancestor taught me, saying, "Until you directly realize the nature of your own mind you cannot discern the true teachings of the sages and Zen masters. Once you awaken to the true nature of your own mind you realize Buddhahood, and attain the buddha-eye that can discern the Treasury of the True Dharma-Eye. You, Louie Wing, are now the Second Ancestor of Zen in the West. You should avoid letting the other students know until you have established yourself somewhere else to liberate beings everywhere."

I said, "What should I do?"

The First Ancestor said, "You should train your buddha-eye on the teachings of the sages and Zen masters, mastering them in practice until their most subtle and profound wisdom has been completely transmitted to you. Then you should continue to make effort to express what has not yet been expressed in order to liberate all beings from suffering."

I said, "I will need to learn how to read then."

The First Ancestor roared with laughter. Then he said, "So, you do not even know how to read? That is something we shall have to remedy. I want you to come to my cabin every morning at three-o clock. I will help you learn to read, and at the same time introduce you to the teachings of the buddhas and masters of yore."

I thanked him and turned to leave, for there were many chores to be done. He called me back and said, "The great Japanese Zen master, Hakuin

Ekaku, used to ask his students to 'listen to the sound of a single hand'. Think about that and let me know what you make of it when you return tomorrow morning."

I said, "What is there to think about? Listen!" I immediately demonstrated the sound of a single hand to the First Ancestor.

The First Ancestor said, "What is the sound of a single hand engaged in sacred spiritual practice?"

I said, "If you want to know about that, teacher, then you should come and watch me clean the outhouse."

He continued to question me about the sound of a single hand for awhile longer. Finally, he laughed saying, "Truly the buddha-dharma will flourish in the world."

For the next three years, I privately met with the First Ancestor every morning at three-o-clock. He taught me how to read and write by having me memorize, recite, and copy the *Shobogenzo*. He also took me through the records of the Zen ancestors' great koan collections, and many of the Buddhist sutras and treatises.

At the end of three years, the First Ancestor presented me with a compilation of records and writings that had been transmitted to him by his own teacher. He said to me, "Louie Wing, it is time for you to go. There is nothing more I can teach you. This record has been transmitted from Buddha to Buddha for over eighty generations. I have added a single verse to the final page. I now entrust it to you."

I began to make nine full bows before the First Ancestor and he said, "You should not bow to a dull old man."

I said, "I am not bowing to a dull old man."

He said, "What is that? What did you say?"

I said, "I am bowing to one that is not a dull old man." Then I finished my bows and thanked him for his kindness.

He then told me that I should leave this place soon and spend a number of years in obscurity, lest people seek me out in order to cause me harm.

The next evening, he accompanied me to the small harbor where the boat for reaching the other shore was kept. Once afloat, he proceeded to take the oars himself. I asked him to rest and allow me to do the rowing.

"It is proper that I should ferry you across," he said.

I said, "Since I am now enlightened, I realize that nobody can deliver me to the other shore but me."

"Yes, that is so," he said and allowed me to row to the other shore.

Upon reaching the other shore, I bowed to my good and great friend, the First Ancestor of Zen in the West. He waved off my show of ceremony with a flick of his hand. "Take good care of yourself," he said, "Stay warm and dry and try to eat a little more. For someone so tall, you're much too skinny." Then he pushed the little boat out into the surf and began to row. I watched him until the darkness swallowed him up.

That was the last time I ever saw him. Three years later I read his obituary in the Seattle Post Intelligencer. It mentioned that he had spent some time as a POW in Japan. It praised his innovative and influential approach to organic farming. It did not say one thing about Buddhism or Zen.

I set out walking south, intending to find a job where I could earn enough money to support myself while deepening and polishing my realization. After three days of walking, I became aware of a group of men that were following me. Pretending to be unaware of their presence, I was finally able to ascertain that they were students of the First Ancestor. I surmised that they were intending to rob me of the record that had been transmitted to me, and that they may have even been intending to kill me.

One of them was a man named Louie Meeng, whose nickname was Crunch. He was a Green Beret in his early life. His deportment was solemn and his determination fierce. Of all those who pursued me, he was the one that would be most difficult to elude. One night, when the other pursuers were sleeping, he overtook me as I was crossing under a bridge. I set the record on a rock, saying, "This text is nothing but a finger pointing to the moon, you need not take it by force." I then hid myself in some trees nearby.

When he got to the rock, he tried to pick up the record, but discovered he could not lift it. He then called out, "Hey kid," (for I was only twenty at the time), "I am after the truth, not a book."

I came out of hiding and sat on the rock. He apologized for chasing me and said, "Kid, please teach me the truth."

I said, "If you really want to know the truth, think not-thinking, and I will teach you."

He said, "How do you think not-thinking?"

I said, "It is nonthinking. Cease conceptualizing about various things, and simply step back and rest in your own fundamental awareness." After he had done this for a long time, I said, "When you are not thinking of good or bad, what is your original face?"

Suddenly, he was enlightened. He asked, "Apart from this, is there any other secret that has been passed on?"

I said, "What all the buddhas and Zen ancestors have taught has never been secret. If you simply step back into your own fundamental awareness you find that all of the secrets are within you."

Louie Meeng said, "I have been sitting in zazen and studying Zen for a long time, but until now I did not realize that my vision was three dimensional. Louie Wing, you are now my teacher."

I laughed and said, "That is a wonderful saying about your vision. I feel the same way. All the things I used to take for granted and regard as ordinary, have become marvels. Since you are thus and I am thus, we are both students of the First Ancestor. Take good care of yourself." He paid homage and departed.

A couple days later I reached Seattle. There, some of the students continued to pursue me with bad intentions. I was finally able to find refuge on an Alaska-bound fishing boat, where I stayed on with a captain for nearly fifteen years.

When occasion permitted, I taught the fishermen in accordance with their understanding. The fishermen once put me to work tying hooks, but I would tie them so the fish could break them loose. Eventually, my job was changed to clearing the lines and nets of animals that could not be kept. I was very good at releasing them with the least amount of injury. Although the work was hard, during the quiet times I had plenty of time for study and meditation.

Finally, I decided that it was time for me to fulfill my obligation to the buddhas and Zen ancestors by expounding the dharma. So I left Alaska and traveled to a popular Zen center in California.

At the time, I was told that a prominent roshi was in attendance giving a series of lectures on Zen koans. As I walked from the reception area to the lecture hall, I saw what appeared to be two Asian monks arguing about a flag that was blowing in the wind. One monk argued that the flag was moving, the other argued that the wind was moving.

As they seemed unable to settle themselves, I said, "Flag and wind are both motionless; moving moves moving."

I soon discovered, the two were not Asian monks (the shaved heads and Asian robes had fooled me), they were American roshis of the Zen center. Accordingly, the whole assembly was startled, not by what I said, but by the mere fact of my saying it. For as I have since discovered, roshis are rarely challenged in western Zen communities unless some proof of sexual exploitation has become incontrovertible.

I was quickly taken aside by the head monk there, and introduced to the proper protocol for presuming to address a "Certified Dharma Heir." He explained that it was important to clarify the motivation of those that wanted to speak directly to the spiritual leaders. If I would like to have an interview with one of them, I would first need to make an application to meet with the Zen Center Dharma Protection Council.

I burst into laughter, but soon realized he was not joking. I said, "How could the dharma possibly be threatened by speaking to a teacher?" I also inquired about another curiosity that kept coming back to my mind, "Can I ask you why all these Americans are dressed up in Asian clothing?"

The head monk, who was wearing an Asian robe, and even had an authentic looking mountain staff, decided that he had heard enough. He stood, gave a short stiff bow, and walked out. A moment later, two very stout looking monks entered the room and offered to escort me off the grounds.

I spent the next six years traveling around the United States, Europe, and Australia visiting the various Zen communities. I also took the opportunity to read the plethora of contemporary "Zen" books. Although an occasional morning star appeared here and there, it did not take long to realize that the Treasury of the True Dharma-Eye was suffering from the types of misappropriation and exploitation that has historically accompanied its transition and absorption into new cultures. During my pilgrimage, I came to realize how truly great my fortune had been in meeting the First Ancestor.

One evening, I arrived in Grant's Pass, Oregon, on my way to meet a man that was rumored to be a true Zen dragon. I paused at a roadside stand to buy a smoothie from the woman working there.

Greeting the woman, I said, "How are you?"

She said, "Selling smoothies."

I could see right away that she was no ordinary vendor. I said, "Will you sell me a smoothie?"

She said, "Why do you want to buy a smoothie?"

I said, "I want to buy a smoothie to refresh my body and mind."

Then she gestured to my pack and asked, "What are those books you are carrying in that bag?"

I said, "There are two books in this bag: one is the *Shobogenzo*, the

Autobiography

Treasury of the True Dharma-Eye by Eihei Dogen, the other is a compilation of writings handed down through over eighty generations of Zen masters."

Hearing that, the woman said, "If that is the case, may I presume to ask you a question?"

I said, "You have not found it necessary to ask my permission thus far, but if it suits you, fine, ask."

She said, "I have heard that Buddhism teaches that there is no such thing as a self; if so, what body and mind do you wish to refresh? If you can say something to the point, I will sell you a smoothie. If you cannot say something to the point, I will not sell you a smoothie."

I said, "If that is how you are, who will sell smoothies or not sell smoothies?"

She said, "You know that smoothies cannot refresh the body and mind, but don't you know that smoothies refresh smoothies?"

I said, "That is true, but it is only saying eighty or ninety percent."

She said, "How would you say it, sir?"

I said, "Smoothies smoothie smoothies."

The woman laughed aloud, and I could not help but join her. She sold me a smoothie, and enjoyed one herself as I stood sipping mine at the edge of the road. After awhile she said, "You must be here to see Dean Frank."

Happy, though not surprised, that she knew of the man that I was seeking I asked, "Do you know him then?"

"He is my son. He told me you might show up here." She said, "He will be happy to see you again."

"There must be some mistake." I said, "I don't believe I have ever met him."

"When you knew him he was called Daniel Dale." She said.

I was overjoyed to hear this. "How wonderful," I said, "Where is he now?"

She said, "He is sailing around in your eyebrows."

"You are a smoothie," I said.

That night the woman, called Lue by those that knew her, led me to the house where she and her son lived. There I met Dean Frank, whom I had known as Daniel Dale, former attendant to Thaitan Mereck. He offered me the seat of honor at his table and we talked deep into the night.

Early the next morning, Dean led me to a small shed near the cabin where we joined Kyla, Jeff, Keanna, Jordan, Parker, and half a dozen others to enjoy a couple hours of zazen. After sitting and walking meditation, I was introduced to the people in the group and invited to give a talk. More than happy for the opportunity to pass on what has been so freely given to me, I gave the following talk:

> The path to authentic liberation is not complicated, mystical, esoteric, or difficult to understand. You do not require supernatural power or some special ability to access it. It is functioning perfectly within each one of you at this very moment. It is the infinite and unnamable, fathomless void, sometimes called buddha-nature; it is the true nature of your own mind. It includes the whole of time and space; it is nothing less than the homeland of the self.

Later that evening, Dean and I sat alone in this very meadow enjoying some excellent tobacco. The full moon rose and its hazy light shone through the branches of an ancient oak. I knew then that my pilgrimage was completed. Ever since that time, I have been expounding the teaching of the sages and Zen masters that I received from the First Ancestor of Zen in the West. Although there have been many hardships it has been a marvelous and fascinating journey. It has been a privilege and an honor to be of service to my fellow human beings.

The teaching I expound has been transmitted by the sages of all time, and though I have also expressed what had not yet been expressed, it was not devised by me. Those who wish to attain liberation should first learn to cease conceptualization. Then your own true nature will be immediately apparent and all doubts will fall away just as happened to all of the sages of the past. Once you have accomplished this initial step, the subtle and profound teachings of the sages and Zen masters will become discernible, and you will discover that all things are constantly expounding the Treasury of the True Dharma-Eye.

Chapter 2:
Meditation

Louie Wing said, "You hear me say that there is not an objective particle in the entire universe and you misunderstand, and immediately start searching inside your body and mind. You sit up day and night in meditation, torturing your knees and straining your backs. What have your knees and backs done to deserve such punishment?

"If you think you are following the teachings of the sages by such a display, you are sadly mistaken. Awakening does bring a certain kind of stillness to body and mind, but literally forcing the body and mind to be still does not bring awakening. An ancient Zen master said, 'When you want the cart to move, do you whip the cart or do you whip the ox?' I say, you had better heed his words, some of your carts don't look like they can take much more whipping."

Then Louie Wing roared with laughter. After a few moments of that, several students walked out, which seemed only to provoke Louie Wing to even deeper fits of laughter, and tears ran down his cheeks.

—From the collected Sayings and Doings of Louie Wing

The next day, Corinne of the White Hair asked the Second Ancestor to give an address on the meaning and method of meditation.

Thereupon, having taken his seat upon the flatbed, Louie Wing asked the assembly to purify their minds. Then he gave the following address.

Good friends, all the sages and Zen ancestors declare that it is only through realization of our own true nature that prajna, the wisdom of practice and enlightenment, can be realized. After each of the sages personally realized their own identity with the unnamable void, they spent their lives helping others to realize this identity. As Buddhism evolved, the *upaya,* or expedient techniques to help others were refined and developed by the succeeding generations of ancestors down through the ages. All the techniques and methods of Zen can be generally defined as meditation.

Learned audience, the various meditation techniques of Buddhism can be divided into the two general, complementary modes of *cessation* and *observation* or stopping and seeing. Cessation is stopping of delusion; observation is illumination of *prajna,* enlightened wisdom.

One of the clearest presentations of cessation and observation is found in the great treatise of Mahayana Buddhism known as the *Ta-ch'eng ch'i-hsin lun,* or the *Awakening of Faith* treatise. The *Awakening of Faith* is a distillation and summarization of some of the most essential teachings of Buddhism.

Good friends, because of its clarity, I will use the words of this text to briefly outline the two basic modes of Buddhist meditation. The *Awakening of Faith* treatise regarding cessation states:

> Should there be a man who desires to practice 'cessation',
> he should stay in a quiet place and sit erect in an even temper.
> His attention should be focused neither on breathing nor on
> any form or color, nor on empty space, earth, water, fire,
> wind, nor even on what has been seen, heard, remembered,
> or conceived. All thoughts, as soon as they are conjured up,
> are to be discarded, and even the thought of discarding them
> is to be put away, for all things are essentially in the state of
> transcending thoughts, and are not to be created from mo-
> ment to moment nor to be extinguished from moment to
> moment; thus, one is to conform to the essential nature of
> Reality *(dharmata)* through this practice of cessation.[ii]

In regard to observation, *The Awakening of Faith* treatise states:

> He who practices 'clear observation' should observe
> that all conditioned phenomena in the world are unsta-
> tionary and are subject to instantaneous transformation
> and destruction...
> After reflecting in this way, he should pluck up his

courage and make a great vow to this effect: may my mind be free from discriminations so that I may practice all of the various meritorious acts everywhere in the ten directions; may I, to the end of the future, by applying limitless expedient means, help all suffering sentient beings so that they may obtain the bliss of nirvana, the ultimate goal…[iii]

Learned audience, you should know that it is of the utmost importance to balance these two modes of meditation. The importance of balancing them, as well as specific instruction on how to do so, constitutes a generous amount of Zen and Buddhist literature. The *Awakening of Faith* affirms the necessity of this, and sums up the reason that balance is essential thus:

> Whether walking, standing, sitting, lying, or rising, he should practice both 'cessation' and 'clear observation' side by side. That is to say, he is to meditate upon the fact that things are unborn in their essential nature; but at the same time he is to meditate upon the fact that good and evil karma. . .are neither lost nor destroyed…
>
> The practice of 'cessation' will enable ordinary men to cure themselves of their attachments to the world…
>
> The practice of 'clear observation' will cure . . . the fault of having narrow and inferior minds, which bring forth no great compassion, and will free ordinary men from their failure to cultivate the capacity for goodness. For these reasons, both 'cessation' and 'clear observation' are complementary and inseparable.[iv]

Good friends, cessation meditation aims at the realization of emptiness. To become attached to emptiness causes disengagement from the real world of everyday life. Observation meditation activates and refines the wisdom of differentiation. To become attached to differentiation causes one to live in turmoil, which blocks off clear perception of reality. Each of these modes of meditation serves to balance the other. Observation works as an antidote for attachment to emptiness. Cessation works as an antidote for attachment to differentiation.

In learning to apply any of the techniques of Zen meditation, sitting in zazen is usually the easiest and most direct method to begin with. Therefore,

I will now describe the method of sitting meditation as the Zen ancestors have transmitted it down through the generations.

For practicing sitting meditation, anywhere you can sit comfortably will suffice. A lighted place that is clean, dry, quiet, and maintained at a comfortable temperature is best.

Before sitting, be moderate in food and drink. It is also good to be well rested. Wear comfortable, loose fitting clothing, and if sitting in a group, dark, solid colors are preferred, in order to lessen the distraction to others.

It is best to sit on a *zafu*, a round cushion that is placed on a *zabutan*, a larger, square cushion. If such cushions are not available, a meditation bench or a chair is adequate, the aim being a comfortable and stable, upright sitting posture.

Sit with the two sit-bones of your buttocks on the zafu, and your legs folded on the zabutan. Sit in either the full or half lotus posture. For the full lotus posture, place your right foot on your left thigh and your left foot on your right thigh. For the half lotus, place your left foot on your right thigh and simply keep your right foot on the zabutan with your right leg folded in close to your left leg.

Sit upright in a stable, symmetrical position. Place the left hand on the right hand, aligning the middle joints of the middle fingers, both palms upward, and allow the tips of your thumbs to lightly touch forming an oval shape, as if cradling an egg. With your hands in this position, allow them to rest in your lap, holding them close to your body just below your belt line.

Hold your head up so that your ears are aligned with your shoulders and your nose is aligned with your navel. Place the tip of your tongue gently against the roof of your mouth just behind your upper teeth, with your teeth and lips together.

Breathe through your nose. Allow your eyelids to relax so they are comfortable, neither wide open nor closed. Let your gaze fall several feet in front of you or if facing a wall, about the level of your chest. Relax your vision, neither trying to focus it nor allowing it to wander.

Once you are comfortable and stable, take several deep breaths then allow your breathing to become quiet and natural.

Allow your mind to completely relax. Disregard intentional thinking; make no effort to suppress thoughts. Mentally step back and rest in the source of your own fundamental awareness. Trust the inherent wisdom of your own mind and let go of all intention. With total, nonjudgmental acceptance, allow thoughts, feelings, sensations, perceptions, and mental formulations to arise from, abide in, and return to the source of your fundamental awareness without interference.

For beginners that find difficulty settling their minds and bodies, the method of breath counting is often helpful. To apply this method, simply count out each breath until you reach the count of ten. If you lose track of your count or find that you have gone beyond the number ten, simply return to one and begin your count over. When you can consistently reach ten, without losing count or going over ten, for fifteen minutes or so, you can let go of your counting and simply rest comfortably in your own awareness.

Good friends, for sitting in meditation, this is the method recommended by all the Zen ancestors.

For practicing cessation in Zen, there are two primary methods. The first is *mindfulness*, often called *shikantaza* (sole sitting). The second method is concentrated focus on an object, such as the breath or an initial type of *koan*. Once you have become proficient in applying these methods during sitting, they may be carried out during nearly any activity or non-activity.

Learned audience, practicing cessation meditation through the method of mindfulness or shikantaza, can be described as mentally stepping back from all your involvements and considerations–that is letting go of all judgments regarding good or bad, right or wrong, abandoning notions about enlightenment and Buddhahood, and simply resting in your own fundamental awareness.

Good friends, this is in accord with the meditation instructions in all schools of Buddhism. Being in accord with the fundamental teaching, the instructions for mindfulness by all the sages and Zen ancestors are nearly indistinguishable from one another.

Learned audience, do not be fooled by teachers that try to draw major distinctions between their own particular sect or lineage and others by reverting to games of semantics. Some like to argue about the differences between Dogen's term of *nonthinking*, and Eno's term of *thoughtlessness*. Some give long dissertations on how 'cessation' differs from 'no-mind'. While these arguments may be of interest to linguists, they have nothing to do with Zen. The Zen ancestors abstained from indulging themselves in that kind of hairsplitting. Remember, although 'going for a stroll' sounds different than 'taking a walk' the actual experience is identical.

Good friends, Master Dogen was very aware that even the simplest guidelines could be turned into dogmatic formulas or commandments. He often warned students about the dangers of becoming attached to the *teachings,* which he called "the carved dragon," that are used to point to reality, and thereby miss that *reality* itself, which he called "the real dragon."

Learned audience, Dogen, more than many masters, recognized the essential role of the teachings or "carved dragon," nevertheless, he urged us to "love the real dragon more." Arguing semantics about minor differences between the terms used by Dogen, Baso, Obaku, Hyakujo, and other Zen ancestors, not only demonstrates a failure to "love the real dragon more," it demonstrates a disdain for the "carved dragon," which is the teaching transmitted by the buddhas and Zen ancestors.

Although modern pseudo-Zen teachers, with their authentic looking costume and "bloodline" certificates may obscure the Zen ancestor's teachings on meditation, with a little effort, you can personally discover the true meaning of authentic meditation. Once you become familiar with the actual practice of meditation, you can apply and compare Dogen's method of nonthinking and Obaku's method of cessation of conceptualization for yourselves. Then you will discover on your own that the *actual experience* is identical. This is how you should test all the teachings: try them and discover for yourself if they work.

Learned audience, the mindfulness techniques of cessation allow your fundamental awareness of reality to calmly shine in the immediate present. When you are at rest in your own fundamental awareness, the habitual conceptualization that goes on in your brain ceases. When you are truly mindful in the present, you are no longer inundated by thoughts, ideas, views, prejudice, associations, memories, and imagination. In true mindfulness, you experience yourself and the world *as they are*; that is, in their *suchness.* Your false notions of self and other, which screen you off from the universal mirror prajna, fall away, allowing you to awaken to the true nature of your own mind.

Good friends, while there are no major difficulties in learning *how* to practice mindfulness, it does require genuine aspiration and sustained practice. Now clear your minds and I will expound on mindfulness so that each of you can put it into practice, achieve cessation, and experience liberation.

Mindfulness only requires you to cease from habitual discrimination so your own luminous awareness can shine through. Simply step back from your tangling, dualistic thoughts. Step back from all your ideas about self and other, right and wrong, gain and loss, joy and sorrow. When thoughts come, step back and let them be; you are not just your thoughts. Do the same thing with all your notions, ideas, and views. If you persist in this practice, you will suddenly cease conceptualization and awaken to your true identity.

Ceasing conceptualization means your mind is not tangled up in views of self and other, even while participating in the activities of the world. When you cease conceptualization, you discover that your own nature and the nature of all things are identical. Awakening to your true identity, you realize that you have always been free from birth and death. Being free from birth and death, you are not hindered by views of self and other. This is called liberation. It is a mistake to believe there is some special doctrine or esoteric teaching apart from awakening to your own true mind.

Good friends, before you awaken to your true nature, you are floating around in delusion. When you identify yourself as your thoughts—that is delusion. You are not just your thoughts. You are also that from which your thoughts come and back into which your thoughts go. Your true mind does not come, stay for awhile, move in circles, become confused, choose this and judge that. Your true mind is motionless and void, yet luminescent, free, and charged with infinite potential. This mind is the vast, unnamable, fathomless void; it defies description and definition. Yet, it can be directly realized by ceasing conceptualization.

If you want to awaken, do not seek outside your own mind here and now. Right now is the time; right where you are sitting is the place. If you cease conceptual discrimination, delusion will dissolve and your pure, clear, luminous awareness will shine forth. This is identification of mind and reality.

Good friends, because mindfulness or shikantaza is not as effective for some individuals as working with koans, many Zen masters, including Dogen and his teacher, Tendo Nyojo, recommended using koans as an alternative method for 'casting off body and mind'. Though many vehemently deny that Dogen ever recommended the introspection of koans in zazen, his own records contradict this claim.

Learned audience, although there is widespread misunderstanding of koans in general, the false notion that koans are mere *devices* for bringing the intellect to an impasse and thereby causing a sort of psychological breakthrough is one of the most prevalent.

As with many false views, this notion contains a kernel of truth. Koans are direct expressions of reality, which, like scripture, reveal their subtler wisdom only upon deep realization by the practitioner. However, some koans, which I refer to as *initial type*, actually can serve as *devices* aimed at the cessation of conceptualization or the realization of nonthinking.

I know some of you are familiar with various teachings regarding mantras. Therefore, before I discuss koans, allow me to offer a brief comparison. The techniques involving the use of mantras differ widely from the technique of using initial types of koans—both theoretically and psychologically.

Most doctrines on the use of mantras are aimed at the *manifestation* of particular cosmic forces or powers that are posited to exist apart from our own true nature. On the contrary, the use of initial types of koans is aimed at *cessation* of conceptualization. In other words, mantras are used to *attain*, while initial types of koans are used to *let go*.

The mindset of a person aiming to attain something is vastly different from that of a person aiming to let go of something. In my experience the methods that emphasize cessation are usually more effective than those emphasizing attainment. Nevertheless, the practical result of either method is identical, and some may find mantras more adaptable to their individual inclinations. As mantras are not part of the traditional teaching of Zen, I am not qualified to teach them.

Good friends, koans are one of the few things that really distinguish Zen from other forms of Mahayana Buddhism. The Zen monastics of our ancestors in China probably worked longer hours than many laypersons do in the modern West. Because there have always been people, including monks and nuns, that do not have the time or the inclination to spend long hours practicing sitting meditation or meticulously pore over tomes of scriptures and treatises, the great masters developed other expedient methods. One such method, unique to Zen, is 'koan-introspection'.

Koans usually consist of recorded sayings or stories of Zen masters interacting with students. Koans and their related literature form the core texts of Zen. They are condensed expressions of essential nature itself. Koan-introspection is the practice of holding a koan within body and mind, examining it, pondering it, keeping it warm until achieving intimacy with it. What I mean by 'achieving intimacy' with a koan is that the wisdom or prajna within the koan effectively evokes the corresponding wisdom within the practitioner. It is similar to the successful communication of thoughts, ideas, and knowledge in the realm of ordinary everyday life; one person has effectively transmitted their meaning, and the other has correctly understood. However, the wisdom that the Zen koans are intended to transmit is ultimately beyond ordinary intellectual understanding. Like scripture, poetry, mythology, and the sacred lore of the ages, if you do not grasp it with the whole of your being you do not grasp it at all.

Good friends, the wisdom that constitutes koans is not unique to Zen or even to Buddhism; it is the wisdom of reality, the wisdom of life, common to all humanity.

There are many special qualities to the Zen koans; one important quality is the amazingly condensed form in which it appears; another is its universal accessibility to those that activate their inherent ability to realize them. The former aspect allows a vast amount of wisdom to be memorized and carried around, allowing you to practice during nearly any activity. The latter means that you need not be highly educated, literate, or even especially intelligent to introspect and achieve intimacy with koans, hence with the wisdom of reality.

For those who are limited in their ability to pursue deep and thoroughgoing study, for whatever reason, the unique Zen method of koan-introspection may be an appropriate alternative. This does not mean that practitioners of koan-introspection can totally dispense with the study of scriptures, treatises, and the records of the ancestors. It can, however, go a long way toward shortening the list of texts, as well as the amount of time and effort involved in such study.

At the same time, because of the vital role that koans have come to play in the Zen tradition, even those who are able to undertake thoroughgoing study also need to become familiar with koan-introspection. Without an intimate grasp of the classic koans, much of the wisdom of the Zen ancestors' remains out of reach, not the least of which includes Dogen's work. In any case, koan-introspection offers a method of practice and enlightenment that is accessible to almost anyone with genuine aspiration. Zen master Hakuin held this method in such high regard that, at times, he claimed a practitioner could reach the deepest levels of enlightenment through the practice of koan-introspection alone.

Now, regarding the use of what I call the initial types of koan for achieving cessation meditation, let me describe some examples. The four most common initial types of koan are 'Joshu's Mu', 'The sound of a single hand', 'Who hears?', and 'What is your original face?' When utilized by beginning practitioners, these koans can and do function primarily as instrumental devices, that is, as aids to 'forgetting the self'.

Many of these initial koans, including Joshu's 'Mu', do contain deeper wisdom, and should be taken up later by the mature practitioner in order to reveal their hidden depths. The 'Mu' koan actually exists in a number of variations, the more elaborate of which contain ongoing dialogue between Joshu and monastics, discussing the why and what of both *Mu* (No) and *U* (Yes).

Good friends, when koans are used as devices aimed at attaining cessation or nonthinking, they are often abbreviated or simplified. The famous 'Mu' koan about the buddha-nature of a dog, when used as an initial type of koan is usually pared down to the single word, "Mu."

In the classic Zen text, *Mumonkan*, compiled by Master Mumon, we find the most well known version of the 'Mu' koan, in one of its abbreviated forms, "A monk asked Joshu, 'Does the dog have buddha-nature?' Joshu said, 'Mu.'"

Mumon's comment typifies the method of using initial type koans for realization of cessation or nonthinking. It reads, in part:

> Concentrate on this one word "Mu"…Day and night, keep digging into it…It is like swallowing a red-hot iron ball. You try to vomit it out, but you can't…
>
> Suddenly Mu breaks open…you find the Great Freedom[v]

Learned audience, Dogen's own teacher, Tendo Nyojo, also recommended using this koan. His instruction on how to employ it is nearly identical to Mumon's. In the face of all the claims that Dogen discouraged koan-introspection in zazen or sitting meditation, it is interesting to note that Tendo Nyojo recommended utilizing this koan while *sitting in zazen*. He said:

> When thoughts are flying around your mind in confusion, what do you do? "A dog's Buddha-nature? No." This word *No* (*Mu*) is an iron broom: Where you sweep there is a lot of flying around, and where there is a lot of flying around, you sweep. The more you sweep, the more there is. At this point where it is impossible to sweep, you throw your whole life into sweeping.
>
> Keep your spine straight day and night, and do not let your courage flag. All of a sudden you sweep away the totality of space, and all differentiations are clearly penetrated, so the source and its meanings become evident.[vi]

Dogen's writings make clear the reverence he felt for Tendo Nyojo and his teachings. Dogen's writings also prove the great significance he personally found in the 'Mu' koan. A number of his writings and talks utilize the 'Mu' koan in some very intriguing ways.

Good friends, once you have achieved some success in cessation meditation, you begin to employ one or more methods of observation meditation in order to maintain balance and realize progression. Cessation or nonthinking is not abandoned, but continues to be the foundation of your practice and enlightenment. Observation meditation is applied by intentionally examining specific aspects of reality under the illumination of your observing prajna or your buddha-eye, which is activated with your initial experience of true nature. When reality is examined through your observing prajna, its true nature is experienced directly.

Continuous practice and enlightenment is enacted through a multitude of techniques and methods in the great spiritual traditions of the world. Scriptural study is one of the more frequently used methods for transmitting wisdom; however, it is also transmitted through song, poetry, ritual, ceremony, drama, and other methods. Zen Buddhism uses these methods; at the same time, Zen employs the unique method of *koan-introspection*.

Learned audience, koan-introspection differs from the practice with initial-type koans, which are used as devices for achieving cessation. Observation meditation in the form of koan-introspection requires sustained focus in the condition of nonthinking or forgetting the self, and allowing your observing prajna or buddha-eye to illumine the wisdom of the koan. Although the human intellect does play a role in this process, enlightened wisdom must be realized by the whole of your being and cannot be grasped by the intellect alone. Trying to understand it or figure it out through ordinary conceptual means is futile

Good friends, this does not mean that koans are not rational—they assuredly are. The rationality or *reason*, that they convey however, includes *and* transcends ordinary intellectual knowledge. As you will discover when you achieve cessation, there is a vast difference between the ordinary rationality of human intellect and the wisdom of the enlightened mind.

If you are to truly actualize the fundamental point, you must do so through the activation and application of prajna. The human intellect is but one aspect of all time and space, and practice and enlightenment on the path of Zen is all-inclusive realization. In *Shobogenzo, Gyobutsu Yuigi*, Dogen describes what it means to discern and actualize enlightened wisdom through engaging the observing prajna within nonthinking, which he refers to there as 'the mountain-still state'.

Good friends, all of the great masters urged their hearers to illumine the teachings of sages and actualize the wisdom of reality through observation meditation. Having awakened to the innate function of nonthinking through the realization of cessation, we can now apply ourselves to observation.

Observation meditation consists of observing the sacred teachings as well as the everyday world of sensation, perception, mental formulation, and consciousness seeing, hearing, smelling, tasting, touching, and thinking through and with the enlightened awareness of nonthinking. This is taking up and letting go without the notions of 'taking up' and 'letting go.' The Zen path of practice and enlightenment is the continuous and ongoing practice and enlightenment beyond all *ideas* and *concepts* of practice and enlightenment.

Learned audience, the classic records of Zen offer many detailed explanations on how to apply observation meditation to the teachings of sages as well as in our everyday activity. Although you will soon find that cessation and observation can be carried out in nearly any activity, initially it may be easier to apply during sitting meditation.

In *Shobogenzo, Sammai-O-Zammai,* Dogen offers some advice on how to go about practicing observation meditation while sitting. He says, "At the very time of your sitting, you should examine exhaustively whether the total world is vertical or horizontal."

Yes! This is exactly how a practitioner applies observation meditation. Looking deeply, examining exhaustively, not only the perspective of the total world, but of all particular things.

Good friends, the eternal quest that is the source of what, who, where, when, how, and why, is the essence and function of the vast, unnamable, fathomless void. Practicing observation meditation shines your own observing prajna upon the wonder and mystery of being alive.

When you are examining a koan in the light of observation meditation, you begin by quietly observing each word. For example, 'Joshu's Mu' koan:

> A monk asked Joshu, "Does the dog have buddha-nature?"
> Joshu said, "Mu."

First you consider "A monk," letting this inquiry simply rest in the realm of nonthinking under your own observing prajna. Without indulging in conceptualization, this process allows you to get deeply into the koan, and examine exhaustively each word. Sitting on the cushion, utilizing nonthinking, you allow "A monk" to clarify itself. Then you continue along this line of observation by considering, "asked," and then, "Joshu."

Learned audience, you should know that in most instances, this method of practice requires regular contact with a teacher and should not be taken up alone, at least until you have worked through a couple hundred of them with a good teacher.

Learned audience, if you continue to apply yourselves to observation meditation, the wisdom embodied in this koan will yield up its treasure. When this occurs, you will meet the same wisdom that all the Zen masters meet. Indeed, you will meet all the Zen masters face to face. Won't that be fun? I can promise you this: you will certainly laugh.

Good friends, post-kensho practice and enlightenment is what taking the path of Zen is all about. If the path of Zen called only for achieving a state of emptiness or pure awareness or some other static condition, it would be the *station* of Zen rather than the *path* of Zen. You should not follow teachings that urge you to cling to the bliss of emptiness, making heroic efforts to detach from the world or sustain 'pure awareness'. That would be what Dogen calls passing time in vain. Once you have awakened to your true nature, you should follow the instruction of all the sages and never waste another day.

Good friends, the truth itself is not separate from you here and now. To fail to continue along the Zen path of practice and enlightenment for the sake of the truth is to fail to realize or make real, your own true self. Once you have awakened to the true nature of your own mind through the re-alization of nonthinking, and learned to use your observing prajna, you should apply it in order to master the buddha-dharma or the truth of reality.

Chapter 3:
Prajna

Louie Wing said, "Ceasing conceptualization is easy to understand, but it is difficult to put into practice. Some students become frustrated and run off to remote areas or mountain retreats to escape the activities of the real world. They sit in dark, quiet temples with their tongues pressed to the roofs of their mouths listening to themselves breathe. Some of them waste away their whole lives like that. That is not ceasing conceptualization; that is ceasing to be human.

"True cessation consists of dwelling in the pure and clear, luminous awareness of your own mind at all times and places. Abiding within the void and participating in the world are not two separate things. All activities are void; the void is all activities. Do not be deluded by false teachers dressed up like ancient Chinese hermits. If they have not awakened to true nature, Americans who shave their heads and wear Asian robes are simply poseurs."

—From the collected Sayings and Doings of Louie Wing

The next day Jordan, high priest of the School of the Tortoise, asked the Second Ancestor to give another address. Specifically, he wanted to learn about the significance of Maha Prajna Paramita, or the great wisdom of perfect enlightenment.

Thereupon, having taken his seat on the flatbed, Louie Wing asked the assembly to purify their minds. Then he gave the following address.

Learned audience, Maha Prajna Paramita is inherent in every one of you.

It is only because of delusion based on conceptualization that you fail to realize it. The buddha-mind is not different in ordinary people and sages. The only difference between them is that sages have realized it, while ordinary people have not. Now allow me to expound on the nature of the enlightened mind so that each of you can directly realize Maha Prajna Paramita.

Good friends, simply reading or hearing about the inherent nature of prajna without actually awakening to it cannot bring you liberation. Even if your understanding and knowledge is wide and profound, without actual experience, you cannot be free. It is like someone learning to play an instrument; music theory and knowledge about the instrument may be helpful, but without actual practice, there can be no music.

You have to put your learning about prajna into practice with your whole body and mind. Knowledge and understanding alone cannot awaken you to the truth of prajna. At the same time, spiritual practice without knowledge and understanding will not do either. If you have aroused genuine aspiration, however, and you put the knowledge that has been transmitted by the sages into actual practice, you will not fail to awaken to your own inherent prajna.

Buddha is nothing other than the true nature of each one of you; there is no buddha outside of your own body and mind. This is the essence of all time and space. It is all-inclusive with nothing outside of it. It is ultimately beyond all limitations and beyond definition and description. It is the vast, unnamable, fathomless void. That is your own true nature and it must be personally experienced to be realized.

Learned audience, when you hear me call it 'the vast, unnamable, fathomless void', please do not conceptualize about non-existence or nothingness. This is very important. Many people have developed wrong views about this, and have fallen into aberrant paths. They sit like rocks or stumps, keeping their minds blank and empty, sitting in an inky black cave of indifference, cultivating detachment, stifling their intellectual abilities and denying their responsibilities, obligations, and creativity with irrational, inarticulate justifications that things "just are as they are." Such are the impotent non-Buddhist teachings of naturalism and quietism; they have nothing to do with Zen.

The vast and fathomless void manifests and absorbs, contains and penetrates all the myriad things: the sun, moon, and stars, the mountains, rivers, and fields, houses, streets, and cities, animals, plants, and people, heavens, hells, gods, and demons, oceans, galaxies, and universes. The void includes all of this and much, much more. Your true nature is identical with the void. Therefore, your mind contains and embraces all things. If you truly realized the vast and fathomless nature of your own mind, how could attachment or aversion persist?

Having pointed out the dangers of becoming attached to doctrines or failing to balance knowledge and practice, I will now expound upon the nature of prajna.

Good friends, one way of talking about Zen doctrine is to break it down into levels, ranks, positions, stages, or other similar forms. The *Ten Ox-herding Pictures,* the *Five Ranks,* and the *Three Stages of Mountains and Rivers* are well known examples of this in the West. Today I will use a formula that has been largely neglected in the West: the *Four Prajnas of Buddhahood.*

Prajna is usually translated as wisdom or knowledge; however, like the terms "buddha" and "dharma", "prajna" connotes much more than the usual English translations. The term *four prajnas* appears in English translations as four cognitions, four wisdoms, and four knowledges. The *Four Prajnas of Buddhahood* is one of the classic doctrines of Mahayana Buddhism used to describe various aspects of the enlightened mind or Buddhahood.

The first prajna is the universal mirror prajna. In English translations it appears as 'great, perfect mirror cognition', 'great mirror wisdom', 'mirror-like wisdom', and other similar terms. The universal mirror prajna is the aspect of your mind that, like a mirror, perfectly reflects the world *as it is.* Through this prajna, the world is experienced in the immediate present, in its 'thusness' or 'suchness'. Unlike an ordinary mirror, however, this prajna is not only *reflective*, but also *luminescent*. Your initial realization of this inherent characteristic of mind actualizes enlightened wisdom confirming your entrance into Zen awakening.

The second prajna is the prajna of equality. It is translated as 'equality wisdom', 'wisdom of inherent equality', 'universal wisdom', 'cognition of equality', 'knowledge of equality', and the like. The prajna of equality is actualized as the experiential realization of the void or oneness of essential nature. Through this prajna, the Buddhist formula that asserts 'form is emptiness' is transformed from an abstract theory to a lived experience. Experiencing the emptiness of all things, you realize the *equality* of all things, that is to say, the oneness of all space and time.

The third prajna is the observing prajna. Also called 'subtle analytic knowledge', 'profound, observing cognition', 'all-discerning wisdom', and so forth. The observing prajna is the actualization or the function of the enlightened mind. By employing this prajna, enlightened wisdom is deepened and refined, and the spiritual methods and techniques or the 'skillful means' of Zen are cultivated and mastered. The observing prajna is the *active* buddha. Realizing the equal or empty nature of all things you should not turn away from the world of differentiation, but instead, apply your realization within it.

The fourth prajna is the practical prajna. Also called, 'knowledge of accomplishing tasks', 'accomplishment of action wisdom', 'practical cognition', 'perfecting wisdom', 'all-performing wisdom', and other similar terms. This is the perfect *actualization* of Buddhahood, eternal peace, nirvana, and complete, perfect enlightenment. It is the condition where enlightenment and practice are in perfect accord; realization and action are simultaneous and spontaneous.

Good friends, the *Four Prajnas of Buddhahood*, like the doctrines of the *Five Ranks*, the *Ten Ox-herding Pictures*, and others, are, of course, conceptual constructs; however, their reference is to the reality of your own true nature, which Buddhists refer to as buddha-nature. The division into four aspects is arbitrary, and you should understand that each one of these prajnas contains, and is contained by, the other three.

Many of the great Zen masters affirmed the profound insight of the doctrine of the *Four Prajnas*. Zen master Hakuin asserted that realization of the four prajnas was essential for all Zen students.

Learned audience, clear your minds and allow me to expound on each one of the four prajnas. If you learn to apply this teaching and master it in practice, it will lead you to accomplishing the task of a lifetime.

First is the universal mirror prajna. In rare instances, enlightenment or realization can occur before formal practice and study; however, most practitioners must begin with pre-realization practice based on the teachings of buddhas and Zen ancestors. This includes the study of basic Zen and Buddhist texts, and some form of meditation practice, usually sitting and walking meditation.

After some effort in pre-realization practice, awareness of the universal mirror prajna suddenly occurs. Zen texts often describe this as *kensho* (seeing into true nature). Dogen Zenji often refers to this as 'body and mind cast off' or 'forgetting the self'. This initial experience can vary widely in depth and scope according to the individual. Though the experience itself usually fades quickly, the insight or wisdom activated through kensho can be truly transforming.

42

With this experience, practice and study shifts from the *conceptual* level to the living reality. This initial experience is the point where authentic Zen practice begins.

Until you actually experience this entry, often called kensho, you cannot grasp the truth of Zen. Bodhidharma, the First Ancestor of Zen in China, taught that seeing your nature *is* Zen.

This awakening reveals an aspect of yourself that–though concealed until the moment of kensho–has always been with you. This newly revealed aspect of your own true nature has been functioning all along. When you awaken, you do not attain some new knowledge or understanding, you simply become aware of what has always been true. It is this awareness itself that activates your inherent ability to access and utilize prajna.

Kensho is experienced when the discriminating mind of conceptualization falls away, revealing the source of your own immediate, true awareness. The temporal, limited boundaries of abstraction yield to the eternal infinity of reality. The condition of this immediate awareness of here and now is that aspect of the enlightened mind called the 'universal mirror prajna'. Reality is perceived directly, without judgment or discrimination, simply *as it is*.

You have always been equipped with this prajna, but once awakened to, through kensho, it becomes accessible to you in a new way. You should not, however, think that it is limited to simply *reflecting*. Your universal mirror prajna is capable of much more than simply *dwelling* in pure awareness. With proper guidance, you learn to consciously apply the function that is uncovered by kensho. It is the foundation of all your subsequent or post-enlightenment practice on the path of enlightenment.

The transition from pre-realization practice to post-realization practice can be compared to learning to read. I remember when the First Ancestor was teaching me. One day I suddenly understood the *meaning* of the symbols, "The Great Way is originally perfect and ever-present." Only a week earlier the words were meaningless squiggles, but I continued to engage in pre-reading practice. Then suddenly my inherent ability to read became activated.

Good friends, you should know that the Zen masters repeatedly warn about becoming stuck at this point on the path. Kensho is a wonderful milestone on your path, but it is easy to become attached to this experience. Attachment is a barrier to further progress and is a clear sign that you have stumbled past your realization. With kensho you realize that you have been okay from the very beginning, that old age, sickness, and death have never had any real hold on you. What more could you hope to realize? Why should you continue to practice?

Learned audience, if you fail to continue with post-realization practice, you will allow your experience to stagnate and fade away. Without continued determination and cultivation, you will, at best, remain at the threshold of awakening. Not allowing yourselves to become stuck here, you should continue to move ever deeper. If you do persist in dedicated practice, enlightenment itself will eventually disappear along with its sister, delusion.

Having uncovered the universal mirror prajna, you are no longer bound to simply trust in the teachings of others. You now have *intimate* wisdom and insight with which to work. You have gone beyond the words–"kensho," "enlightenment," and "true-nature"–to the reality that these terms indicate.

Good friends, if your initial insight is to be of any real and lasting value, you must learn to apply it. Although cultivation still requires you to make sustained effort, you will find that your experience has inspired you with deeper confidence and competence. With even the shallowest of kensho experiences, you will be amazed at your new ability to grasp teachings that have eluded you. By continuing to cultivate practice and enlightenment, you can deepen your realization endlessly.

Once my capacity to read was activated, the First Ancestor gradually exposed me to more and more words in various contexts and higher degrees of difficulty. With his guidance, and my own continuous practice, my ability to read progressed. As my ability to read progressed–sometimes slow and steady, sometimes with sudden leaps–the ability to process what was being read also advanced.

The First Ancestor pointed out how enlightening my mind through the practice of reading demonstrated the *nondual* relationship of practice and enlightenment. He helped me realize that the transference of meaning from the books to my mind was *simultaneously* practice (reading) and enlightenment (discerning). They only occur together, yet they maintain their separateness; reading is not discerning, and discerning is not reading.

Good friends, this is similar to discovering the innate working of your own true nature. You must learn to apply your newfound ability to the various teachings of buddhas and Zen masters. As your skill increases–sometimes slow and steady, sometimes with sudden leaps–your ability to enact the wisdom of practice and enlightenment advances. This is the true meaning of the Zen tradition of *mind to mind transmission*, which is the *nondual* activity of practice and enlightenment. The transmission of wisdom from the buddhas and Zen masters to the Zen practitioner is *simultaneously* practice and enlightenment. They only occur together, yet they maintain their separateness; practice is not enlightenment, and enlightenment is not practice.

Learned audience, the second prajna is the prajna of equality. It is activated by focusing the luminous awareness of your universal mirror prajna on yourselves, the world, and the daily activities and non-activities of your lives. Through this practice you awaken to the reality that everything you experience—trees, pebbles, the babbling of the stream, the coolness of the breeze, the fragrance of flowers, your memories and thoughts, all of it—is your own true self. The prajna of equality is the experience of the truth that all things are empty, that is, equal.

Good friends, the Zen masters urge you to avoid becoming stuck at this level of realization. Awakening to the prajna of equality, you may become enamoured by the blissful condition of quietude and fail to make effort to advance and actualize the third and fourth prajnas. Without ongoing, progressive practice toward these latter two, even the prajna of equality will not become fully actualized. The buddhas and Zen masters consider any teaching that encourages students to remain dwelling within the second prajna as an aberration of the true path.

I have observed pseudo-Zen teachers who claim that Zen practice and enlightenment is aimed only at realizing this condition, and learning to expand and sustain it. Such teachers are what the authentic masters sometimes refer to as, 'dust-wiping' or 'mirror-polishing' adherents. Attached to the notion of continuously wiping away defilements, adherents of this practice are unable to advance and experience the true path of Zen.

Learned audience, many popular "Zen" books advocate the experience of the universal mirror prajna and the prajna of equality, but fail to acknowledge, much less encourage students to realize, the deeper levels of wisdom beyond these partial aspects of the enlightened mind. The authors of such books sometimes assert that progress on the path of Zen consists only in expanding the *duration* that the conditions of 'oneness' or 'pure awareness' can be sustained.

Such aberrant teachings, by failing to recognize the wisdom of differentiation, can effectively bar students from the true wisdom of the buddhas and Zen masters. The overall effect of practicing such teachings actually fosters a non-Buddhist disdain for the world of things and events. If such teachings were true, the highest realization of Zen would consist of nothing more than living in a detached state of pure awareness all the time. To become fixated on this aspect of the enlightened mind is to abstain from the zeal, the passion, the joy, and the heartache that gives life its flavor.

Good friends, the realization of emptiness, equality, or oneness is a necessary first step into the vast and fathomless realm of the bud-dha-dharma, and should be continuously deepened and refined. However, there is much more to Zen Buddhism than experiences of oneness or pure awareness. The practice and enlightenment of Zen includes the wisdom of differentiation, infinite variety, and joyful participation in the world.

Becoming attached to or fixated on the blissful conditions of oneness, or pure awareness is a disease that causes practice and enlightenment to stagnate and become foul. The profound wisdom and skillful techniques of the buddhas and Zen ancestors are beyond the reach of practitioners that stop here. Failing to awaken to the wisdom *beyond* emptiness and equality, they remain powerless to help others in any truly meaningful way.

The Zen ancestors have all lamented the appropriation of the name of Zen by those who advocate escapist teachings of naturalism and quietism by encouraging attachment to the experiences of pure awareness or one-ness. Now, people are free to become "founders" of monasteries, schools, and meditation techniques; however, such teachings should not be posited as the doctrines of "Zen." Those who postulate their own versions of religion under the name of Zen are simply prostituting it for their own personal gain.

Both the awareness of the universal mirror prajna and, through it, the realization of the prajna of equality, are necessary for the ongoing practice and enlightenment on the path of Zen. Consequently, the records of Zen contain much exhortation as to the significance of the realization of pure awareness, or 'mirror-like awareness'. It is important to understand, how-ever, that to become stuck here is simply swapping one form of delusion for another.

The First Ancestor taught me that my newfound ability to read was not the *ends* but the *means* to gaining knowledge. Similarly, the Zen practitioner's newfound ability to realize immediate awareness and equality are the *means* to the ongoing fulfillment of wisdom and compassion.

With the realization of the second prajna, you experience the reality of the unnamable void as it truly is. You know for yourselves that all things are equal; when one is raised, all are raised. However, what is the use of activating this wisdom if you do not *apply* it?

If you avoid becoming fixated in the prajna of equality and continue to hone your skill through continual practice, your ability to utilize the mirroring and equality prajnas will gradually become more powerful. The next step is to apply this ability to the wisdom and teachings of the buddhas and Zen ancestors. Through this practice, the third of the *Four Prajnas,* the observing prajna, is actualized.

Good friends, the observing prajna is also known as the dharma, or 'buddha-eye'. It is through observing prajna that the Zen tradition of *transmission* occurs. Contrary to the opinions of many, authentic transmission has nothing to do with lineage charts or certificates. Nor does it refer to any kind of supernatural technique where a teacher transmits something from their mind to the mind of a student. Transmission is the communication of wisdom or prajna–the wisdom for living an authentic life, as well as the wisdom for helping others. Sometimes this wisdom is transmitted through direct personal association, sometimes through enlightened awareness in ordinary activity, sometimes through the records of the masters, sometimes by devices or doctrines like *The Five Ranks* and *The Four Shouts,* and written treatises of all kinds.

Dogen frequently uses phrases like, "Sometimes one is enlightened through a teacher, sometimes one is enlightened through scriptures." The widely held notion that enlightenment is a sudden, one-time event has caused some misunderstandings in this area. If enlightenment was an *event* rather than a *process* you might read Dogen's statements as meaning that some people become enlightened one way, and others become enlightened in other ways. Since enlightenment is not an event, but an ongoing process, you can understand the true meaning of his words; you are enlightened through a teacher, at some times, and through scriptures at other times.

Learned audience, having awakened to your inherent wisdom, you become open to the wisdom of those who have awakened before you. For ultimately, as the phrase "mind to mind" implies, transmission is wisdom communicated *to* wisdom *from* wisdom. In addition to this marvelous opportunity to learn wisdom from others, you are also free to explore realms not yet discovered. For now you will be walking in the same realm as the ancients, and even they have left some stones unturned. Moreover, the actualization of prajna does much more than simply hone your abilities to cope with life on life's terms.

Soon after the First Ancestor taught me to read, I discovered a tattered old book that had fallen behind a cabinet in the bunkhouse. The cover was torn and faded and I could just make out the title: *Watership Down*, by Richard Adams. Curious, I read the first sentence, then another. When I finally looked up from the book, I noticed that half the day had gone by! As I set about my chores, I realized that the fictional characters in Mr. Adams' book were no less real to me than the other characters in my life. They exerted an influence on me that was just as significant. I missed them and desired to return to the book and see how things were going with my new friends: some fictional rabbits and a bird!

The actualization of my inherent ability to read opened whole new worlds to me. Not only did a vast store of information and knowledge suddenly become accessible to me, so, too, did the wonders and marvels of the creative imagination. After living as a rabbit, I became a riverboat pilot with Twain, then a whaler with Melville, a wolf-dog with London. I discovered more than I ever could have expected. William Blake even gave Dogen a run for his money, and Shakespeare, oh, Shakespeare! Have no doubt about it, the buddha-mind rejoices in creativity.

Yet, I could not truly appreciate, or even imagine how learning to read would enrich my experience of life. Similarly, when prajna is actualized and you experience it for yourselves you will discover how pale my words are, how pale are even the words of Buddha. This is something that should not be missed. When the observing prajna begins to function within you, you will not be able to miss it. The world will take on a whole new significance. Some things that seemed important before, like personal wealth or prestige become meaningless, while the most unlikely, ordinary things, like rocks, the barking of dogs, a cup of tea, are suddenly experienced in almost supernatural splendor.

The flower, the oak tree, and the dry clump of dirt, as well as the call of the dove, the scent of newly mown grass, even a slice of bologna, are experienced in their reality as particular aspects of all time and space coming forth here and now. The vast and fathomless universe, the infinite void, referred to as *emptiness*, is manifested as each speck of dust.

Emptiness can be likened to a tree, the many things of the universe, as the flowers of that tree. As plum trees only generate plum tree flowers, so emptiness only generates emptiness flowers. The universe generates flowers of the universe. A world is a flower of the universe, a flea is a flower of the universe; dreams, fears, houses, books, and all the many things are flowers of the universe, flowers of emptiness. You read with the eyes of the universe, speak with the voice of the universe, love with the love of the universe.

Good friends, through observing prajna, the universe or buddha-nature experiences and knows itself. When practitioners intimately experience themselves as that from which all things come, and back into which all things go, fear and greed naturally fall away. As all true sages teach, however, this experience is only the beginning of authentic practice and enlightenment.

On the authentic path of Zen, your own particular manifestation here and now, that is, your present body and mind is not to be abandoned, ground down, and overcome, but to be fully actualized. The great scholar, mythologist, and *bodhisattva* (enlightening being) Joseph Campbell, referred to this actualization of your own true nature as becoming transparent to transcendence. The realm of life and death or samsara *is itself* the realm of joyous serenity or nirvana. The quiet and peaceful experience of emptiness becomes a dark, uneventful cave of death for those who turn their backs on the world of the myriad things and cultivate dispassion for the flowers of emptiness.

Good friends, it is here that the authentic path of practice and enlightenment is distinguished from the false. For the "All is empty" adherents of quietism, personal salvation, through the realization of emptiness, is the final goal. Having saved themselves from the anguish of fear and greed, they detach from the world and cultivate quiescence. Unwilling and *unable* to *use* their realization in the world of differentiation, declining the opportunity to develop wisdom and help others. The authentic student, however, learns to use the realization of emptiness, by cultivating wisdom and compassion, and participates in the world helping all beings. The true Zen master is active in the world of life and death while remaining within the realm of serene emptiness.

Once you have deeply experienced and realized the oneness of yourselves, the universe, and the many things, the Zen path calls you to the forge of the ancestors. By using your buddha-eye, that is, your observing prajna, you apply yourselves to discerning the wisdom of buddhas and Zen ancestors. That is how you become proficient in the skills of helping all beings, which is now your true task.

Good friends, the study of the verbal teachings of buddhas and Zen ancestors has always been an integral part of Zen. Unfortunately, Zen has often been maligned as anti-scholastic, and even anti-rational. This has resulted partly from institutions and false teachers with agendas other than the spiritual promotion of the community.

Prajna

You are fortunate to live in a time when many of the classic Zen texts are available to you in your native language. The translators of these texts have done much to carry the message of Zen, that is, to *transmit* Zen to the west. The people who have spent their lives deciphering and presenting you with the records of the ancient masters are true bodhisattvas working toward the salvation of all.

Unfortunately, some contemporary teachers assert that reading and study are non-essential to Zen. Some even go so far as to imply that reading and study are detrimental to practice and enlightenment, often insisting that sitting meditation is all that is important. This is not a new phenomenon; it has been a recurring plague on Zen down through the ages. Many of the great masters have pointed out the fallacy of this teaching.

Learned audience, you use teachings, expressed and discerned through words, before kensho to guide you to awakening. You apply teachings, expressed and discerned through words, after kensho to polish your realization and develop your insight. Of course, you learn to meditate while sitting, standing, walking, and lying down. The actual practice of meditation or zazen is a vital and integral part of practice and enlightenment. However, without the doctrines expressed through texts and teachers, you could not even learn *how* to meditate.

Of course, there is a wide variation of opinions on what the Zen and Buddhist scriptures and treatises consist of. Opinions as to what constitutes the essential Zen texts range from the entire Buddhist cannon, said to consist of 5,049 scrolls, to a handful of scriptures and Zen records. In addition to this, modern Zen practitioners consist of people from a wide range of lifestyles and capacities. Many practitioners simply cannot immerse themselves in continuous, thoroughgoing study. Time and circumstances limit many practitioners: families, jobs, and other responsibilities make deep and prolonged study impossible. Others simply do not have the mental capacity to delve deeply into the complexities of "The Three Bodies of Buddha" or "The Principal and Satellite" theory of the Huayen School. Some, like the legendary Sixth Ancestor, Eno, may be illiterate. There are as many differing circumstances as there are practitioners.

That does not mean however, that the practice and enlightenment of the path of Zen is out of reach for anyone. How *far* along the path you travel is not nearly as important as the *direction* in which you are traveling. On the Zen path there is no such thing as standing still: you are either moving deeper into enlightenment or deeper into delusion. The Zen adherent that lolls by the roadside, content to rest on their laurels, will find the luster and sparkle of reality begin to fade.

Good friends, as I mentioned before, Hakuin occasionally claimed that koan-introspection alone could bring one to the most profound depths of Wisdom. Of course, Hakuin specifically referred to the 'difficult to penetrate' type of koan. These are the so-called *nanto* koans, which are distinguished from others by their uniquely formidable resistance to resolution. The depth of insight that results when resolution finally occurs compensates for the high level of difficulty of this type of koan. After taking a good hard look at some of these difficult-to-penetrate sayings, some of you may prefer to delve into the 5,049 sutras and shastras instead!

Learned audience, if you truly persist in applying the observing prajna to thoroughly penetrate the teachings of the ancestors, you may come to realize the fourth prajna. The fourth prajna, practical prajna, arises with the fulfillment of the third prajna–that is to say, fulfillment of the third prajna, and actualization of the fourth is *simultaneous*.

Realization of practical prajna defies any manipulation by conscious intent; nevertheless, it is not beyond realization. The fourth prajna, like the first three prajnas–and everything else in the entire universe, including walls, tiles, grasses, and birds–is not apart from you right here, right now. It is only your delusion and preoccupations that keep you from realizing it.

The term *practical prajna* is one of the many provisional names for the spontaneous dynamism of the universe itself. Here, the nondual reality of action and agent, knowledge and known, practice and enlightenment, self and other, finite and infinite, buddha and ordinary being, and so on, are experienced and activated *as they are*, beyond all names and conceptual constructs. We have come to the very limit of relative terms. Practical prajna is a reference to the actualization of nondual wisdom, where wisdom and the agent of wisdom are not two things. 'Knowing it' is 'being it'.

Practical prajna is a reference to the highest wisdom, transcending all duality, including that of right and wrong or good and evil. This wisdom is not subject to any rule, law or precept, for it is the very source of all such codes and formulations. Practical prajna is the nondual essence *and* function of perfect, pure, unbiased righteousness itself. Under the guiding influence of practical prajna, which includes all four prajnas, the awakened practitioner is released from the bonds of literal adherence to ethical codes. Notions of right and wrong are displaced by the spontaneous enactment of what Dogen calls, "good doing." This is the highest meaning of the term "responsibility" that is, to *respond*, in the present, with *ability*.

It was from this wisdom that Zen Master Nansen acted in the famous Zen koan about killing a cat.

> The monks of the eastern hall and the monks of the western hall were arguing about a cat.
>
> Nansen happened along and snatched up the cat saying, "If you can say something, the cat will be spared. If you cannot say anything I will cut off its head."
>
> Nobody could say a word, and Nansen cut the cat into two.
>
> Later that evening, Joshu returned to the monastery and Nansen related what had happened. Joshu immediately removed his sandals, placed them on his head, and walked out.
>
> Nansen said, "If you had been here, the cat would have been spared."[vi]

To claim that conscious intention was involved by purposefully breaking the precept not to kill misses the whole point of this koan. Because the precepts themselves are *drawn* from this realm, to say that Nansen violated the precepts by killing the cat is like saying that a night watchman is violating the curfew. Nansen, the cat, the action of killing, and the precept not to kill all find their source in the wisdom of practical prajna. It was also from this realm that Joshu, hearing of Nansen's action, placed his sandals on his head and walked out.

Good friends, any aspiration that falls short of the realization of practical prajna cannot be considered genuine aspiration. Without such aspiration, you will not even be able to help yourselves, much less others. While genuine practice and enlightenment on the path of Zen is not dependent on achieving any particular level of realization; it does require genuine aspiration. *The Four Great Vows*, which all Mahayana practitioners take up, illustrate this attitude of mind:

> The many beings are numberless; I vow to save them.
> Greed, hate, and ignorance arise endlessly; I vow to abandon them.
> Dharma-gates are countless; I vow to wake to them.
> Buddha's way is unsurpassed; I vow to embody it fully.

This attitude of willingness and determination for full and complete enlightenment is the manifestation of buddha-nature, or ultimate reality itself. It is the zazen of Zen and the Zen of zazen; it is prajna enacting prajna.

Learned audience, until you achieve complete realization and fulfillment of the third prajna, intentional effort in cultivation is required. You need to apply yourselves to practice in order to progress along the path. In other words, your *intention* to practice is essential *and* effective. Regarding the fourth prajna however, intention is *not* essential or even *effective*.

In Buddhism, the simile of a raft is often used to illustrate the function of verbal teachings and doctrines. The Buddhist practitioner is likened to a person using a raft to cross a body of water from this shore of samsara to the other shore of nirvana. Once the person reaches the other shore, the raft is left behind, rather than being carried around. Practical prajna is where the "raft" of the verbal teachings of buddhas and Zen masters, is left behind. "Buddha," "Zen," "practice and enlightenment," and all such terms fall away, and even the notion of "falling away" falls away. The Zen master, Ummon, called this 'going beyond'. Going beyond is up to you alone. Hakuin, Dogen, and all the buddhas and Zen ancestors cannot do it for you. They have taken you to the very cliff edge, but only alone can you make the final leap.

The realization of practical prajna is the experience of unexcelled, supreme, perfect enlightenment, even if only experienced for the fraction of a second. One second contains eternity; one atom contains all of space. One person in one instance of enlightenment is all space and time *as* one instance of unexcelled, supreme, perfect enlightenment.

The vast world-system is completely inside a speck of dust. The mystery of the fourth prajna is the highest, most profound level of practice and enlightenment. One person realizing a single moment of enlightenment is one moment of complete Buddhahood.

Good friends, as Zen practitioners, are you not the descendants of Eno, Dogen, Hakuin, and Obaku? Can you trust their words, their verbal teachings as your guides? If you cannot trust their words, then whose can you trust? There is an easy way to test these old masters: You can put their words into practice, look within yourselves, and find out the truth.

In order to actualize the fourth prajna of Buddhahood, you just continually apply the observing prajna to the buddha-dharma, the verbal teachings, as well as the reality of your present circumstances, devoting your lives to the *Four Great Vows*. Persisting in your practice, you will be amazed at how a story that you thought you thoroughly understood will suddenly yield up whole new levels of subtle wisdom. You will discover the joy of each new moment as life continuously unfolds an infinite ever-changing wonder.

The path of Zen is the *path* of Zen. Whether you have just gotten your first glimpse or you have plumbed the very depths; you are all traveling on the same path. You can take heart in the knowledge that whether or not you ever experience the fourth prajna of Buddhahood your journey will not be dull—or lonely. Even in the first glimmer of the universal mirror prajna you find that you are walking shoulder to shoulder with all of the buddhas and ancestors. You will be closer than breathing. So close, in fact, that Dogen himself takes a nap when you get tired.

Good friends, *here* is the place, *now* is the time where all things are *realized*.

Chapter 4:
Some Questions on the Four Prajnas

A student asked, "What is the difference between delusion and reality?"

Louie Wing said, "Delusion is a misperception of reality. Reality is correctly perceiving delusion."

The student asked, "What is the difference between people who are deluded and those who are awakened?"

Louie Wing said, "Deluded people seek liberation through conceptualization; awakened people realize liberation in their own pure and clear awareness. Deluded people act with expectation of reward; awakened people act in accordance with reality. Deluded people function in delusion and create more delusion; awakened people function in wisdom and create more wisdom. Deluded people experience themselves as separate from the rest of the universe and fall into fear and greed. Awakened people experience the oneness of all and realize fearlessness and fulfillment. Deluded people enjoy some activities, are indifferent to some activities, and loathe others. Awakened people enjoy the mystery of awareness in all of their activities."

—From the collected Sayings and Doings of Louie Wing

After the Second Ancestor finished his talk on Maha Prajna Paramita, he offered to respond to questions from the assembly.

Nic, master of the Fast Hand Zendo, asked, "Teacher, if prajna is inherent in each one of us, what is the use of studying all the various Buddhist scriptures, treatises, and other writings and verbal teachings? Or if writings, doctrines, and spiritual practices are necessary, how can it be that prajna is already inherent within us?"

Louie Wing said, "Learned audience, prajna is inherent in each one of us, but if it is not practiced it cannot be realized. Just as the ability to read, though inherent in each of us, must be practiced to be realized."

John, a priest of One Log Erik Zen, asked "Is there any particular method or teaching that you recommend for someone that has not yet experienced kensho?"

Louie Wing said, "Good friends, all the various techniques for attaining initial awakening are aimed at achieving cessation. Cessation means to put a stop to conceptualization. When you truly achieve cessation, your true nature is immediately experienced. In Zen and Buddhist texts, cessation is called no-mind, mindfulness, stopping, freedom from thought, nonthinking, and other similar terms. The most reliable method for achieving cessation is zazen, which is usually translated as sitting meditation. There is however, much more to true zazen than just sitting. Once a practitioner has achieved true zazen, it can be practiced in nearly any activity or non-activity."

Travis, of the Fifty Ways Dharma, asked, "Some teachers exhort us to strive diligently, and others insist that trying to attain enlightenment is a mistake, that we should just sit without any goal. What is the right approach, when it comes to effort and intention?"

Louie Wing said, "Good friends, when the buddhas and Zen ancestors urge you to make great efforts, while also advising you not to try to become buddhas, they are not teaching two separate things. You must make great effort, but you need to do so in a way that leads to truth. Since each one of you is originally Buddha, trying to become Buddha would be like trying to turn gold into gold. A person that did that would clearly be acting from delusion and wasting their efforts. If you are unaware of your own buddha-nature, any notion you have about enlightenment or Buddhahood will necessarily be false, hence any "goal" you conceive of will only lead you astray. For these reasons, the sages urge you to dismiss conceiving goals aimed at becoming Buddha, and simply make diligent effort in zazen or cessation.

"Those who would teach should be skilled in the various expedients which lead others to enlightenment. Unfortunately, many so-called Zen teachers in the West do not know the expedient skills for teaching students about where and how to apply effort. Having failed to achieve great enlightenment themselves, many preach a non-Buddhist doctrine of naturalism, claiming that sitting meditation itself is enlightenment. I have seen

---

Ted Biringer

hundreds of students sitting on round cushions letting things 'be as they are,' and making no effort to accomplish the task of a lifetime. It is truly regrettable.

"Good friends, learn from the ancestors of the past. Which of them did not make great effort? Shakyamuni studied diligently, and then sat under the bodhi-tree for six years. Eka cut off his arm for the truth. Dogen underwent years of study and practice, finally risking a perilous journey to China. Look at Hakuin's autobiography. His whole life is a testament to the priceless value of genuine, ongoing effort."

Vikki, Taoist master of Sixes, asked, "Teacher, you have made references to zazen that seem to indicate your disapproval of the technique of shikantaza or 'just sitting'. Is that not the method Master Dogen recommended? Why do you disagree with it?"

Louie Wing thought for a moment, straightened himself and began.

Learned audience, this is one of the most insidious and persistent deceptions regarding Dogen's teaching. The notion that he regarded sitting meditation as the ultimate point of Zen is an aberrant teaching. Both shikantaza and sitting meditation are basic techniques practiced in nearly all Schools of Buddhism. Learning and applying both shikantaza and sitting meditation had been basic practice for most Buddhists in Japan long before Dogen was ever born. If the authentic path of Zen consisted in the mere act of sitting cross-legged or applying the simple method of "just sitting," Dogen's journey to China and all of his subsequent teaching would be useless.

Sadly, I have personally witnessed this ridiculous notion functioning as the foundation of a number of cultic communities that identify themselves as "Zen" centers or monasteries. The superstitious notion that simply sitting '*like* Buddha' is itself '*being* Buddha' is openly expressed by a number of westerners sporting shaved heads and dressed in gorgeous Asian robes.

Although the various centers that propagate this teaching vary about the details, they commonly assert a kind of supernatural notion of zazen that magically transforms ordinary mortals into buddhas. In some versions, it is important to sit in just the proper posture. For others, it apparently makes no difference how one sits. Some self-proclaimed authorities of Dogen assert that simply sitting cross-legged is the complete manifestation of Zen.

Part of this nonsense is due to a certain grandiosity accorded to Zen masters or roshi's in the West. Some American "Zen masters" touting themselves as "Dharma successors" apparently consider themselves equal in significance with Shakyamuni, the historical Buddha. As self-supposed fully enlightened beings, they believe they have absolute spiritual authority and disregard the transmitted wisdom of tradition. Like self-righteous zealots throughout history, they promote themselves as founders of Zen monasteries or other exclusive communities. Others describe themselves as founders of new schools or unique lineages. Some of these "masters" go so far as to trademark their own peculiar methods, often guaranteeing fast, easy enlightenment—for a fee, of course.

Good friends, such teachers often maintain exclusive communities, screening and denying applicants that do not meet their preconditioned requirements. In some popular, though widely divergent "Zen" centers, students are subjected to years of graduated study and practice based, not on Zen tradition, but on strange, rigid curriculums devised by their founders. As the students progress through the unique curriculums, they may be awarded titles or even insignia of status to proudly wear on their Asian-style robes. It is truly lamentable. One cannot help but wonder when someone will open a drive up window selling "Fast enlightenment," all packaged up in Styrofoam boxes!

Learned audience, when you examine the explanations of zazen espoused by some of these quacksalvers, things often get extremely convoluted. Their "teachings" are often expressed with deliberately irrational language, apparently intended to make the writer sound mystical or wise.

I came once to a "Zen" center located in the foothills of a mountain. I had been walking for many days and was dressed as usual in jeans and a flannel shirt. During that time in my life I wore a beard and seldom cut my hair.

Two bald-headed, very clean-looking American monks met me at the gated entrance. They wore undecorated, but very finely made black Asian robes. Neither made any effort to disguise their disapproval of my appearance. After a bit of wrangling, they allowed me to enter.

I was escorted to a room where a pleasant, smiling nun and a wiry, pinch-faced monk met with me. Both were shaved headed, and both wore fine, ornamented robes. Pointing to one of the official looking badges pinned to the monk's robe, I asked what it meant.

"That one is for passing all the koans in the Mumonkan," he said, "I earned that several years ago, of course."

"Of course," I said.

The nun asked me where I had come from and what it was I wanted.

58

I said, "I have walked here from Boise. I stopped to meet the teacher."

"Boise!" The monk said, "That's over a hundred miles." His face expressed obvious disbelief, pinched or not.

"Yes," I said, "It is about three hundred and twenty miles, give or take." He bowed, gave me a sideways pinched look and left.

The nun explained that this center was for residents only and the policy did not allow "walk-ins." If I wanted to meet the teacher here, I would have to send in an application. Then she explained that I could go to one of his "public" three-hour workshops. The fee was only two hundred dollars, and sometimes the roshi permitted a few questions at the end.

As I was about to respond, a bald man wearing a gorgeous blue and cream, elaborately ornamented Asian robe swept into the room.

The nun bowed deeply. "M-Master," she said.

He ignored her and turned his attention to me. "Hello," he said. "Norman tells me you walked all the way from Boise just to see me. Is this true?"

I bowed politely, then said, "Partly true-"

"Skip the 'Zen talk'," he said, "'Partly true', bah! Just speak ordinary."

"It is true that I walked here," I said, "but it was not just to see you. I am on my way to Florida and heard about this place yesterday and it seemed appropriate to pay you a visit."

"Appropriate?" he said, "Are you a Zen practitioner then? A student?"

"Yes," I said, "I am a-"

Interrupting me, he asked, "What lineage do you follow?"

"I follow no particular lin-" I began, but was interrupted again.

"Bah!" He said, then he produced a small, carved stick from somewhere inside his many-layered robe, and tossed it at me.

I caught it, held it out and said, "You dropped your stick."

"Bah! You haven't a glimmer," he said and abruptly departed.

About two years later, I was again in the same area as that "Zen" center. I went to a local thrift store where I purchased an old set of heavy, gold-colored drapes, some fancy sandals, and a gnarly looking cane. I cut and sewed the drapes into an intricate, gorgeous robe. I shaved my head and beard. Then, I hired a limousine and traveled to the center where the roshi himself opened the gate

The driver opened the door and I got out with a glare in my eye.

The roshi made three deep bows.

I said, "Can you say a word of Zen?"

His Adam's apple bobbed a few times, then he said, "Just this is it."

"Good!" I said, and bowed. "Now you test me."

He hesitated a moment then said, "What is the sound of a single hand?"

I immediately removed one of my sandals and slapped him across the face with it, which was of course, a meaningless gesture.

He bowed again saying, "I have dreamed about you, wise Master."

I said, "I am Sajavoni Roshi, of the Wokfumboise lineage. I have heard about you, Master, and your great Zen center and have come to learn your methods."

After he finished lavishing me with flattery, I was led to a private cottage and assigned two novice monks as "attendants." I stayed on for three weeks. Finally, I went to the roshi's suite, where two of his young female "attendants" escorted me in. As he made bows, I dropped the carved stick he had given me two years earlier, turned my back on him and walked out.

While I was there, I learned how the students were screened based on financial status and professional skills. I learned how "non-conformists" were quietly shunned until they "chose" to move on. I learned how members were encouraged to provide information on potentially valuable friends and family members that might be recruited.

Saddest of all, I saw how those who were lured in, were instructed to "just sit." This, they were told, is wisdom. Although this is an extreme example, I saw the same kinds of practices being carried out to a lesser degree all over the United States, Europe, and Australia. The majority of these cults advocate some variation of the formula that "sitting meditation" is the only essential message of Zen.

Make no mistake about it—such teachings have nothing to do with Zen. Simply sitting like a buddha cannot awaken you to Buddhahood. True zazen requires you to make particular, concentrated effort.

Good friends, Dogen, like all the true Zen masters, implores you to wholeheartedly practice zazen. He consistently affirms the nondual relationship of practice and enlightenment. He goes to great lengths however, to define exactly what he means by zazen.

In *Shobogenzo, Zazenshin,* which is his most incisive teaching on zazen, Dogen points out two common fallacies about zazen that were prevalent in his own time. The first wrong view is the notion that zazen is "just sitting" and understanding that there is nothing to realize, just sit and attain peace of mind.

Learned audience, popular teachers are espousing variations of this aberrant Zen path in our own time. The authors of some popular "Zen" books exalt the notion that Zen practice is about achieving a 'natural state of mind'. This is very different from master Dogen's teachings, which exhort us to, above all else, 'achieve the bodhi mind'.

Good friends, the second aberration that Dogen denounces manifests in various forms as the notion that 'everything is Zen'. This is commonly espoused by expressions like, "Everything is One-essence, so do whatever you want; it is all okay."

Contrasting this kind of "teacher" with Dogen, who approached life as an eternal quest for meaning and experience—discovering whole worlds in each moment, in each drop of water—we can understand his disdain for the perverted 'nothing to realize' and 'everything is it' notions of false Zen. Dogen constantly focused on the truth that aspiration and effort are *essential* to genuine practice and enlightenment.

Learned audience, Dogen urges those who have already attained enlightenment to continue to go ever-deeper, attaining enlightenment upon enlightenment. Enlightenment without practice is not authentic enlightenment; practice without enlightenment is not authentic practice.

The necessity of wholehearted effort and focused, dedicated practice is a basic teaching of Buddhism, and a hallmark of Zen. This teaching has always been susceptible to misunderstanding and misappropriation. In fact, some of the most pernicious divisions in the history of Buddhism have been caused by arguments around what this teaching means. The confusion between *sudden realization* (original enlightenment) and *gradual cultivation* (acquired enlightenment), has been the most visible and persistent manifestation of this argument in the Zen tradition.

For Dogen, the apparent contradiction between original enlightenment and acquired enlightenment became the *barrier to* and eventually the *catalyst of* his own great awakening. Resolving this conflict became the central focus of his spiritual quest. It was through his personal resolution of the seeming contradiction between the doctrine of original enlightenment and the need for spiritual practice that allowed him to—in his own words from *Shobogenzo, Bendowa*—"complete the task of a lifetime."

What happened in Dogen's case was like this:

> A monk fell asleep in the meditation hall. Tendo Nyojo, Dogen's teacher, shouted at the sleeping monk, "True zazen demands that we cast off body and mind. Why are you sleeping?" These were the turning words that opened Dogen's heart. He went to Tendo Nyojo's

61

room, burned incense, and made bows. Tendo Nyojo asked, "Why are you doing this?" Dogen said, "Body and mind are cast off!" Tendo Nyojo replied, "Body and mind are cast off, cast off are Body and mind." Dogen said, "Do not affirm me lightly teacher." Tendo Nyojo said, "I do not." Dogen said, "What is not affirmed lightly?" Tendo Nyojo said, "Casting off is cast off." This is how Tendo Nyojo testified to Dogen's great enlightenment.

After such a powerful experience, it is only natural that the nondual nature of practice and enlightenment became such a central theme in Dogen's teaching. By "nondual" I mean empty of duality, I do not mean that practice and enlightenment are one, as is propagated by some. Practice and enlightenment in Zen are *two aspects* of one reality. It is important to understand that though they always go together, they each maintain their distinctive aspects.

Dogen's earliest teachings are full of wonderful expressions that convey this principle. The *very first* paragraph of his *very first* teaching, *Fukanzazengi,* is constructed of four lines—each variations of this fundamental truth.

> Now, when we research it, the truth originally is all around: why should we rely upon practice and experience? The real vehicle exists naturally: why should we put forth great effort? Furthermore, the whole body far transcends dust and dirt: who could believe in the means of sweeping and polishing? In general, we do not stray from the right state: of what use, then, are the tiptoes of training?[viii]

Learned audience, this is not simply a series of rhetorical statements, but an expression of spiritual realization, urging us to deep contemplation. Dogen is not saying, "the truth is all around: we do not need to rely upon practice, put forth great effort, etc." Rather, he is saying, "the truth is all around: *why* do we need to practice, *who* could believe in the means, of *what* use, and so on." His statements are neither rhetorical, nor are they conventional questions wanting answers. Master Dogen is indicating, at once, the revelation of a spiritual truth *and* giving an indication of the appropriate attitude for Zen practitioners to employ in their efforts.

Learned audience, Dogen taught what all the true buddhas and Zen ancestors taught; enlightenment is the *essence* of authentic practice, practice is the *function* of authentic enlightenment. The duality of practice and enlightenment is actualized and transcended, not eradicated or annihilated. Dogen frequently uses the term zazen in reference to the nondual nature of practice and enlightenment, not just as a reference to sitting meditation.

In *Shobogenzo, Genjokoan,* Dogen outlines the fundamental teachings of Zen. Near the end of this essay, he uses a Zen koan to illustrate the nondual nature of practice and enlightenment. The koan runs:

> Zen Master Hotetsu, of Mount Mayu is using a fan.
>
> A monk comes up and says, "The nature of air is ever-present, and there is no place it does not reach. Why then does the Master use a fan?"
>
> The master says, "You understand that the nature of air is ever-present, but you do not understand the truth that there is no place it does not reach."
>
> The monk says, "What is the truth of there being no place it does not reach?"
>
> At this, the master just continues to use the fan.
>
> The monk does prostrations.

Dogen goes on to say, "The actualization of the buddha-dharma, the living way of authentic transmission, is like this."

It is worth noting that the word "zazen" does not appear even once in this vastly popular, and often misrepresented, treatise.

Learned audience, the term zazen, like dharma, buddha, bodhi, and the like, has different meanings depending on the speaker, audience, and context of its expression. Just as the most common use of the term "Buddha" is as a reference to the historical Shakyamuni Buddha, so the most common use of the term "zazen" is as a reference to sitting meditation. Once you develop a working knowledge of the records and koans of Zen, it will be clear when Dogen is using the term zazen strictly in reference to sitting meditation, and when he is using it in its higher sense: the nondual nature of practice and enlightenment.

Good friends, it is truly deplorable that Dogen's profound expressions on practice and enlightenment have been, and continue to be, twisted into shallow, naturalistic views. Dogen's amazing teaching that practice *is* practice-and-enlightenment, and enlightenment *is* practice-and-enlightenment, has been mutated into practice *is* enlightenment, and enlightenment *is* practice.

If we were to revise the koan about the master using a fan and the ever-present nature of air to illustrate the false notion foisted upon Dogen's teaching, it would read:

> Zen "Master" Contemporary so-and-so, founder of Zen Center such-and-such is using a fan. A student comes by and asks, "The nature of air is to be ever-present, and there is no place that air cannot reach. Why does the master use a fan?"
>
> The "master" says, "You have wrongly understood that the nature of air is something real, and you do not yet know the truth that there is no enlightenment."
>
> The student says, "What is the truth that there is no enlightenment?"
>
> At this, the "master" puts a glare in his eye and continues using the fan. The student does prostrations and donates money to the Zen Center. --*Blind Dharma-Eye Treasury,* Roshi So-and-So, pages, 1-5000

Learned audience, any teaching that posits practice as a term indicating something other than *the enactment of* enlightenment, as in practice-and-enlightenment, or as a term *synonymous with* enlightenment, is false teaching. Unlike Dogen's works, many contemporary "Zen" books avoid the word "enlightenment" altogether–except as something to be challenged. The word "practice," however, is profuse. They ramble on about Zen practice this and Zen practice that. Sadly, in such cases practice is often divorced from enlightenment and diminished to a simple catchphrase of pseudo-Zen cults.

Good friends, this misrepresentation of practice is often married to a literalist interpretation of zazen, consequently reducing great enlightenment to ordinary sitting meditation. The final creed for this abomination of Dogen's teaching is; "there is no enlightenment to seek, have no goal except to only sit, which is itself full and perfect enlightenment." Is this not a truly reprehensible state of affairs?

Chapter 5:
The Five Ranks

Louie Wing said, "The unnamable void transcends explanation, yet explanations are used to guide you to the unnamable void. Words do not reach the vast, unnamable, fathomless void, yet through words it is revealed."
—From the collected Sayings and Doings of Louie Wing

The next day the nun, Lisa of the DT school, asked the Second Ancestor to address the assembly. She wanted to learn the significance of the Zen doctrine of the *Five Ranks*.

Thereupon, having taken his seat upon the flatbed, Louie Wing asked the assembly to clear their minds. Then he gave the following address.

Good friends, Tozan Liang-chieh, who lived from 807 to 869, was an exceptionally ingenious master of Zen expression. Very few masters before or since have matched his skill at presenting the subtle wisdom of the enlightened mind. His disciple, Sozan, through his elucidation and refinement of Tozan's teaching, proved his inclusion among these few.

The teaching of the *Five Ranks* is one of the most essential doctrines of Zen. Hakuin Zenji considered the realization of the *Five Ranks* indispensable to authentic Zen practice and enlightenment. He believed that the teaching of the *Five Ranks* was expounded to awaken students to the *Four Prajnas of Buddhahood*. The importance that he placed on the *Five Ranks* is evidenced by his inclusion of them as the completion of his systematic approach to koan-introspection. Hakuin considered the actualization of the *Five Ranks* to be simultaneous with the activation of Buddhahood.

Good friends, the essence of what the *Five Ranks* represents has always been an integral aspect of Mahayana Buddhism, including Zen. However, the presentation of it by Tozan, further refined by Sozan, marks the point at which it reaches the level of true Zen expression.

Learned audience, many Zen expressions serve to indicate the relationship between the relative and the absolute. These two aspects of reality appear in the Buddhist texts in many guises: form and emptiness, phenomena and real, finite and infinite, temporal and eternal, and the many and the one.

One of the most methodical expressions of this order of reality was achieved in the Huayen Buddhist teachings of *shih* (thing, event, etc.) and *li* (principle, absolute, etc.). The philosophy of Huayen is truly astounding in its depth and scope. The study of the Huayen texts is a worthwhile venture for anyone who wants to understand the many implications of the inter-penetrating characteristics of reality. For anyone wanting to approach the subtle teachings of the Zen ancestors a general grasp of the fundamental teachings of Huayen is essential.

Good friends, Tozan and Sozan were both thoroughly familiar with Huayen metaphysics, as were most of the great Zen masters. Their ability to assimilate the wisdom of these doctrines through personal realization, and present it to Zen students was exceptional. Tozan was already displaying this mastery of expression in his earliest moments of realization.

Once, following a dialogue with his teacher, Ungan, Tozan was still harboring some doubt in his mind when, crossing a stream, he saw his image reflected in the water and experienced a great awakening. He then composed this verse:

> Earnestly avoid seeking without,
> Lest it recede far from you.
> Today I am walking alone,
> Yet everywhere I meet him.
> He is now no other than myself,
> But I am not now him.
> It must be understood in this way
> In order to merge with Suchness.[ix]

Already in this early expression, the seeds of the *Five Ranks* can be seen. The immediate and *intimate* words about "hearing with the eye" and "meeting him everywhere while walking alone" are pure blood and guts Zen. Though Zen does not shirk philosophy, it prefers 'direct pointing at the human mind'. Tozan is one of the all-time masters of this 'direct pointing'.

Good friends, one thing that sets Zen apart from other spiritual traditions is its directness of expression. True Zen expression is so direct it is *immediate*. I am using the term "expression" here in its highest, most inclusive sense; *to communicate, manifest, depict, convey, squeeze out, disclose, implicate, expose, and indicate.* This is the realm of Zen's mind-to-mind transmission. The wisdom of enlightenment, prajna paramita, is transmitted through expression and realization.

Like Zen koans, *The Five Ranks* is one way that this wisdom is transmitted. True Zen expressions are direct expressions *of* wisdom, which can only be realized *by* wisdom. When we take up a koan, we are taking up specific wisdom, realized and expressed by the buddha-mind. When we have become intimate with the koan, that is, when its wisdom is realized in us and has become our wisdom, transmission has occurred.

Learned audience, although a great amount of wisdom can sometimes be transmitted by a single expression, it nevertheless takes many expressions and realizations to transmit the vast store of the wisdom of the buddhas and Zen ancestors. We, as human beings, have the extraordinary opportunity to receive this transmission.

Good friends, each of the five ranks, like each koan, is unique; each expression transmits a *particular* aspect of wisdom. For those who would set out to realize authentic Zen practice and enlightenment, wholehearted dedication and long-term commitment is necessary. The resolution of the one great matter of life and death is no easy task; yet, there is no task as worthwhile.

Learned audience, as electricity will not transfer without a ground, so Zen cannot be transmitted without a receiver. As soon as a ground is provided, however, electricity flows. As soon as you become a receiver, Zen transmits.

Dogen frequently points out that this transmission only occurs from Buddha to Buddha. For, if we do not receive it with our buddha-mind, we do not receive it at all. Zen expression comes from buddha-mind and goes to buddha-mind. Buddha expresses Buddha, and thereby realizes Buddha.

Buddha awakens Buddha. One meaning of "Buddha" is "awake." Hence, we can say, Buddha *Buddhas* Buddha.

Good friends, it is vital to follow through completely if we are to realize the freedom to respond equally in every direction. The *Five Ranks* are among the best Zen methods of progressive transcendence. Nevertheless, each rank, if not fully penetrated and transcended, can become a bond or a sticking point itself.

Learned audience, all true Zen expressions come from buddha-nature, or the enlightened mind. Some transmitters, however, are more powerful than others are. The Zen doctrine of the *Five Ranks* is one of the most powerful Zen transmitters, and one of the most profound. Like the best koans, the *Five Ranks* contain layers and layers of wisdom, we will find, like *Gutei* (Chu-chih) did with his "one finger Zen," we can use them our whole life but we will never use them up.

The first of the *Five Ranks* is called: Individual within the Universal. The verse for this rank is:

> At the beginning of the night's third watch, before there
> is moonlight,
> Don't be surprised to meet yet not recognize
> What is surely a familiar face from the past.[x]

Learned audience, the first of the *Five Ranks*–Individual within the Universal–refers to the world of things and events as they are experienced from *within* the world of the absolute. This is the reality behind the teaching that "form is emptiness." For a practitioner at the first rank, all particular things are experienced as empty, and seemingly unreal.

Good friends, you can reach some understanding of this by focusing your attention on any particular thing or event in such a way as to discover that it does not exist as a separate entity. This is described as 'empty of self-nature' that is, void of independent existence.

Lifting a large, yellow pear from a bowl of fruit that someone had placed on the flatbed, Louie Wing said, "For example, this pear is one aspect of many things: a pear tree, sunshine, water, earth, time, and so on. What we call a 'pear' is not really a pear, but is just one aspect of all these various things, ultimately including all of time and space. If we took away any one of the things that make up this particular pear, this pear could not

68

exist. I am sure all of you would agree that would be a pity." Then, closing his eyes, Louie Wing began to eat the pear. Eating slowly, as if to memorize each bite, he consumed all but the stem, which he set aside as he continued his sermon.

Good friends, while such philosophizing can lead you to insight and knowledge, it remains an abstract theory until its reality, which this conceptual framework attempts to indicate, is intimately experienced. Talking about or describing the taste, texture, and refreshment of eating pears can only be truly understood by someone that has eaten pears. Zen is not concerned with abstract theorizing and philosophical erudition. It is the *direct experience* of reality or buddha-nature that Zen is interested in engendering within you. Once this is realized, the true power of words and doctrines become accessible in a meaningful, useful way.

Learned audience, when you have been cultivating practice based on the teachings of buddhas and Zen masters, you experience the first rank as an utterly still, quiet, purposeless, and meaningless condition. Here, you are actually face to face with your own true nature, however, for the moment you remain unaware of this fact. As one Zen saying puts it, "He has opened the door and is looking at it, but does not yet see it."

Good friends, as Tozan's verse points out, this is the night's *third* watch. During the first two watches, you have been practicing zazen, seeking the host of seeing and hearing, becoming intimate with Mu or applying a similar technique. You do not realize it, but you are on the brink of sudden enlightenment. Yet, everything is dark, shadowy, and dreamlike. This is what Tozan indicates in his verse by, "before there is moonlight."

Learned audience, in the first rank everything from the practitioner's point of view has ceased to exist in any *significant* way. Both the world and yourself are experienced as insubstantial and seemingly nonexistent. It is important to understand that while you are in this condition you still see, hear, and interact in the world. It is not as though you are blind, deaf, and mute; everything is still here, but in a dreamlike, *insignificant* manner.

Good friends, there are two pitfalls you must avoid when you come to experience this condition. One is the danger of falling into a sense of melancholic dejection. Having worked hard to reach this promising condition, you may surprisingly find yourself becoming suddenly discouraged. This arises from the mistaken conclusion that you are actually experiencing some kind of realization. "This is it?" you may ask yourself. "All that time and energy pursuing the truth only to discover that everything is nonexistent? Enlightenment is nonexistent, delusion is nonexistent, Zen is nonexistent, and I am nonexistent. What is the use?"

If you continue your practice, however, this experience of empty dullness will not last too long. You should be aware of it in order to avoid becoming discouraged and failing to persevere with your practice. It is also important to understand that although this is an experience of "emptiness" it is not the true experience of "vast emptiness." That truly liberating experience of the vast and fathomless void occurs when you arrive at the third rank. Dullness and obscurity mark the experience of emptiness in the first rank.

Good friends, the other danger associated with the initial experience of the first rank is also a result of concluding that you have come to some kind of realization. Only here, it does not manifest as disappointment or discouragement, but as indolence. For some, the experience of dull emptiness, because it brings relief from the vicissitudes of life, becomes an object of attachment. Because things are experienced as insubstantial, insignificant, and nonexistent you may feel you have no more obligations or responsibilities; that you are free to do as you please; after all, it is *just* a dream, and it is not anything special.

Good friends, if this disease is allowed to take root it is very difficult to overcome. It can be extraordinarily damaging, to you as well as to those around you. Take heed of the teachings of your good and great friends the true Zen masters of yore. Then, experiencing the first rank will prove to be your entry into true enlightenment. You can experience the conditions of melancholy or indolence in their moments of fullness, letting them come, then go as you continue to stay focused on your practice.

Learned audience, allowing the experience of dull emptiness to come and go as you move deeper into your practice, you may discover a remarkable sense of *impending realization*. This is quite an extraordinary experience. An awareness of the brink of some kind of realization sets in solidly, and without doubt. Often a serene sense of joy accompanies this sense of impending realization. You have been working hard, and you are beginning to see the loom of light just over the horizon. It is similar to seeing a familiar face right before remembering who it is or like looking at one of those pictures with a hidden image just before it becomes clear.

Of course, the ranks are not simply "stages" you pass through, but aspects of practice and enlightenment. What I am calling a "sense of impending realization" will become a common companion on your travels along the ancient Way.

You should also know that not only are the ranks not stages, but they are also not separate from each other. As long as you do not fixate on them, they flow naturally into each other. The initial experience of the first rank is the point at which the aspect of enlightenment, sometimes referred to as the universal mirror prajna, becomes partially realized. The full realization of this prajna is fulfilled as you move into the experience of the second rank–the Universal within the Individual.

Good friends, it is in the first rank that the potential for sudden realization becomes manifest. You need only persevere in your practice and the inevitable moment when the filter of conception and discrimination drops away, delusion dissipates, and buddha-nature appears at once. At that time, even if for only the fraction of a second, you will see with Tozan's ear, you will hear with Dogen's eye.

This experience occurs simultaneously with your initiation into the second of the *Five Ranks*: the Universal within the Individual. The verse for this rank is:

> An old crone, having just awakened, comes upon an ancient mirror:
> That which is clearly reflected in front of her face is none other than her own likeness.
> Don't lose sight of your face again and go chasing your shadow.[xi]

Learned audience, this rank is described by variations of the formula "emptiness is form." You learn through applying yourselves to the Zen path of practice and enlightenment that emptiness is *itself* form. The very same truth that "form is emptiness" is here perceived from the opposite perspective.

"Good friends," Louie Wing said, lifting the pear stem he had set aside earlier and holding it up for all to see, "you saw how the pear was empty of self-nature; being only one particular aspect of many things, and therefore void of an independent self. Shifting to the opposing standpoint, you discover that the *emptiness*, which seemed to nullify form, is itself the very *reality* of form. That is to say, the *relationship* between the many things that made up the pear, were precisely the pear itself. In fact, *all* of emptiness manifests *as* each particular thing or event."

Louie Wing then tossed the stem into his mouth, chewed it up and swallowed. With a broad smile, Louie Wing continued.

As you see, not only is this particular pear the whole of space and time, the pear is simultaneously one of the many things that makes up the whole of me.

Learned audience, the experience of the second rank–the Universal within the Individual–is particularly resistant to expression with the relative terms of language. Nevertheless, in his verse, Tozan manages an expression that demands our respect and our gratitude. His verse on the second rank actually pushes language beyond its usual relative limits to the very brink of the absolute. Tozan's verse not only describes the experience of the Universal within the Individual; it *evokes* it. Since the 'universal' is true nature, and the 'individual' is you, Tozan's verse, like the Zen koans, evokes your inherent true nature.

One koan that demonstrates the nature of the second rank in a marvelous and very direct manner is Joshu's Cloth Shirt.

> A monk asked Joshu, "All things return to the One, where does the One return?"
> Joshu said, "When I was in Seishu, I made a cloth shirt. It weighed seven pounds."

Good friends, Joshu is not known as the master of "the Zen of lips and tongue" for no reason. You can see why Dogen Zenji often refers to him as "the eternal buddha." The monk in this koan is no slacker either. We should all be grateful for his daring question.

Another koan demonstrates the nature of the second rank by approaching it from an entirely different angle; listen to this koan from the *Mumonkan*:

> Gettan asked a monk, "The cart-maker made a hundred carts. If you take away the wheels and the axle, what is clearly apparent?"

Initially, this koan might seem to be revealing a facet of the first rank of the Individual within the Universal; but if you mull it over and master it in practice and you will discover the underlying pattern in all its elaborate detail.

Learned audience, in Tozan's verse, the "old crone" that has "just awakened" is you. You *are* old, too, very old! The "ancient mirror" in which she catches her reflection is no more ancient than she is. It is the universal mirror prajna. This mirror has been right in front of your face from the very beginning, and even before that. Not only *in front* of your face, as Zen master Rinzai said, "Right here, in this lump of red flesh there is a True Man with no rank. Constantly he is going in and out the gates of your face. If you still do not know this, look! Look!"

Good friends, the True Man with no rank is very ancient indeed. In and out through the gates of your eyes, ears, nose, tongue, body, and mind, he goes. This master of seeing and hearing does have a particular age though, as Wu Yeh said:

> Your nature of seeing, hearing, and being aware is
> the same age as the universe, which is birthless and
> deathless.[xii]

Good friends, the "old crone" and the "ancient mirror" go together in perfect harmony. Sometimes the mirror reflects the old crone; sometimes the old crone reflects the mirror. You may remember how master Joshu likened the mirror to a clear jewel:

> The Master entered the hall and said, "This fact is
> like a clear jewel in your hand. If a barbarian comes, it
> reveals a barbarian. If a Chinese [sic] comes, it reveals a
> Chinese."[xiii]

Dogen took up Joshu's jewel and unfolded its vision even more thoroughly:

> What all the buddhas and all the patriarchs have re-
> ceived and retained is the eternal mirror. They have the
> same view and the same face, the same image and the
> same cast; they share the same state and realize the same
> experience. A foreigner appears, a foreigner is re-

flected—one hundred and eight thousand of them. A
Chinaman appears, a Chinaman is reflected—for a moment and for ten thousand years. The past appears, the
past is reflected; the present appears, the present is reflected; a buddha appears, a buddha is reflected; a patriarch appears, a patriarch is reflected.[xiv]

Learned audience, is this a divine mirror? Look around and see if there is
anything mundane anywhere. This mirror's true power lies not only in its
marvelous *essence* however, but in the demonstration of its wondrous *function*.

All people who practice develop illumination by cultivating the supreme correct path of unobstructed perfect
awareness. All the buddhas, all the *tathagatas*, begin with
their own cultivation and end by transforming other beings. There is nothing that they do not achieve.[xv]

Good friends, your initial experience of the second rank reveals and
awakens what you have unseeingly been gazing at all along. Together the
first two ranks overlap kensho—awakening to your own true nature. By
"overlap" I mean that the border or demarcation between the first rank and
the second rank is not a separation, but a connection; not a barrier, but a
joint. In this sense, the kensho experience can be understood as the joint
between the first and second ranks. In the first rank, you partially experience the universal mirror prajna. When this prajna suddenly becomes fully
actualized, you have entered the second rank.

When you enter the second rank, you will discover the oneness of the
entire universe and yourselves. From there you can say, "I and the universe
are one."

Good friends, with your first experience of the second rank, a great shift
occurs in your practice; you no longer need merely rely on the teachings of
others. You will now have actual experience and insight into what you have
hitherto only heard about. Although you will still rely on teachings to guide
you in deepening and refining your realization, your practice will be *based* on
your own experience. Furthermore, your experience will have confirmed
the truth of the *dharma* and thus strengthened your faith.

It is important to understand clearly that this is not a final realization; it
is where true Zen practice and enlightenment *begins*.

Learned audience, in the second rank, you uncover an aspect of yourselves that you had previously been unaware of. This aspect, the universal mirror prajna, is the new foundation for your practice. It is through this prajna that you experience life as it is *before* naming and conceptualization. It is the experience of *suchness* or *thusness*. The universal mirror-mind spontaneously reflects all that you see, hear, smell, taste, touch, and think in its suchness. As we have already observed, *reflection* is not the only aspect of this prajna. It is also imbued with self-luminescence. It is with this self-generating *light* that you begin to explore and en-*light*-en the wisdom of the universe. As you learn to focus this luminescent mirror-mind in all of your activities and non-activities, you begin to discover the marvels of the vast and fathomless realm that is at once the universe and the self.

It is at the borderland of the second and third ranks that the second prajna, that is, the prajna of equality, is realized. When this prajna becomes fully manifest, you have entered the third rank—Coming from within the Universal. The verse for this rank is:

> Amidst nothingness there is a road far from the dust.
> If you are simply able to avoid the reigning monarch's personal name,
> Then you will still surpass the eloquence of previous dynasties.[xvi]

Good friends, it is within the third rank that you fulfill the second prajna—the prajna of equality—and partially awaken to the third prajna—the observing prajna."

Remember, the Prajna of Equality is the realization of vast and fathomless, empty oneness; no-thing-ness—"a road far from the dust." It is the realm of tranquility, peace, and atonement. Through cultivation, you have honed your ability to use your own inherent universal mirror prajna in all conditions, which brings you into direct insight of equality or emptiness.

In this rank, your understanding and your actions begin to accord with each other. The third rank is where the separation between your self and your experience dissolves. A capping phrase illustrates this nicely:

> The wild geese do not intend to leave traces,
> The water has no mind to absorb their image.[xvii]

The water-geese! Learned audience, you may ask, "What about when the geese are not flying over? When there is nothing reflected where is the self then?" Look at this classic koan and see how Ryutan helps Tokusan discover the light inside the dark, and the dark inside the light. This koan is: Ryutan Blows Out the Candle:

> Tokusan questioned Ryutan late into the night. Finally Ryutan said, "Why don't you retire?"
>
> Tokusan made his bows then lifted the blinds to leave, but was met by darkness. He turned back and said, "It is dark outside."
>
> Ryutan handed a lighted candle to Tokusan. When Tokusan was about to take it, Ryutan blew it out. Tokusan experienced sudden enlightenment and made bows.
>
> Ryutan said, "What did you see?"
>
> Tokusan said, "I will never again doubt the words of the old priest who is renowned everywhere."

When Tokusan lifted the blinds, how did he know it was dark outside? When Ryutan blew out the candle, was it still dark outside? As one Zen saying goes, "In a cauldron of boiling water, there is no cool spot."

Good friends, Ryutan was simply pointing out the obvious. You, like Tokusan, have nothing to *gain*, you need simply become aware of what has always been true: namely, you are, *as you are*, Buddha. Tokusan *is* darkness, darkness *is* Tokusan.

It is said that Shakyamuni Buddha attained enlightenment when he saw the morning star. How is that? When Shakyamuni Buddha saw the morning star, the morning star saw Shakyamuni Buddha. Shakyamuni Buddha, the morning star, the seeing, and the seen, are not separate things—they are "far from the dust."

Shakyamuni Buddha sees the morning star. The morning star sees the morning star. Shakyamuni Buddha sees Shakyamuni Buddha. Seeing sees seeing. When the candle is blown out, Tokusan realizes darkness, the darkness realizes Tokusan, darkness realizes darkness, Tokusan realizes Tokusan.

Now, how do you follow Tozan's instruction to "avoid the reigning monarch's name"? To "name" anything is to categorize, conceptualize, philosophize, intellectualize, and all the other "izes." This is dividing what is indivisible. Through the prajna of equality, you are able "to avoid using the monarch's personal name." A *tacit* understanding suffices.

Good friends, one of the most wonderful illustrations of the "eloquence that surpasses previous dynasties" is the story of Bodhidharma transmitting his, skin, flesh, bones, and marrow:

> He said to his disciples, "The time has come [for me to go back home]. I want each of you to show your understanding."
>
> One disciple, Tao Fu, answered, "According to what I understand, function of the Tao cannot be grasped through literal knowledge, nor is it apart from literal knowledge."
>
> The Master remarked, "You have gained my skin!"
>
> A nun, Tsung Ch'ih, said, "What I understand now is like Ananda's glimpse of the realm of Aksobhya Buddha. It may be seen in oneness, but never in duality."
>
> The Master said, "You have gained my flesh!"
>
> Tao Yu said, "The four great [elements] are originally empty, the five aggregates (physical form, sensation, perception, impulse, and thought) do not exist, and in my comprehension there is not a single thing to be found."
>
> The Master declared, "You have gained my bone!"
>
> Finally Hui K'o bowed, and remained standing at his seat.
>
> The Master said, "You have gained my marrow."[xviii]

Learned audience, the actual realization of emptiness is not what you might imagine. It is not an experience of nothingness or nonexistence. It is the experience of *perfection*. The great scriptures of Buddhism that deal most intensively with the teachings of emptiness are the prajna paramita sutras. Prajna paramita is often translated as "*perfection* of wisdom."

You must remember though, that I am using words to describe something that is finally beyond description. Reality transcends all names and forms. It cannot be described or figured out.

Good friends, when you come to experience this clear vision without doubts, you will find that everything has been okay from the very beginning; in fact, everything has been *perfect*.

The third rank also includes the partial realization of the observing prajna, the vehicle through which enlightened wisdom functions. The prajna of equality can be understood as the cognizing of the *essence* of buddha-nature, while the observing prajna can be understood as the cognizing of the *function* of buddha-nature.

Learned audience, to get a sense of what this 'function of buddha-nature' is, you can look at some of the other terms that have been used to translate the words "observing prajna." It has been translated as "profound observing wisdom" by John Blofeld, "the all-discerning wisdom" by A. F. Price & Wong Mou-lam, and "the subtle observing wisdom" by J.C. Cleary. Thomas Cleary used to translate it as the "subtle analytic knowledge" and has recently translated it as "Observing Cognition." These various translations should give you some understanding as to the implications of this prajna.

This prajna, which is partially realized in the third rank, is the enlightened wisdom that allows you to actualize or be actualized by the wisdom of *upaya*, or skillful means of Zen. That is the knowledge or wisdom of the bodhisattva.

Good friends, the reality that is symbolized by the ideal of the bodhisattva is of the utmost importance to the authentic practice and enlightenment of Zen. Indeed, the ideal of the bodhisattva is a better representation of the Zen ancestors, than even the ideal of the Buddha.

Learned audience, you should remember that Zen is not a school or sect *of* Buddhism, Zen is the authentic transmission of Buddhism itself. It is not my intention to delve into the history of Buddhism or Zen; I only remind you that Zen did not suddenly spring, full-blown, out of the ground. Zen is the natural evolution of a living, dynamic reality. As soon as we try to define it we stop it in its tracks and murder it.

Buddhism, like all living things, *evolves*. All things that evolve leave behind fossils. Some of these fossils continue to function. As the alligator has remained unchanged for eons, so too, some earlier forms of Buddhism. In the cases of both the alligator and the earlier forms of Buddhism, evolution has been arrested. The alligator eats; the 'dust-wiper' escapes the difficulties inherent in the human condition; the 'no enlightenment' Zennist lolls in a dream of self-absorption, and the 'everything is Zen' adherents neglect wisdom and exploit those around them.

Good friends, the vitality of Zen demands evolutionary potential if it is to remain authentic. As one Zen saying goes, "a dragon does not live in stagnant water."

When Baso, noticed that his teaching of 'Mind is Buddha' was becoming stagnant, and students where becoming fixated, he started teaching 'not mind, not buddha'. The genuine masters are always ready to pivot.

Dogen was one master that really knew how to pivot. In some talks, he says that enlightenment is as accessible to the lay Buddhist as it is to the monastic; in others, he says that lay Buddhists have never realized enlightenment. Master Dogen praises Rinzai as a master of the dharma in one text, and chastises him as a fraud in another.

Good friends, these examples are the everyday food and drink of Zen expression. Dogen, like all the great Zen masters, *used words* rather than allowing himself to be used by words. Zen doctrines are often like fingers pointing to the moon. Do not become stuck to the finger and miss the moon. At the same time, do not become attached to the moon and fail to realize the value and significance of the finger. In the end, you may discover that moon and finger are not the same, not different.

Learned audience, let me give you one example of how Zen fossils are created. Dogen, noticing that sitting meditation was being abandoned by droves of monks due to an overemphasis of textual study and intellectual pursuit, vigorously exhorted the practice of zazen. Later, "one method fanatics" used this as an excuse to exclude all other practices. Many fossilized schools of pseudo-Zen are still attached to this teaching.

Good friends, you should know that dogmatically asserting notions of only one right or true lineage or form of practice is false teaching. Being attached to *formal* doctrines or *forms* of practice denies the very reality to which these concepts are trying to direct you. The prajna paramita literature gives clear guidance regarding the authentic buddha-dharma:

> Not in any perfections, not in their name or their form, not in the body of a Bodhisattva, nor in any of the Five Eyes, or the superknowledges, or the eighteen kinds of emptiness; not in Suchness, the Reality limit, nor the Element of Dharma; not in the maturing of beings, the purification of the Buddha-field, nor in skill in means. And why? Because he who could settle down,

or whereby or wherein he could settle down, all these
dharmas do not exist.[xix]

Good friends, the bodhisattva represents the *continual transcendence* of
enlightenment. When you take up Zen, you take up the *Four Great Vows*.
The first great vow is: The many beings are numberless; I vow to save them.
Unless you are truly committed to this task, your practice will not be authentic. One of the ways that you go about the task of saving all beings is by
enacting the third great vow: Dharma-gates are countless; I vow to wake to
them.

Learned audience, as many of you know, the ideal of the bodhisattva is
often used to illustrate the difference between Hinayana and Mahayana
Buddhism. This is accurate as far as it goes; however, there is more to it
than that. According to Zen tradition, the bodhisattva is really the defining
difference between *authentic* Buddhism, and *inauthentic* Buddhism, authentic
Zen, and pseudo-Zen.

Good friends, if you allow yourselves to linger in the realm of the third
rank or prajna of equality, you will fail to enact or be enacted by the wisdom
of the bodhisattva. You will then find yourself in a place that the Zen
masters call a "skull-littered field." You might as well go hide in a cave
somewhere for all the good it would do others or yourselves.

If you continue to cultivate your realization, however, you will begin to
function in harmony with reality. In the rank of Coming from within the
Universal, your observing prajna, also called the buddha-eye or the 'eye to
read scriptures' begins to function. The transmission of the wisdom of
buddhas and Zen ancestors begins to be received by you. Like an old radio,
the signal may at first be weak and scratchy, but as you learn to adjust it, the
transmission becomes clearer.

Good friends, as you approach the fourth rank the wisdom transmitted
through scriptures, koans, treatises, records, living human beings, and the
universe itself becomes the expression of your lives. The expression of this
wisdom is the activity of the bodhisattva.

Having actualized the prajna of equality and realized the essence of
reality, you now begin to awaken to its marvelous *function*. As you apply
yourselves to the teachings of the buddhas and Zen ancestors, you begin
to realize the infinite potential of this vast and fathomless universe. The
fourth of the *Five Ranks* is called Going within Together. The verse for
this rank is:

Ted Biringer

> Two crossed swords, neither permitting retreat:
> Dexterously wielded, like a lotus amidst fire.
> Similarly, there is a natural determination to ascend the
> heavens.[xx]

Learned audience, when the subtle observing prajna begins to manifest with vitality, you have crossed into the fourth rank–Going within Together. Your discernment and insight into the teachings of buddhas and Zen ancestors becomes smooth and powerful. The more wisdom you realize, the greater your capacity to realize wisdom becomes.

Good friends, in the fourth rank the activation of the bodhisattva is in full swing. The "two crossed swords" of Tozan's verse represent the *expression* and *reception* of wisdom, as well as the harmonious dance of emptiness and form, self and other. You are seamlessly engaged with each moment, thing, and event.

Using the power that is actualized through cultivation and realization, the bodhisattva demonstrates a skill as rare as "a lotus amidst fire" and "dexterously wields" the "two crossed swords" in spontaneous action appropriate to the circumstances of the moment. The reality that the metaphor of the "two crossed swords" indicates is sometimes expressed in Zen texts as the "double-edged sword"–the sword that kills, and the sword that gives life. It is the same sword wielded by Manjusri, the bodhisattva of wisdom. In one of the truly great koans, Joshu praises a hermit who wields the double-edged sword:

> Joshu went to the hut of a hermit and called out, "Anybody in, anybody in?"
> The hermit raised one fist. Joshu said, "The water is too shallow for a ship to anchor." Then he left.
> Joshu went to the hut of another hermit and called out, "Anybody in, anybody in?"
> This hermit also raised one fist. Joshu said, "Freely you give, freely you take away, freely you kill, freely you give life." Then he made three bows.

The observing prajna, which becomes fully actualized at the rank of Going within Together, allows you to realize the wisdom of Joshu and the hermits in this koan. In his comment, Wu-men says:

81

If you say that one hermit was superior to the other, you do not yet have the eye of reflective study. And if you say there is no difference between them, you do not yet have the eye of reflective study.[xxi]

Using your "eye of reflective study," or observing prajna, you see Joshu's sword flashing in this koan—as well as the sword of *both* hermits. Not only do you see the sword, you heft it in your own hands. Enlightenment and delusion are fused in the sword that has been sharpened in the forge of buddhas and Zen ancestors. Dogen says it is easy to cut something in two, but difficult to *cut into one*. Emptiness and form are cut into one by the "two crossed swords" which is also the razor-sharp sword of case one hundred in the *Blue Cliff Record*.

> A monk asked Haryo, "What is the razor-sharp sword?"
> Haryo said, "Each branch of coral supports the moon."

How wonderful to discover that you have been using it all along.

Master Tozan went around visiting the teachers of his day after he left his own teacher. He did so to test and sharpen his own realization. When he was taking leave of Nan-yuan, they had the following dialogue:

> Nan-yuan said, "Make a thorough study of the Buddha Dharma, and broadly benefit the world."
> The Master said, "I have no question about studying the Buddha Dharma, but what is it to broadly benefit the world?"
> Nan-yuan said, "Not to disregard a single being."[xxii]

Good friends, as you become more dexterous at wielding this sword, you will discover "a natural determination to ascend the heavens." This inspiration is the inevitable effect of the infusion and activation of buddha-nature.

Your "determination" will manifest as zeal and affirmation for the dharma. This is not the zeal of ambition or personal gain. It is the true joyous realm of what Dogen calls self-fulfilling samadhi. It is the "play" (in both senses of the word) of the universe itself. It is 'dharma enacting dharma'. In the words of the *Large Sutra of Perfection of Wisdom*:

Ted Biringer

> What is the liking for the Dharma? The wish, the
> eagerness for Dharma. What is the delight in Dharma?
> The pleasure in Dharma. What is fondness for Dharma?
> The appreciation of its qualities. What is devotion to
> Dharma? The developing, the making much of that
> Dharma.[xxiii]

Learned audience, this "developing" and "making much of that Dharma" is
the life and death of the unnamable void, the life and death of the universe.
Actualizing your realization, you refine and deepen your realization.

Good friends, you cannot help but rejoice at the freedom and boundless
wealth you will have realized in the fourth rank, yet, another marvel remains
to be discovered. In the borderland of the fourth and fifth ranks, the fourth
and final prajna of Buddhahood–practical prajna–begins to function. This is
the realm of total and absolute liberation. Dogen is indicating this when he
refers to, "When Buddhas are Buddhas, they do not know they are Buddhas."

In practical prajna, wisdom and compassion are *spontaneously* manifested
beyond intention, and convention. The fifth of the *Five Ranks* is called
Arriving within Together. The verse for this rank is:

> Falling into neither existence nor nonexistence, who
> dares harmonize?
> People fully desire to exit the constant flux;
> But after bending and fitting, in the end still return to sit
> in the warmth of the coals.[xxiv]

Learned audience, any comment about the fifth rank–Arriving within
Together–is going to fall far short of the unnamable reality Tozan so elo-
quently expresses. This is the realm of spontaneous, unconventional, absolute reality. Many commentators, in their efforts to explain the unex-
plainable, have missed the mark.

"Falling into neither existence nor nonexistence." With these words,
Tozan takes you into familiar territory–or so it would seem. Then he says,
"Who dares harmonize?" This pitches you out of any conventional understanding. This is the eye of the first line. When you come to realize
"who" would dare to harmonize, both existence and nonexistence will have
melted away like dew before the bright sun.

Good friends, Tozan says, "People fully desire to exit the constant flux." People want enlightenment, salvation, peace, serenity, and on and on. If only they had this or that…If only others would behave properly…If only, If only…

What does all this wanting and wishing finally achieve? "But after bending and fitting…" What is "bending and fitting"? Doing zazen for thirty years! Studying all the *sutras* and *shastras*! Going through the difficult-to-penetrate koans, over and over again! And then what? "…in the end still return to sit in the warmth of the coals." Ahhhh, nice and warm. And some tea too? How lovely.

Learned audience, the true meaning of the often-cited, and widely misunderstood Zen story about the *Three Stages of Mountains and Rivers* is revealed in passages like this. "Before learning Zen, mountains were mountains and rivers were rivers. While studying Zen, mountains were no longer mountains, and rivers were no longer rivers. After learning Zen, mountains are mountains and rivers are rivers." The fifth rank–Arriving within Together–is mountains are mountains and rivers are rivers. This, good friends, is "returning to sit in the warmth of the coals."

Good friends, we should be careful to avoid misunderstanding this. As Dogen says, "These words do not say that 'mountains' are mountains; they say that mountains are mountains."

Yes, this is the realm of "everyday mind" or "ordinary mind," but it is far from "no enlightenment." It includes and transcends both enlightenment *and* no enlightenment. Joshu once asked his teacher, Nansen:

> "What is the Way?"
> Nansen said, "Ordinary mind is the Way."
> The master said, "Then may I direct myself toward it?"
>
> Nansen said, "To seek [it] is to deviate [from it]."
> The master said, "If I do not seek, how can I know about the Way?"
> Nansen said, "The Way does not belong to knowing or not knowing. To know is to have a concept; to not know is to be ignorant. If you truly realize the Way of no doubt, it is just like the sky: wide-open, vast emptiness. How can you say 'yes' or 'no' to it?"
> At these words the master had sudden enlightenment. His mind became like the clear moon.[xxv]

Ordinary mind turns out to be very special. Much later Joshu expressed his gratitude for Nansen's introduction to it:

> The master asked Nansen, "Where does a person who knows what there is to know go to?"
> Nansen said, "They go to be a water buffalo at the house of a lay person at the foot of the mountain."
> The master said, "I am grateful for your instruction."
> Nansen said, "At midnight last night, the moonlight came through the window."[xxvi]

Learned audience, was this moonlight ordinary moonlight or divine moonlight? Perhaps Joshu can shed some light on this for you:

> A monk said, "In the day there is sunlight, at night there is firelight. What is 'divine light'?"
> The master said, "Sunlight, firelight."[xxvii]

Good friends, the warmth of the coals is a nice cozy place to be.

The fifth rank transcends knowing and not knowing, practice and realization, Buddha and Zen. You have done your work, 'bending and fitting' and you are ready to go to the bottom of the mountain and become water buffaloes. Does a water buffalo know it is helping others? Does it know when it is helping itself? A water buffalo water buffalos a water buffalo.

Do you want to know where Joshu and Nansen are now? They are Arriving within Together. Arriving within what? A water buffalo. Where does a water buffalo flow forth from? How long does it last? Can a water buffalo be used up? Master Engo responds to all these questions:

> Everywhere everything becomes its Great Function, and every single thing flows forth from your own breast. The ancients called this *bringing out the family treasure*. Once this is attained, it is attained forever. How could it ever be used up?[xxviii]

Chapter 6:
Final Instructions

Louie Wing said, "Sometimes the sages compare the pure and clear, luminous awareness of your true mind to a still pool or a clear mirror; it reflects all things as they are, without changing its essential nature. This is true as far as it goes; yet, the luminous awareness of your own mind is much grander than a still pool or a clear mirror.

Once your mind has reflected something you are able to recall it at will, even years later. How marvelous! Moreover, though a mirror can perfectly reflect the pages of a novel, only the human mind can conceive a character there. How many times has Captain Ahab's wooden leg thudded across the wooden decks of human minds? Not to mention the human mind that put Ahab's leg into that book in the first place. A mirror can reflect as many wolves as are presented to it, yet only human minds can work and accomplish the task of reintroducing them into the wild. A still pond can perfectly reflect a Bald Eagle soaring above it, but only a human mind can go 'ah'!"

—From the collected Sayings and Doings of Louie Wing

On the morning of June 21, 2007, Louie Wing sat upright on the flatbed and asked the assembly to gather in close around him.

He then said, "Long ago I borrowed the elements that make up this massive body, now in gratitude I will return them. "First, I want to tell you all a wonderful secret. Are you listening?"

The assembly quietly responded, "Yes, we are listening."

Louie Wing said, "It is this…"

As the students leaned in, Louie Wing said, "The moon, the trees." As he finished speaking, he closed his eyes and passed away. He was 52 years old.

Part II
Commentaries of Louie Wing:
A Deeper Examination of Zen

Commentary 1:
The *Genjokoan*

Louie Wing said, "There is a common misunderstanding about spiritual practice and worldly activity. Many people say that worldly activity is a hindrance to spiritual practice. Alternatively, some people say that worldly activity teaches you spiritual practice. What do you think about that? I say, worldly activity is you teaching yourself spiritual practice. What have you been teaching yourself?"
—From the collected Sayings and Doings of Louie Wing

The celebrated *Genjokoan* is one of the most widely known and highly praised essays of the thirteenth-century Japanese Zen master Dogen. There is a very good reason for this; *Genjokoan*, literally meaning "actualization of the fundamental point," is a masterpiece of Zen expression.

One thing that places Dogen in the company of the greatest of Zen masters is his magnificent skill for Zen expression. Few masters before—and none since—have matched his skill for expressing the profound and subtle wisdom of the enlightened mind. Two of his early predecessors, Tozan and his disciple Sozan, earn their inclusion among these few through their elucidation of the classic Zen teaching of the *Five Ranks*.

The doctrine expressed as the *Five Ranks* is one of the most influential Zen expressions of all time. The subject of that doctrine—the function and essence of the enlightened mind—is, and has always been, the summum bonum of Buddhism. Every genuine Buddhist expression is grounded on this central principal. The presentation of this principal by Tozan, further refined by Sozan as the *Five Ranks,* marks one point where the expression of the central truth of Buddhism *evolved.*

Dogen's *Shobogenzo* marks another such point.

Dogen's genius for expression is displayed nowhere better than in *Shobogenzo, Genjokoan.* His views, on every major aspect of the buddha-dharma, are revealed, either explicitly or implicitly, in this extraordinary essay. *Genjokoan* is a skeleton key that can be used to unlock the *Shobogenzo,* literally "Treasury of the True Dharma-Eye."

The opening lines of *Genjokoan* outline the fundamental aspects of reality: the interdependence and interpenetrating aspects of the one and the many, the individual and the universal.

> When all things are seen as the buddha-dharma, then there is delusion and enlightenment, there is practice, there is life and there is death, there are buddhas and there are ordinary beings.

This line affirms the relative aspect of reality. Here, "the buddha-dharma" denotes all-inclusive reality. "When all things are seen as the buddha-dharma" indicates one way of perceiving the buddha-dharma (reality). In this way of perceiving the buddha-dharma, "all things" (the myriad dharmas) are seen. That is, reality appears as a multitude of separate individual things. From this perspective of reality, there is "delusion and enlightenment, there is practice, there is life and there is death, there are buddhas and there are ordinary beings." There are people, animals, houses, stars, and all the other kinds of things.

Dogen, more than most Zen masters, delves deeply into the implications of this aspect of reality. While many Zen masters and Buddhist texts give short shrift to the relative aspect of experience, often simply dismissing it as the experience of delusion, Dogen methodically articulates how this aspect of reality *affirms* the ultimate significance of every particular thing. The *Shobogenzo* repeatedly directs us to this truth; because everything is the buddha-dharma, the buddha-dharma is every *thing.* For Dogen, *every* thing has ultimate significance as the buddha-dharma; including even such things as broken tiles, pebbles, dreams, illusions, and doubts.

The next lines of the *Genjokoan* read:

Ted Biringer

> When all things are seen as empty of self, there is no
> delusion and no enlightenment, no buddhas and no or-
> dinary beings, no life and no death.

These lines acknowledge the truth of the universal or empty aspect of reality. "When all things are seen as empty of self" refers to another way of perceiving the buddha-dharma (reality). The experience of reality from this perspective is the experience of absolute oneness. In the experience of oneness, there are no separate individual things; the buddha-dharma is totally undifferentiated. From this perspective, all things (the myriad dharmas) cease to appear as distinct entities (empty of self) and are there-fore *not* distinguishable as things. That is to say, oneness is truly oneness, without anything left over. When there is no-thing that can be distinguished from any other thing, "there is no delusion and no enlightenment, no buddhas and no ordinary beings, no life and no death." There are no people, no animals, no houses, no stars, or any other *particular* things.

In the *Shobogenzo*, Dogen reveals the meaning of this aspect of reality in some startling and ingenious ways. Without resorting to innuendo or "mystical" language he exposes the truth of the universal nature of emp-tiness, or the void, excepting nothing, not even emptiness itself. Dogen, perhaps more than any other Zen master, makes *rational* the profound rationale of the truth of emptiness, making the emptiness of *emptiness* as self-evident as the emptiness of form.

The *Genjokoan* continues:

> Buddha's truth includes and transcends the many
> and the one, and so there is life and death, delusion and
> enlightenment, ordinary beings and buddhas.

The *Buddha's truth* is not in reality divided into *the many* (the myriad dharmas) and *the one* but includes and transcends both. Since the Buddha's truth (true nature of reality) is all-inclusive, there is "life and death, delusion and enlightenment, ordinary beings and buddhas." There are people, ani-mals, houses, stars, and all the other particular things.

The point Dogen makes in this short line, forms the topic of thousands of pages of Buddhist literature. It is also the subject of the most popular Mahayana Buddhist scripture, The *Heart Sutra*. The *Heart Sutra* was the subject of the very first commentary Dogen wrote for the *Shobogenzo: Sho-*

93

bogenzo, Maka-Hannya-Haramitsu, the second or third thing he wrote upon his return from China. Though commentaries on emptiness are myriad, the profound implications of this sublime doctrine are extremely subtle and difficult to penetrate. Dogen's illumination on the topic of emptiness is extraordinarily clear, provocative, and *evocative.*

Dogen's expressions in the first three sections of *Genjokoan* are a succinct overview of the nature of the universe; first as perceived from the contrasting perspectives of the universal and the individual, then as transcending those perspectives. Transcending these opposing perspectives is sometimes referred to as the mutual interpenetrating and non-obstruction of the one and the many where each thing and event, and all things and events, contain, and are contained by, each other. This is expressed in the Buddhist literature by the doctrines of form and emptiness, the particular and the absolute, the universal and the individual, and so on. This mutually inclusive aspect of the one and the many is expressed in Zen koans in an intimate and direct manner; for instance, in the classic koan, Two Monks Roll Up the Blinds:

> Master Hogen raised his hand and pointed to the
> blinds. Two monks went and rolled them up in the same
> way. Hogen said, "One gains, one loses."

Upon resolution of this koan, you will intimately realize that master Hogen's words "One gains, one loses" apply to each of the two monks. Indeed, his words apply to *every* thing and event in all of time and space.

Throughout his works, Dogen consistently affirms the vital position of verbal expression in the buddha-dharma (the authentic teaching of Buddhism), and at the same time, clearly defines its limitations. The next line of *Genjokoan* is one of the finest examples of this.

> And though it is like this, it is simply that flowers,
> while loved, fall; and weeds, while hated, flourish.

This line may be the most direct expression in the whole *Shobogenzo.* It may also be the most misunderstood. It is often interpreted as a simile, which completely misses, and even subverts the point Dogen is making. In fact, Dogen points out that the *previous* three points are similes with the words, "And though it is *like* this." In this line, he points out that reality is not *like* anything: it is simply reality; that is, "flowers fall...weeds flourish."

This teaching corresponds with the true meaning of the often-quoted Zen dictum "a separate transmission outside the scriptures, not dependent on words and letters." This does not mean that Zen disregards scriptures and texts, but that the reality the scriptures indicate is separate from the scriptures themselves, and not dependent on the words and letters that are used to indicate it.

Zen teachings require you to see into and through the words, while avoiding becoming attached to the words. You cannot "learn" Zen through reading and study, but you cannot disregard reading and study either. To use an analogy: reading a recipe for chocolate cake will not result in producing a chocolate cake—you must possess the ingredients and follow the instructions. At the same time, simply possessing the ingredients without the knowledge provided by the recipe will not do either.

In the first three statements, Dogen illustrates what reality is *like*; in this line, he presents it more directly, "and though *it* is like this, *it* is only that flowers, while loved, fall; and weeds while hated, flourish." This kind of expression, common in Zen literature, is meant to convey the truth that reality or enlightenment is not produced by words, knowledge or even spiritual practice; reality is reality, as it is here and now.

After laying the foundation in the first four lines of *Genjokoan*, Dogen methodically builds the structural framework upon which he spent the rest of his life fleshing out: the function and essence of "the rightly-transmitted buddha-dharma."

Next, the *Genjokoan* begins an examination of delusion and enlightenment:

> That people drive the self to actualize awareness of
> the many things is delusion. That the many things actu-
> alize awareness of the self is enlightenment.

Here Dogen gives a precise definition of the important Buddhist concepts of delusion and enlightenment, outlining their most basic aspects with clear precision. Delusion or enlightenment is what distinguishes a "buddha" from an "ordinary being." A buddha is someone who is enlightened about delusion, that is, to the reality of his or her own true nature. An ordinary being is someone who is deluded about enlightenment (the reality of his or her own true nature). Because delusion and enlightenment are nondual, meaning they are not two separate, independent entities, we come to the understanding that differences between them are differences of perspective only.

First Dogen says, "That people drive the self to actualize awareness of the many things is delusion." The very idea that you can "drive the self" to enlightenment implies that you must be experiencing your self as separate from enlightenment. Because in reality you are both separate and not separate from the many things, experiencing your self as only separate is delusion.

Awakening to the truth that "the many things actualize awareness of the self" is the function of Zen practice; your true nature is the true nature of the universe. The Buddhist formula for salvation, liberation, enlightenment, or any of the other terms used to indicate the ultimate truth of religion consists of personally realizing that you are one with all things including both enlightenment and delusion. Continuing on, the *Genjokoan* states:

> Those who are enlightened about delusion are buddhas.

In the *Shobogenzo*, being "enlightened about delusion" means awakening to the *reality* of delusion. That is, realizing what delusion truly is. It is like when, for example, a person is shown the cause of a magician's illusions: mirrors, wires, hidden compartments, and so on. The person can then grasp the *reality* of the illusion. The reality of the illusion, the mirrors, wires, hidden compartments, is *existent*, and the illusion is a real *characteristic* of its existence. Similarly, when you realize the cause of delusion: misperception or partial perception, of true nature, you realize the *reality* of delusion. The reality of delusion, misperception or partial perception of our own true nature is existent, and delusion is a *real* characteristic of its existence. Those who are "enlightened about" this are called "buddhas."

Next, the *Genjokoan* says:

> Those who are deluded about enlightenment are ordinary beings.

To be "deluded about enlightenment" is to view enlightenment as being something outside or apart from you or the everyday world. This is not a judgmental statement; it is a simple observation. When you are aware of your true nature, you are called buddhas; when you are unaware of your true nature, you are called ordinary beings. Flowers fall, weeds flourish; cocks crow, dogs bark. The *Genjokoan* goes on:

> There are people who continue to realize enlight-
> enment based on enlightenment.

Dogen's emphasis on post-kensho practice and enlightenment is rarely matched in Zen literature. He insists that attaining enlightenment is just the beginning of genuine practice and enlightenment. In fact, enlightenment for Dogen is only authentic as practice *and* enlightenment. In all his works, he repeatedly urges you to realize enlightenment *based upon* enlightenment, often using the Zen ancestors of the past as examples of how to approach the lifetime process of deepening and refining your realization. The *Genjokoan* continues:

> There are people in the midst of delusion adding to
> delusion.

Dogen is not simply repeating his previous point but indicating something else. In *Shobogenzo, Keisei-Sanshiki*, Dogen uses the same phrase in a manner that suggests its deeper implication:

> When [a person] tells people who do not know the
> will to the truth about the will to the truth, the good
> advice offends their ears, and so they do not reflect upon
> themselves, but [only] bear resentment towards the
> other person. As a general rule concerning actions and
> vows, which are the bodhi-mind, we should not intend
> to let worldly people know whether or not we have es-
> tablished the bodhi-mind or whether or not we are
> practicing the truth; we should endeavor to be unknown.
> How much less could we boast about ourselves? Be-
> cause people today rarely seek what is real, when the
> praises of others are available, they seem to want
> someone to say that their practice and understanding
> have become harmonized, even though there is no
> practice in their body, and no realization in their mind.

"In delusion adding to delusion" describes exactly this.[xxiv]

In this passage, Dogen defines the condition of "increasing delusion in the midst of delusion" as the *denial* of delusion. That is to say, when people in delusion deny they are deluded (or assert they are enlightened) they are "in delusion *adding to* delusion."

Looking at case one of the *Blue Cliff Record* can shed some light on this particular condition. The koan reads:

> Emperor Wu asked Bodhidharma, "What is the ul-
> timate meaning of the holy truths?"
> Bodhidharma said, "Vast emptiness, nothing holy."
> The Emperor asked, "Who is facing me?"
> Bodhidharma responded, "I don't know."
> The Emperor did not understand. After this Bo-
> dhidharma crossed the Yangtse River and traveled to the
> kingdom of Wei.
> Later the Emperor asked Master Chih about it.
> Master Chih asked, "Do you know who this man is?"
> The Emperor said, "I don't know."
> Master Chih said, "He is the great bodhisattva,
> Avalokitesvara, transmitting the confirmation of the
> buddha-mind."
> The Emperor was regretful and wanted to send an
> envoy to bring Bodhidharma back.
> Master Chih said, "Don't say you will send someone
> to bring him back. Even if everyone in China went after
> him, he would not return."

Commenting on the line "The Emperor did not understand," Engo says, "Too bad! Still, he's gotten somewhere." The meaning of Engo's comment, "Still, he's gotten somewhere," illumines what Dogen means by "in delusion adding to delusion." In following the reasoning here, Emperor Wu was "adding to delusion" when he *thought he knew* something (asserted his enlightenment). However, (although he is still in delusion) after his meeting with Bodhidharma, he admits that he does "not understand," that is, he does not *deny his own delusion.* The Emperor is in delusion (not enlightened), but he is no longer *adding* to delusion (by asserting his enlightenment).

Recognizing and acknowledging the reality of your own delusion is a prerequisite to enlightenment. For arousing the necessary will for enlightenment is only possible when you recognize and acknowledge your own delusion. For Dogen, recognition and acknowledgement of your delusion is simultaneous with enlightenment. Throughout the *Shobogenzo*, Dogen remains ever-aware of the nondual nature of delusion and enlightenment. For as we read above, buddhas are those "who are enlightened about delusion." Dogen does not say that buddhas are *free* from delusion, as is sometimes proclaimed by people without a clear understanding of Zen.

The *Genjokoan* goes on to say:

> When buddhas are buddhas, they do not know they are buddhas.

This line points out that when buddhas are experiencing the condition of Buddhahood, there is nothing but Buddha in the whole universe. This is the condition that is sometimes described in Buddhist literature as the state where the *known* and the *knower* (or actor and action) are one. Obviously, for a buddha to have the thought, "I am a buddha," they would have to perceive themselves as something (buddha) in opposition to something else (not buddha), hence; they would not be in the condition of Buddhahood. That does not mean there are no buddhas, as the *Genjokoan* points out next:

> Nevertheless, buddhas are buddhas and continuously actualize Buddhahood.

The condition of Buddhahood is not something that is *gained*, but something that is discovered and activated; that is, the nature of delusion is illumined and your original Buddhahood is *realized*. Of course, this experience is only called Buddhahood to differentiate it from delusion. When you speak of a state beyond delusion you call it "Buddhahood." However, in the absolute sense, as in Dogen's opening lines to *Genjokoan*, there is nothing to be grasped (no buddhas, no ordinary beings, etc.) and in the transcendent sense, buddhas and ordinary beings always contain and include each other.

In the actual experience of Buddhahood all names and labels are meaningless; for from the perspective of oneness or emptiness, *differentiation* does not exist. Even "oneness" is a relative term—that is, oneness is relative and only valid in contrast to multiplicity. Therefore, when differentiation is truly dissolved so, too, is oneness or Buddhahood.

One wonderful Zen expression of this principle is a verse attributed to Ananda, one of Buddha's disciples and the traditional Second Ancestor of Zen in India:

> When we are awake to the truth, even the non-
> dharma does not exist.[xxx]

The simple fact that the *Genjokoan* goes to such lengths to describe the nature and actual experience of Buddhahood is enough to put Dogen in a very exclusive minority. When the experience of Buddhahood *is* described, it is usually simply described as "indescribable." In *Genjokoan*, Dogen not only describes characteristics like "buddhas do not know they are buddhas" and that buddhas "continuously actualize Buddhahood," he also describes *why* and *how* that is. The *Genjokoan* explains:

> Mustering the whole body-and-mind to look at
> forms, and mustering the whole body-and-mind to listen
> to sounds, they perceive them directly; not like an image
> reflected in a mirror, and not like the reflection of the
> moon on water.

This is a description of the condition called Buddhahood. "Buddha" describes a person in the activity or condition of authentic practice and enlightenment, the deeper meaning of zazen. The keystone of Zen practice is not "sitting meditation" (though that is where it is often first discovered), it is "mustering the whole body-and-mind" and perceiving the world directly.

Seeing and hearing (as well as smelling, tasting, feeling, and thinking) sights and sounds (smells, tastes, sensations, and thoughts) with the 'whole body-and-mind' means truly being one with them. When you are truly one with them, there is no sense of *I* see that or *I* hear that. Hence, buddhas do not know they are buddhas. "It is not like an image reflected in a mirror, and not like the reflection of the moon on water" because there are not two things (e.g. moon *and* water). When you are authentically engaged in practice and enlightenment you do not hear a bell, there is simply, *booooonngg–boooooongg*. The classic Zen koan about escaping heat and cold illustrates this point wonderfully:

> A monk asked Tozan, "When cold and heat come, how can we avoid them?"
>
> Tozan said, "Why don't you go to the place where there is no cold or heat?"
>
> The monk said, "What is the place where there is no cold or heat?"
>
> Tozan said, "When it's cold, the cold kills you; when it's hot, the heat kills you."

This is not advice to "accept" your situation, as some commentators have suggested, but a direct expression of authentic practice and enlightenment. Master Tozan is not saying, "When cold, shiver; when hot, sweat," nor is he saying, "When cold, put on a sweater; when hot, use a fan." In the state of authentic practice and enlightenment, the cold kills you, and there is only cold in the whole universe. The heat kills you, and there is only heat in the whole universe. The fragrance of incense kills you, and there is only the fragrance of incense in the whole universe. The sound of the bell kills you, and there is only *"boooong"* in the whole universe.

This is the true significance of Dogen's notion of zazen. In spite of the convoluted arguments by some pseudo-Zennists, Dogen's use of the term "zazen" is not simply concerned with your physical posture, but with mustering your whole body-and-mind. Sitting in a meditation posture without mustering your whole body-and-mind is not zazen; brushing your teeth or raking leaves while mustering your whole body-and-mind is zazen. Dogen often refers to this state or condition as nonthinking, and sometimes as no-mind. When you have become proficient at this, all places and times are illuminated by the power of zazen.

Dogen was once asked, "What is Buddha?" He replied by directly indicating the realm of seeing and hearing while mustering the whole body-and-mind:

> Someone [in the assembly] asked, "What is Buddha?"
>
> The teacher Dogen said, "Finally, future births are prevented with the special attainment of cessation not arising through analysis."
>
> The monk said, "Master, don't teach people using Lesser Vehicle Dharma."

Dogen said, "I am not teaching people using Lesser Vehicle Dharma."

The monk asked: "What is Buddha?"

The teacher Dogen said, "Finally, future births are prevented with the special attainment of cessation not arising through analysis."

Then Dogen said, "Heaven is not high; the earth is not dense. Mountains and rivers, and the sun and moon, are not separated. The radiant light of each place penetrates each place. A Persian riding on a white elephant enters the Buddha hall; Handan people with bare feet circumambulate the monks' hall. What principle can we rely on to be like this?"

After a pause Dogen said, "The bright moon follows someone as if there were a reason. Naturally white clouds provide rain with no mind."[xxxi]

Next, the *Genjokoan* presents the experiential realm of true zazen:

As one side is revealed, the other side is concealed.

In Hee-Jin Kim's *Mystical Realist*, this line is translated as, "As one side is illumined, the other is darkened."[xxxii] The implications of this simple statement run deep. In the opening lines of *Genjokoan* Dogen treated us to some of the practical, experiential implications of this through three perspectives of reality: the relative, the empty, and the all-inclusive. Each one of these perspectives is a real aspect of the universe. All three of them are complete and simultaneous; they are interdependent and non-obstructive. When one of these aspects is revealed, the others are concealed. When "cold" (one side) is revealed, "hot" (the other side) is concealed. Using Kim's translation we could paraphrase thus: "as cold is illumined, hot is darkened." This does not mean that "hot" is not present or does not exist; on the contrary, it makes "hot" an essential aspect of cold. Not only "hot," but also everything else in time and space are included within "cold" (or any other experience of seeing, hearing, etc. with whole body-and-mind).

Next, the *Genjokoan* brings us to the whole point of practice and enlightenment:

Ted Biringer

To realize the buddha-dharma is to realize your self.

This is the fundamental point of Zen. Buddhism is not about a teacher or holy man of long ago and far away, it is not about metaphysical doctrines, it has nothing to do with objective knowledge; it is about you, a real, live human being here and now. Enlightenment, wisdom, Buddhahood, Zen, true-nature, etc. are provisional terms employed for directing you to the truth about yourself. "Buddha" is simply a term for an awakened human being. If there is one thing that all the great Zen masters agree on, it is that buddha is not separate from ordinary people. In order to illustrate the high level of conformity by the Zen masters on this point, I will cite a number of examples from the classic Zen Records:

> Through endless kalpas without beginning, whatever you do, wherever you are, that's your real mind, that's your real buddha. *This mind is buddha* says the same thing. Beyond this mind you'll never find another buddha.
> —Bodhidharma[xxxiii]

> You should know that so far as buddha-nature is concerned, there is no difference between an enlightened man and an ignorant one.
> —Eno[xxxiv]

> You have always been one with the Buddha, so do not pretend you can *ATTAIN* to this oneness by various practices.
> —Obaku[xxxv]

> If you want to be no different from the patriarchs and buddhas, then never look for something outside yourselves.
> —Rinzai[xxxvi]

> This real Buddha is none other than the heart of all beings, the master of seeing, hearing, and perceiving.
> —Bassui[xxxvii]

103

After reminding us that "To realize the buddha-dharma is to realize your self," the *Genjokoan* tells us what it means to "realize our self":

> To realize your self is to forget your self.

Learning the Buddha's truth (your truth) is to *forget* your self. Forgetting your self is what occurs when you truly achieve mustering your whole body-and-mind, which is zazen, the keystone of Zen. In his works, Dogen uses a number of terms and phrases to refer to this forgetting; besides 'mustering your whole body-and-mind' he uses 'casting off body-and-mind', 'no-mind', 'nonthinking', 'the still-still state', and a variety of similar terms. This is why he said that in the experience of Buddhahood, there is no sense of being Buddha. When you forget the self, grasping and aversion no longer bind you to abstract notions and conceptualizations. Theories, concepts, and knowledge are then seen and utilized within their proper sphere and context, not as unbending metaphysical laws, but as rational and dynamic methodological principles for living in the real world. This kind of "forgetting," says the *Genjokoan*, reveals a fascinating implication:

> To forget your self is to be actualized by the many things.

A skier mustering whole body-and-mind, totally absorbed in the activity of skiing down a mountain, forgets his or her "self" and is actualized by the myriad dharmas (the many things). With no ideas of self and not self, there is simply *swoosh, swoosh, chunk, swoosh, swoosh*. There is no "snow" there is *whiteness, coldness*. There are no "sounds" there is *shoo, shoo, tweet, weeee!* There is no "thinking" there is *left, right, straight, watch out*. In *Shobogenzo, Hossho*, Dogen gives us a delightful expression of this experience:

> In the Dharma-nature there is no "non-Buddhist" or "demon," but only "Come for breakfast! Come for lunch! And come for tea!"[xxxviii]

The *Genjokoan* continues:

> To be actualized by the many things is to allow the body-and-mind of your self and the body-and-mind of other than your self to fall away.

This expression reveals the essence and function of the universal mirror prajna, the dynamic quality of immediate awareness in the present moment. When the body-and-mind of "your self" and the body-and-mind of "other than your self" both fall away, there is only, "Come for breakfast! Come for lunch! And come for tea!" This is why people often laugh upon their initial enlightenment experience; all along your inherent awareness, that is, your buddha-nature or true-nature, has been functioning perfectly. A couple explanations from Zen literature may help to clarify the meaning of this:

> Q: What is implied by 'seeing into the real Nature'?
> A: That Nature and your perception of it are one. You cannot use it to see something over and above it-self.
> —Obaku[xxxix]

> The nature of perception being eternal, we go on perceiving whether objects are present or not. Thereby we come to understand that, whereas objects naturally appear and disappear, the nature of perception does neither of those things; and, it is the same with all your other senses.
> —Daibai[xl]

One Buddhist scripture, the *Surangama Sutra,* contains a passage that presents this point so directly that it is included as case ninety-four of the *Blue Cliff Record*:

> The *Surangama* scripture says, "When I do not see, why do you not see my not seeing? If you see my not seeing, naturally that is not the characteristic of not seeing. If you do not see my not seeing, it is naturally not a thing—how could it not be you?"
> —*The Blue Cliff Record*

The Rinzai Zen master, Hakuin, comments on this koan in part:

> Because it is not a thing, it must be your own awakened mind. The realm that is not a thing is your true

vision; true vision is your essential nature. That's the message.[xli]

The Soto Zen master, Tenkei, comments in part on the same case:

> The point is that of all the myriad things, none is not you. You are you; I am I. One can only know oneself. That's what this means.[xlii]

Dogen's words "To be actualized by the many things" are an original and marvelous expression of the same truth that Master Tenkei makes here as "of all the myriad things, none is not you."

Now the *Genjokoan* explains:

> All traces of enlightenment fall away, and the falling away of all traces of enlightenment is continuous.

Dogen is here expanding on the point he alluded to earlier with the words "There are people who continue to realize enlightenment based on enlightenment." Realization of enlightenment is not a static event but a vigorous, dynamic condition of continuous manifestation. On the authentic Zen path of practice and enlightenment, each moment is experienced as the continuous unfolding of the entire universe, perpetually fresh. Engo calls this "continuous awareness from mind-moment to mind-moment":

> When there is continuous awareness from mind-moment to mind-moment that does not leave anything out, and mundane reality and enlightened reality are not separate, then you will naturally become pure and fully ripe and meet the Source on all sides.
> —Engo[xliii]

Compare these words with Dogen's own wonderful expression in *Shobogenzo, Gyobutsu Yuigi*:

> [To research] this truth of moment-by-moment utter entrustment, we must research the mind. In the mountain-still state of such research, we discern and under-

stand that ten thousand efforts are [each] the mind being evident, and the triple world is just that which is greatly removed from the mind. This discernment and understanding, while also of the myriad real dharmas, activate the homeland of the self. They make immediate and concrete the vigorous state of the human being in question.[xliv]

No thing, event, or experience can escape the momentary nature of existence. Dogen points out in his essay *Shobogenzo, Uji* (being time) that one quality of time is its ever-changing flow. He says:

The entire world is not unchangeable, is not immovable. It flows.[xlv]

Dogen expresses the ever-changing, ever-renewing aspect of reality throughout his works in startlingly provocative and creative ways. For example, in his essay, *Shobogenzo, Tsuki,* Dogen says you should master in practice the fact that tonight's moon is not yesterday's moon:

So although the moon was there last night, tonight's moon is not yesterday's moon. We should master in practice that the moon tonight, at the beginning, middle, and end, is the moon tonight. Because the moon succeeds the moon, the moon exists and yet is not new or old.[xlvi]

At the same time, Dogen reveals that the very fact of its momentary existence demonstrates its inevitability, that is to say, its *inevitable* existence as an aspect of the whole of time and space (being time).

Each moment is all being, is the entire world. Reflect now whether any being or any world is left out of the present moment.[xlvii]

With the body-and-mind of self and other cast off (in nonthinking or forgetting the self) each moment is experienced as *all being,* "the entire world with nothing left out of the present moment." Each moment, each thing, including even such things as *worry*, and *surprise* contain and are contained by the whole of time and space. According to Dogen, "there are myriads of forms and myriads of grasses throughout the entire earth, and yet each grass and each form itself is the entire earth.

> "Even worry itself is just *the matter which is it,* and so it is beyond worry. Again, we should not be surprised that *the matter which is it* is present in such a state. Even if *it* is the object of surprise and wonderment, it is still just *it.* And there is it about which we should not be surprised."[xlviii]

The *Genjokoan* continues:

> The first moment you seek the dharma you are far removed from the environs of dharma. The first moment of true dharma transmission your originally-true nature is realized.

These two lines need to be read in the context of the Zen teachings of original (or sudden) enlightenment and acquired (or gradual) enlightenment.

Nearly all schools of Mahayana Buddhism, including Zen, affirm that all beings are originally Buddha, and ultimately there is really nothing to attain. Accordingly, the Zen masters often point out that to actively *seek* enlightenment is, itself, a barrier *to* enlightenment.

Herein lies the crux of the problem. On the one hand, if you are already buddhas, what need is there for practice? On the other hand, if practice is the cause of Buddhahood, what do the Zen ancestors mean when they say you already are buddhas? It is precisely the apparent contradiction of these two Zen axioms ("there is nothing to seek" and "you must strive diligently") that Dogen resolves with these lines.

The first line, "The first moment you seek the dharma, you are far removed from the environs of dharma," simply points out the fact that if you are *seeking* it (the dharma, truth of reality), you are obviously *unaware* (far removed from) of it.

To "seek the dharma," which is always immediately present, is like looking for your glasses, unaware that you are, in fact, *wearing* your glasses. It is only the *notion* that your glasses are somewhere else (which is delusion) that causes you to be "far removed from the environs of dharma" (deluded).

Yet, at the very "first moment of true dharma transmission your originally-true nature is realized" is what you discover or uncover upon your initial insight (kensho) into reality; your buddha-nature or true-nature has been immediately present ("originally") all along.

When you realize you have been looking for your glasses while you were wearing them, you realize that you have been looking *for* your glasses *with* your glasses. There has never been any real separation–only a confused assumption (the confused assumption, "I am not Buddha," or "My glasses are somewhere else").

In the next section of *Genjokoan*, Dogen amplifies the implications of the doctrine that delusion is not actually separate from enlightenment, but merely a *confused assumption* based on a partial (hence inaccurate) perception.

> A person sailing along in a boat looking at the shore might have the illusion that the shore is moving. However, if they look closely at the boat they realize the boat is moving. Similarly, when they try to understand the many things based on deluded notions about body-and-mind they might have the illusion that their minds or nature are stationary. However, if they step back into fundamental awareness they realize nothing has a fixed self.

Here, Dogen uses a simile to illustrate how delusion acts. The illusion that the shore is moving, when seen from a boat, can be quite convincing. If, however, you pay close attention to the facts, "look closely at the boat," you will realize the truth that "the boat is moving."

"Similarly," he says, "when they try to understand the many things based on deluded notions about body-and-mind they might have the illusion that their minds or nature are stationary." If you pay close attention to the facts, "step back into fundamental awareness," through Zen practice and enlightenment, you will see through this illusion (be enlightened about delusion). The truth will become obvious and you will "realize nothing has a fixed self" (all things are empty, equal, one, void).

The particular deluded notion here, that your "mind or nature is stationary," indicates the confused assumption of yourself as a separate, *inde-*

pendent entity. Of course, even science recognizes the fallacy of a being that is independent of its environment, but even with an intellectual grasp of this point the illusion can be very convincing. The first step on the Zen path of practice and enlightenment is to see through this delusion, in the *Gen-jokoan's* terms, to "become enlightened about delusion." This does not mean *eradicating* delusion; because of the nonduality of delusion and enlightenment, that would also eradicate enlightenment. In order to see through such mistaken views, Dogen recommends "dropping off body-and-mind" (forgetting the self, letting the body-and-mind of self and other fall away):

> My late teacher Tiantong [Rujing] said, "Sanzen (practicing Zen or zazen) is dropping off body and mind." Already having dropped body and mind, definitely you will not have mistaken views, attachments or arrogance. I sincerely pray on behalf of all of you."[xlix]

Even the words "mistaken views," however, can become an object of attachment, and ultimately become a mistaken view of its own. As Dogen stated earlier, buddhas do not need to "know they are buddhas." Any view, if taken as absolute truth, is a mistaken view. Zen master Hogen expresses this point succinctly:

> What is disturbing you and making you uneasy is that there are things outside and mind inside. Therefore even when the ordinary and the holy are one reality, there still remains a barrier of view. So it is said that as long as views remain you are ordinary; when feelings are forgotten you're a buddha. I advise you, don't seek reality, just stop views.[l]

Next, the *Genjokoan* proclaims:

> Firewood becomes ash; it can never go back to being firewood. Nevertheless, you should not take the view that ash is its future and firewood is its past. Remember that firewood abides in the dharma position of firewood. It has a past and it has a future.

Here Dogen uses an analogy of firewood and ash to illustrate the interdependence and non-obstruction of things *and* times. He begins with, "Firewood becomes ash; it can never go back to being firewood." This affirms your everyday experience; a child becomes an adult, and cannot become a child again, an apple blossom becomes an apple, and cannot become a blossom again, and so on.

Next, he says, "Nevertheless, we should not take the view that ash is its future and firewood is its past." The reason he says you should not take this view is that it posits an *independent* entity, something with a *separate* "self." In this wrong view, "it" was firewood, and now "it" is ash; but in reality, there is no-thing to call "it."

Dogen is not saying that firewood and ash are *nonexistent.* "Remember that firewood abides in the dharma position of firewood." What is called "firewood" is a provisional name for one particular aspect of all-inclusive space and time. Accordingly, the quality of firewood is both "particular" *and* "all-inclusive." As "tonight's moon is not yesterday's moon," today's ash is not yesterday's ash, much less yesterday's firewood. That which is called "firewood" at any particular space and time, is simply that particular aspect of all of space and time.

Accordingly, "It has a past and it has a future." If you look deeply at the *firewood of today* from the perspective of emptiness (equality, oneness, the absolute, etc.) you realize that it is *one particular aspect* of *all* space and time. Its non-separation with all of space and time necessarily includes all things and times in the past, present, and future. For instance, the *firewood of today* necessarily includes *the firewood of yesterday,* and *the firewood of yesterday,* has to include *the firewood of today.* Since it is so, the firewood of yesterday could not have *become* the firewood of today, because then the firewood of yesterday could not be *included* in the firewood of today.

This may sound complicated, but it is important to get a handle on this in order to understand Dogen's teachings in the *Shobogenzo.* Dogen recognized the inseparability of time and existence or time and space, hence, when he speaks of *either* time or existence, he assumes *both* of them. When he refers explicitly to this unity of time and existence (space-time), he usually uses the term *Uji* (being time). Dogen explores this concept in detail in *Shobogenzo, Uji.*

The *Genjokoan* continues:

Commentary 1: The Genjokoan

> Although it has a past and a future, the past and the
> future are cut off.

Here Dogen makes the point from the relative perspective (the particular, the individual, etc.). When you look at today's firewood from this
perspective, today's firewood is unique. That is, today's firewood is distinctively *today's* firewood. It is, always has been, and always will be *today's*
firewood.

This aspect is demonstrated philosophically by the Huayen doctrine of
"principal and satellites." When any particular thing, time, or event is posited
as the "principal," all other things, times, or events are seen as "satellites." For
instance, look at an apple that has fallen from a tree. As the "principal"
everything else in the universe can be seen as its "satellites," including the
apple that was on the tree, the apple falling through the air, and the rotten
apple of next month. Now if you shift your focus and take the rotten apple as
the "principal" the fallen apple is now a "satellite" of the rotten apple. In this
way, each thing, time, and event can be seen to include every other thing, time,
and event. This applies to apples, firewood, ash, or any other particular thing,
time, or event, including you at this very moment.

Next, the *Genjokoan* says:

> Ash exists in the dharma position of ash. It has a past
> and it has a future.

Here, Dogen makes the same point with ash that he just made with
firewood. Since both ash and firewood "abide" or "exist" in their own
particular "place in the dharma," their own unique "place" in all of space
and time, one cannot *become* the other.

Now this section of the *Genjokoan* comes full circle:

> The firewood, after becoming ash, does not again
> become firewood."

The first line of this section of *Genjokoan* referred to your everyday
experience, after taking you through the implications of what this statement
means, Dogen repeats the first line. While it still carries the common sense
meaning of your practical experience, this time it *also includes* the implications that he illustrated through his analysis.

112

As you become more familiar with these implications as they apply to yourself and to all things in the universe, Dogen's expressions begin to reveal some extraordinary marvels. Here are a few examples from the *Shobogenzo* that this teaching helps to illumine:

> Since there is nothing but just this moment, the time-being is all the time there is.[li]

> Know that among the infinite things in oneself, there is life and there is death. One should calmly think: is this present life, along with the myriad things concomitant with life, together with life or not? There is nothing at all, not so much as one time or one phenomenon, that is not together with life. Even be it a single thing, a single mind, none is not together with life.[lii]

> How joyful it is! From kalpa to kalpa is the Flower of Dharma, and from noon to night, even though our own body-and-mind grows strong and grows weak, it is just the Flower of Dharma itself. The reality that exists *as it is*, is a treasure, is *brightness*, is *a seat of truth, is wide, great, profound, and eternal*, is *profound, great, and everlasting*, is *mind in delusion, the Flower of Dharma turning*, and is *mind in realization, turning the Flower of Dharma*, which is really just the Flower of Dharma turning the Flower of Dharma. [sic] [liii]

Next, the *Genjokoan* examines this aspect of reality as it relates to the human realm:

> Similarly, human beings, after death, do not become alive again. This being so, it is the established teaching of Buddhism to deny that life turns into death. This is why Buddhists speak of no appearance. In addition, it is the established teaching of Buddhism that death does not become life. This is why Buddhists speak of no disappearance. Life is an instantaneous situation, and death is an instantaneous situation. It is like winter and spring. You do not think

that winter becomes spring, and you do not say that
spring becomes summer.

"Similarly," Dogen says, "human beings, after death, do not become
alive again." This line carries the implications of the *second* reading of, "The
firewood, after becoming ash, does not again become firewood" (i.e. human beings have a past and future, *and* they are cut off from past and future,
and they abide in the dharma position of human beings).

Then Dogen explains, "This being so, it is the established tradition in
the buddha-dharma (Buddhist teachings) to deny that life turns into death.
This is why we speak of no appearance." "No appearance" in Buddhism
means "no-birth" or "unborn." Dogen is directing your attention to the
fact that because each thing, time, and event is one aspect or characteristic
of all space and time (being time), there is the teaching of "no appearance."
That is to say, because each thing, including each human being, already
abides in its "dharma position," things do not "appear," because they *already
exist* in their dharma position (as individual, and *inevitable*, aspects of all time
and space (being time)).

This same reasoning of appearance applies to disappearance, "In addition, it is the established teaching of Buddhism that death does not become
life. This is why we speak of no disappearance." "No disappearance" means
"no-death" or "imperishable." Because human beings abide or exist in the
dharma (i.e. all of time and space) there is the teaching of "no disappearance." In other words, things do not "disappear" because they are *integral
aspects* of all time and space (being time).

Dogen drives his point home with, "Life is an instantaneous situation,
and death is an instantaneous situation." Life and death are each an instantaneous situation of all time and space (being time). That is to say, what
is called life, and what is called death, are not separate entities, but are
simply particular aspects of all time and space (being time).

Finally, Dogen uses an analogy to clarify his meaning, "It is like winter
and spring. We do not think that winter becomes spring, and we do not say
that spring becomes summer." When we are experiencing springtime, we
do not think of it as a new condition of winter. When we are experiencing
summertime, we do not say that it is a new form of spring.

The implications of what Dogen has thus far explained about the path
of Zen practice and enlightenment may sound astonishing. According to
the reasoning of *Genjokoan*, each one of you is, has always been, and always

Ted Biringer

will be the entirety of space and time (being time). That is, you are, *as you are*, nothing less than the entire universe. At the same time, *every* other particular thing, moment, and event also is, has always been, and always will be the entire universe. Moreover, according to Dogen, there is an experience whereby you can personally achieve verification of this truth.

Dogen is not presenting some new and unique perspective; all of the points he has made are implied in the traditional doctrines of Zen. However, Dogen's emphasis, succinct manner of expression, and rational, methodical presentation of these principles is striking in its originality.

Many of his statements may sound contrary to your own everyday experience. How could the teachings of no birth and no death be true when you see birth and death all around you? How can things both have a before and after, and yet be cut off from before and after? How could you embody the entire universe? These kinds of questions naturally occur when you hear these statements.

Dogen confronts and resolves these doubts with an amazingly succinct and profoundly illuminating presentation of the Buddhist doctrine of mutual interpenetration and non-obstruction. This complex teaching is one of the cornerstones of the Huayen School of Buddhism. In a remarkable demonstration of his mastery of expression, Dogen presents the very heart of this labyrinthine doctrine with a simple analogy that illustrates what it is like for a human being to embody the entire universe. He says, a person "contains" the whole universe (all time and space) like a single drop of water reflects (contains) the whole sky. In the words of the *Genjokoan*:

> A person experiencing enlightenment is like the moon being reflected in water: the moon does not get wet, and the water is not broken. Though its light is wide and great, the moon is reflected in a puddle of water an inch wide. The whole moon and the whole sky are reflected in a dewdrop on a blade of grass and are reflected in a single drop of water.

If you go out into a field on a clear night with a magnifying glass and look closely at a single drop of water, you will see that it "contains" the moon, the stars, and all the space in-between. Likewise, each thing and each person contains all the many things of the universe. You cannot see them with an ordinary magnifying glass; however, you can see them with the magnifying glass of Zen practice and enlightenment. In fact, seeing that reality *is* Zen. The *Genjokoan* continues this analogy:

> Enlightenment does not break a person, just as the moon does not pierce the water.

The reflection of the moon (and sky) does not "pierce" the drop of water. In other words, the drop of water is not altered (does not expand or change into something else) by containing the whole sky. It is in fact an inherent quality of the true nature of water drops to "contain" the moon. Similarly, "enlightenment does not break a person;" to contain all of space and time is an inherent quality of "a person." The *Genjokoan* continues:

> A person does not constrict enlightenment, just as a dewdrop does not constrict the sky and moon.

The moon and sky do not "pierce" the drop of water, nor does the drop of water "constrict" the moon and sky. In Huayen Buddhism, the quality of "containing" is called "mutual interpenetration," and the quality of "not constricting" is called "non-obstruction." The sky and the moon seen within the drop of water are seen *as they are*. In the same way, an individual (person) contains, but does not constrict, the whole of space and time (and in fact, this is true of every particular thing, time, and event). The *Genjokoan* continues:

> The depth of the drop is the height of the moon.

Looking at the drop of water with the magnifying glass you see that all the space between the stars and moon is contained within it, so too the space between the drop of water and the moon. In other words, although the drop of water is a fraction of an inch, you can see "down into" it for thousands, even millions of miles. You see the moon, then millions of miles (and light-years) deeper in the drop of water, there is the Big Dipper. As Dogen is using this analogy to illustrate the nature of a person experiencing enlightenment (oneness with all of space and time), the depth and height of enlightenment (all time and space) are contained within a person. As the *Genjokoan* says:

> Whether large or small, and whatever the length or
> shortness of its duration, the whole sky and the whole
> moon are discerned in each body of water.

As with each "body of water," each person, wise or deluded (large or
small), whatever "its duration," a one hundred-year-old man or a
one-day-old baby, contains all space and time (the whole sky). Therefore,
Dogen exhorts you to "discern" the myriad aspects of this reality. The
moon, the sky, and the Big Dipper are just the beginning; there are whole
galaxies to explore. Not only that, but the "longness and shortness of its
moment" reminds you of the ongoing newness or unfolding of it all. That is
to say, the moon, the Big Dipper, and all the galaxies of today are not
yesterday's moon, Big Dipper, and galaxies.

Next, the *Genjokoan* states:

> When the dharma has not yet filled the whole
> body-and-mind people feel already replete with dharma.

When you are, in Dogen's earlier words, "ordinary beings" in "delusion" you feel replete with the dharma. In other words, when you are still
deluded you do not *feel* as if you are in "delusion." In fact, if you *realized* your
delusion you would be buddhas, enlightened beings. One sure sign of
delusion is thinking that you know who and what you are. Remember,
buddhas do not know they are buddhas. So, the *Genjokoan* says:

> When the dharma fills the body-and-mind people
> feel something is lacking.

When you realize your identity with the universe, you naturally sense a
lack. There is nothing lacking in *all* of space and time (being time), yet
Dogen says you feel something to be lacking. If you realize your oneness
with all of space and time, how can this be? He gave you a clue when he
explained that "whatever the length or shortness of its duration, the whole
sky and the whole moon are discerned in each body of water." In the following paragraphs of *Genjokoan*, Dogen explains his reasoning in detail:

> For example, when a person sails out beyond the
> mountains into the ocean, and looks around in the four

directions, the ocean appears only to be round; it does
not appear to have any other characteristics at all.

Clear enough; if you sail out beyond the sight of land, no matter how
keen your eyesight is, the ocean appears to be round.

The *Genjokoan* continues:

Nevertheless, this great ocean is not round, and it is
not square.

Though the ocean appears round to you, and there is nothing wrong
with your vision, the ocean is not round. Obviously, if you adjust your
position (your perspective) so that you can see the shoreline, you will realize
that it is not round. As you sail along the shoreline, the shape of the ocean
will appear to change with your perspective. In the words of the *Genjokoan*:

There are an infinite number or qualities to the ocean:
to fish it is like a palace; to gods it is like a string of pearls.

Indeed, the qualities of the ocean are inexhaustibly many. To fish, the
ocean is like a palace; to gods it is like a string of pearls. To a jet skier, it is
like a playground. From the perspective of a diver, the very same ocean you
see as round, is quite different. From the perspective of a person on the
shore, other qualities are seen; from the perspective of a bird flying over-
head other qualities are apparent. Yet, as the *Genjokoan* says:

Nevertheless, as far as someone's eyes can see, it just
appears to be round.

Though all of these qualities exist at the same time, for the time and
place where you are (here and now) it just seems round.

The *Genjokoan* continues:

As it is for the ocean, so it is for the many things.

As the ocean has a multitude of qualities beyond what you can see at any
particular place and time, so it is with all things and times (being time).

The *Genjokoan* explains:

> There are a multitude of qualities in the world of
> form and the world of the void, but you see and under-
> stand only as far as your eyes of practice and realization
> are able to reach.

Both the individual (relative, particular, etc.) perspective of the world
(of form) and the universal (empty, equal, etc.) perspective of the world (of
the void) encompass numerous qualities. However, you only see and understand what your "eyes of practice and realization are able to reach." In
other words, when you glimpse—even for the fraction of a second—the true
nature of reality, you are seeing *all* of reality from *one* perspective; therefore,
you do not see all the multitudinous qualities and details of that reality.
When you look at a mountain from an airplane, you may see the whole
mountain in a single glance; however, you could spend lifetimes exploring
its many dimensions.

This is why you "feel that something is lacking;" the universe is full of
an infinite variety of qualities and possibilities. It is also in a constant condition of flux and unfolding so that even if you were able to take it all in at
once, the next moment it would be entirely new. The Zen path of practice
and enlightenment is the ongoing exploration, discovery, and embodiment
of the universe, which is your own true self. As Dogen indicated earlier,
enlightenment about delusion is not the eradication of delusion, but the
realization of it.

The *Genjokoan* goes on:

> If someone wants to know how the many things
> really are, they should remember that besides appearing
> square or round, the qualities of the oceans and qualities
> of the mountains are infinitely numerous; there are
> worlds in the four directions. Not only the periphery is
> like this; remember, the immediate present and a single
> drop of water are also like this.

This then, is the reason why throughout the *Shobogenzo*, Dogen is so
vehement about continuous, ongoing practice and enlightenment. The
buddha-dharma that is the universe is full of numerous qualities and
wonders without end. There are "*worlds* in the four directions," even in this
present moment, and in a single drop of water. Your enlightenment is the

enlightenment of the universe. Your awareness is the awareness of the universe. The Zen path of practice and enlightenment is the universe aware of *itself*, exploring *itself*, and experiencing *itself*.

Next, the *Genjokoan* uses a number of similes to further illustrate the interpenetrating nature of the universe and the practice and enlightenment of human beings:

> When fish swim in the ocean, no matter how far they swim, there is no end to the water. When birds fly through the sky, no matter how far they fly, there is no end to the sky. While this is so, fish and birds have never left the water or the sky.

When a fish swims in the Pacific Ocean, it swims in the *whole* Pacific Ocean. If the part of the ocean that the fish is not swimming in were removed, the part the fish is swimming in would also be removed. Likewise, for a bird flying through the sky.

The *Genjokoan* continues:

> Simply, when their ability is great, their usage is great, and when their ability is small, their usage is small.

When a fish or a bird travels a great distance, it travels a great distance within the *entirety* of the ocean or sky. When a fish or a bird travels a small distance, it travels a small distance within the *entirety* of the ocean or sky.

The *Genjokoan* explains:

> Thus, each realizes its full potential and each experiences its full realm. If a bird leaves the sky, it will die at once; and if a fish leaves the water, it will die at once.

A fish or a bird performing fish or bird "activity" (swimming/flying in the water/sky) never fails to "realize its full potential" (is always within the whole ocean/sky). Likewise, each particular moment is always within the whole of time; each particular thing is always within the whole of space. Each thing, each time realizes its full potential (lives, moves, and has its being) in the whole universe ("experiences its full realm"). If a bird or fish leaves the sky or water, it dies at once. If a minute were removed from an hour, it would "die" at once (it would cease to be a minute)–so, too, the hour from which it was removed would "die" (it would no longer be an hour).

The *Genjokoan* continues:

> Therefore, you know that water is life and you know
> that sky is life. Birds are life, and fish are life. Hence, life
> is birds and life is fish.

One of the many qualities of water is fish-life; an aspect of the sky is bird-life. A quality of birds is sky-life; an aspect of fish is water-life. Water-life and sky-life are fish and birds. One quality of the universe is human life; one quality of human life is the universe.

Furthermore, the *Genjokoan* says:

> Beyond this, there may still be further progress.

The whole ocean is a fish's skin; the whole sky is a bird's coat. The whole earth is an earthworm's sweater. The whole hour is a minute's home. The whole pine tree is a pine needle's extension. The whole earth is a pine tree's foundation. The whole Milky Way includes the solar system. The Milky Way moves in the whole universe. The whole universe is your homeland. "And beyond this, there may still be further progress."

The *Genjokoan* continues:

> The existence of their practice and enlightenment,
> and the existence of their life, are like this.

The reality of the fish and bird's actualization (practice and enlightenment) and the reality of their existence are like this (non-separate from the whole of time and space (being time), while perfectly adapted to the particular abilities and needs of each unique being). Therefore, *the Genjokoan* says:

> This being so, a bird or fish that tried to move
> through the water or the sky only after getting to the bot-
> tom of the water or the sky, could never find its way or
> find its place in the water or the sky.

A bird or fish that intended to move through its element, only *after* completely understanding all of its qualities, could not even realize its present circumstances. A bird that intended to realize the sky would be demonstrating its own delusion (that the sky was separate from the bird itself). A fish that set out to discover water would only do so if it was under the delusion that water was something apart from itself. People aiming to discover their buddha-nature (their own true nature) can only do so by failing to realize their own identity with buddha-nature.

The *Genjokoan* points out this astonishing point:

> When people find this place, this action is *itself*, the actualization of the fundamental point (genjokoan). When people find this way, this action is *itself* the actualization of the fundamental point (genjokoan).

The very action of *finding* this place (awakening to your true nature) is the universe *itself*. The very action of *finding* this way (the buddha-dharma) is the universe *itself*. In other words, discovering your own true nature is inevitably the universe discovering *itself*. When Jane Doe suddenly overcomes amnesia and recalls her identity as Jane Brown, Jane Brown *simultaneously* realizes her identity with Jane Doe.

The *Genjokoan* goes on to explain:

> This way and this place are not great or small; not subjective or objective; they have not existed since the past, nor do they arise in the present; they are simply as they are.

The entire activity of the buddha-dharma ("this way") and each particular point of this universe ("this place") transcend verbal and intellectual limitations, and are unnamable and inconceivable. Concepts, such as great and small, subjective and objective, etc. cannot describe the vast, unnamable, fathomless void. Reality here and now (this way and this place) transcends all conceptual views like "existed since the past" or "arises in the present." Reality is *as it is*. Flowers fall, weeds flourish, cocks crow, dogs bark.

The *Genjokoan* continues:

122

> When a person is experiencing the practice and
> enlightenment of the buddha-dharma, each practice
> is complete practice, and meeting each thing is
> mastering it.

For a person that is "experiencing the practice and enlightenment of the buddha-dharma," each particular practice (moment, thing, or event) is the complete practice *of* that particular practice. When a human being stands up, the whole universe stands up *as* that particular human being.

Next, the *Genjokoan* states:

> Here, the place exists and the way unfolds, and
> therefore the area of enlightenment is not conspicuous.
> For this enlightenment and the buddha-dharma mani-
> fest simultaneously and are experienced simultaneously.

The "area of enlightenment is not conspicuous" (i.e. has no *real* de-marcation, is not distinctively described) *because* "the place exists" and "the way unfolds" are the *whole* of space-time manifesting *as* each particular "here" (and now). That is to say, the *existence of* the buddha-dharma, and the *realization of* the buddha-dharma is simultaneous. Practice and enlighten-ment are two aspects of a single reality that, like water and waves, are dis-tinct, yet not two.

Now the *Genjokoan* says:

> Do not assume that what is realized will be grasped
> by consciousness or will be recognized by the intellect.

Here, Dogen warns you to avoid conceptualizing and creating a view (assume) that "what is realized" will be understood by your ordinary human consciousness or "recognized by the intellect." Such an assumption posits a duality between "what is realized" and your "self." The following passage of *Genjokoan* explains why that assumption is untenable:

> Although the experience of the ultimate state is re-
> alized immediately, its mysterious existence is not a
> manifest realization. Realization of the inconceivable is the
> inconceivable itself.

123

Here, in a fresh and provocative way, Dogen again indicates the non-dual nature of practice and enlightenment. The *experience of* the ultimate state is *itself* the ultimate state.

In the actual experience of practice and enlightenment, the inconceivable nature of reality ("its mysterious existence") does not become an intellectual understanding ("a manifest realization"). "Realization *of* the inconceivable *is* the inconceivable itself." When the inconceivable is experienced it is not "constricted," but experienced *as it is,* which is *inconceivable.*

Having set out the canvas, prepared the brushes, and demonstrated the colors and textures of the paints, Dogen now presents a Zen koan to bring the whole essay to its fundamental point.

The koan begins:

> Zen Master Hotetsu, of Mount Mayu is using a fan.

It may be hot; the Zen master, Hotetsu, is using a fan to cool himself. Perhaps he is sitting in the shade with a glass of iced-tea on a little table, a book in one hand, and a paper fan lightly sweeping air over his face in the other.

Now the koan says:

> A monk comes up and says, "The nature of air is ever-present, and there is no place it does not reach. Why, then, does the Master use a fan?"

Maybe a lot of monks have passed by, seeing the old master relaxing in the shade with his fan, they might have thought it would be rude to interrupt him. One monk however, is serious about his quest and notices an opportunity to settle a question that has been bothering him for years. His question is intimately familiar to Dogen. The same question drove him to undertake a dangerous journey to China.

Buddha-nature is already present; it is everywhere and everything, including us. Why then, is it necessary to engage in spiritual practice?

As the koan states:

> The master says, "You understand that the nature of air is ever-present, but you do not understand the truth that there is no place it does not reach."

The master immediately understands where this monk is stuck. He then articulates the monk's immediate obstruction. "Your *understanding* of the ever-present buddha-nature is correct; however you have not yet *realized* the way its ever-present nature manifests itself everywhere."

The koan continues:

> The monk says, "What is the truth of there being no place it does not reach?"

The monk follows the master's line of reasoning and asks him how to take the next step. "How does the ever-present nature of buddha-dharma manifest everywhere?" The koan shows how:

> At this, the master just continues to use the fan.

The experience of the cool air of the fan is simultaneous with the fanning. The *realization* of the state of buddha is simultaneous with the *functioning* of buddha. Although distinct from the experience of air, fanning and the experience of air always go together. Although distinct from Buddhahood, practice *and* the experience of Buddhahood always go together.

The koan says:

> The monk does prostrations.

This monk, having cleared up his confusion, immediately uses a fan. Authentic spiritual practice (such as the monk's prostrations) and Buddhahood manifest simultaneously. So, the *Genjokoan* states:

> The actualization of the buddha-dharma, the living way of authentic transmission, is like this.

This is *not* the "actualization of the buddha-dharma, the living way of authentic transmission," but it *"is like this."* Flowers fall and weeds flourish. The *Genjokoan* explains further:

> A person who says that because the nature of air is ever-present they don't need to use a fan or that without

> using a fan they can know the ever-present nature of air,
> does not know ever-presence or the nature of air.

To think that "knowing" or "understanding" that all things are bud-dha-nature, and therefore conclude that spiritual practice is not necessary, is merely to demonstrate your delusion about buddha-nature. As the *Gen-jokoan* concludes:

> Because the nature of air is ever-present, the air of
> Buddhism manifests the gold of the Earth and ripens the
> Long River into fragrant cream.

Since buddha-nature is ever-present, authentic practice ("the air of Buddhism") causes the whole universe to manifest as the way of complete, unsurpassed, perfect enlightenment.

Commentary 2:
Bodhidharma's Vast, Unnamable, Fathomless Void

Louie Wing said, "The vast, unnamable, fathomless void is not activated by some kind of spiritual practice; just cease screening it off through conceptualization. When perceptions, feelings, and thoughts arise, simply act accordingly without attachment or aversion. All of the myriad things are identical to the vast, unnamable, fathomless void, which is identical to your own mind. There is not a single objective particle anywhere."
—From the collected Sayings and Doings of Louie Wing

Introduction

When you see smoke rising from behind a hill, you know right away there is a fire; when you see ox-horns sticking up from behind a fence, you know right away there is an ox. Understanding three when one is raised, discerning clearly with a single glance is the everyday food and drink of a Zen adept. Arriving at cessation of conceptualization, you are free to rise in the east and set in the west, to oppose or to affirm, in all directions, you are free to give or to take away. However, when such actualization occurs, whose actions are they? Look into Setcho's entangling vines.

When you see smoke, you know—even without seeing flame—there is fire; when you see ox-horns sticking up from the other side of a fence, you know there is an ox. This is ordinary everyday experience; Engo is not presenting some great mystery here. Why is he making such an obvious statement?

What if he had said that when you see smoke, you know there is an ox? I say that when you see smoke, an ox knows right away that there is fire.

There is a wonderful Buddhist teaching about a vast, fathomless net called the *Net of Indra*. Every point of this net is fashioned with a clear, perfect jewel. Each one of the infinite numbers of jewels in this vast and fathomless net contains the reflection of each and all of the other jewels in the net, while simultaneously being reflected in every other jewel. If you look closely at any one jewel, you will see every other jewel; and if you look at the reflections in "your" jewel, you will see "your" jewel reflected in each one of the reflected jewels, and in each of those reflections, ad infinitum.

In his marvelous book, *Wholeness and the Implicate Order*, physicist Professor David Bohm proposes that the whole of space and time "is *enfolded* within *each region* of space (and time). So, whatever part, element, or aspect we may abstract in thought, this still enfolds the whole and is therefore intrinsically related to the totality from which it has been abstracted."

Engo says, "Understanding three when one is raised, discerning clearly with a single glance; this is the everyday food and drink of a Zen adept." What if a Zen adept eats rice and drinks water? Are each grain of rice and each drop of water a jewel in the vast net of Indra? How about the pencil in your hand, can you see that it *enfolds the whole*?

If so, you are on the authentic path of practice and enlightenment; grasping or discarding nothing, "you are free to rise in the east and set in the west, to oppose or to affirm, in all directions, you are free to give or to take away."

Engo will not affirm you lightly, "However, when such actualization occurs, whose actions are they?" Can you meet his challenge? If not, he offers you some guidance, "Look into Setcho's entangling vines."

The Koan

> Emperor Wu asked Bodhidharma, "What is the ultimate meaning of the holy truths?"
> Bodhidharma said, "Vast emptiness, nothing holy."

The Emperor asked, "Who is facing me?"

Bodhidharma responded, "I don't know."

The Emperor did not understand. After this Bodhidharma crossed the Yangtze River and traveled to the
kingdom of Wei.

Later, the Emperor asked Master Chih about it.

Master Chih asked, "Do you know who this man is?"

The Emperor said, "I don't know."

Master Chih said, "He is the great bodhisattva,
Avalokitesvara, transmitting the confirmation of the
buddha-mind."

The Emperor was regretful and wanted to send an
envoy to bring Bodhidharma back.

Master Chih said, "Don't say you will send someone
to bring him back. Even if everyone in China went after
him, he would not return."

"Emperor Wu asked Bodhidharma." The Emperor did not know who
Bodhidharma was, but he could see that there was *something* about this
red-bearded barbarian. Therefore, he took the opportunity to ask a most
important question, "What is the ultimate meaning of the holy truths?"
What is most important?

"Bodhidharma said." Like a mirror, Bodhidharma responds instantaneously to what is placed before him. This is an example of "discerning
clearly with a single glance."

"Vast emptiness, nothing holy." That is the ultimate meaning of the
holy truths. That is what is most important. Pointing directly to the dimensionless human mind, Bodhidharma says it is clear all the way through
to the very bottom.

"The Emperor asked, 'Who is facing me?'" Caught off guard, the
Emperor has not achieved enough humility to admit he does not understand. Instead, he challenges Bodhidharma. Although the Emperor has
stumbled, his words are not ordinary. "Who is facing me?" His question
should not be taken lightly. Empty, without holiness? *Who* says vast emptiness? If all things are void, why do we get hungry?

Vast *emptiness*? *Nothing* holy? Then *who* is facing me? How do you respond to this challenge?

The Emperor asked about the ultimate meaning, the most important thing in life. Did he think he already knew the answer? Was he trying to test Bodhidharma? Was he truly trying to discover if he was going to be okay when death came calling? Could the merit resulting from good karma free him from old age, sickness, and death?

Clearly discerning at a glance, Bodhidharma removes all the Emperor's options. Later, Sosan, the Third Ancestor of Zen in China, would confide that, "The Great Way is not difficult, just avoid picking and choosing." If the Emperor had mastered this skill, would he have been free to rise in the east and to set in the west? Yet, how can you avoid picking and choosing?

In case thirty of the *Blue Cliff Record*, we find Joshu confronted with a similar situation. He also demonstrates his skill for "discerning clearly with a single glance." Look how Joshu avoids picking or choosing.

> A monk asked Joshu, "Master, is it true that you have personally seen Nansen?"
> Joshu said, "Chinshu Province produces giant radishes."

This monk is not being polite; there is a sharp needle inside the fluffy cotton ball. His question about personally seeing Nansen is like the Emperor's question about who is facing him. Have *you* personally seen Nansen? *Who* is facing me?

"Bodhidharma responded." Again, it was not intentional, really he could not help himself. "Mommy, a bee!" *Smack!* "Who is facing me?" "I don't know." Engo, demonstrating excessive compassion, says, "Bodhidharma's compassion was excessive." Excessive or not, *who* responded? *Who* does not know? Is Bodhidharma's response the same as Joshu's?

"The Emperor did not understand." He did not get it. Engo says, "Too bad. Still, he's gotten somewhere." What is he saying; if the Emperor did not understand, where could he have gotten? The Emperor *thought* he knew, but now he *does not* understand. The Emperor's *not understanding* is not as good as Bodhidharma's *not knowing*, but it is better than *thinking he knows*.

"After this Bodhidharma crossed the Yangtze River and traveled to the kingdom of Wei." Bodhidharma continued onward. He was not fixated. When the universe contracted, Bodhidharma expanded; when the universe expanded, Bodhidharma contracted. Engo praised him highly saying, "This wild spirit of a fox! How shameful; crossing from west to east and from east to west." Yes, look at that foxy-smelling, red-bearded barbarian rising in the east, setting in the west.

"Later, the Emperor asked Master Chih about it." The Emperor has some doubts–the seeds planted by Bodhidharma, have sprouted nicely. Who says Bodhidharma was unable to transmit confirmation of the buddha-mind to Emperor Wu?

Master Chih asked, "Do you know who this man is?" Master Chih likes to play the role of the Emperor. *Who* is facing me? He invites the Emperor to play the starring role. Forget about the script, Emperor, just turn around, then say it in your own words. Lights, camera, action! "Who is facing me?"

The Emperor said, "I don't know."

Cut! Forget the script. Get into character and put it in your own words! Joshu said, "Chinshu produces giant radishes," Bodhidharma said, "I don't know." Even though the Emperor's "I don't know" is not the same as Bodhidharma's, it is better than, "I know."

Master Chih said, "He is the great bodhisattva, Avalokitesvara, transmitting the buddha-mind seal." It seems Bodhidharma and Engo are not the only ones indulging in excessive compassion. Engo complains that Master Chih explained it haphazardly, giving away the secret about the elbow not bending backwards. However, we see that Engo was just setting a trap when he goes on to ask, "If Bodhidharma is Avalokitesvara, and Master Chih is Avalokitesvara, which is the real Avalokitesvara?" Is it the Avalokitesvara familiar to us from the *Heart Sutra*? If so, why mention one or two? The myriad hands and eyes of Avalokitesvara outnumber all the superstrings in a billion universes by at least three by three in front, three by three in back.

Avalokitesvara is the bodhisattva of compassion that can manifest as a male or female, a saint or a sinner, a sage or a fool, all depending upon the needs of any particular being. She is constantly deepening and refining her skills to liberate all beings. Long after Emperor Wu had been safely delivered to nirvana, she continued to hone her skill. Manifesting as the Zen master Hakuin, she tried to outdo even Engo's willingness to trail mud and drip water. Hakuin said, "Everything, meadows, mountains, and all, is the *Mahasattva Avalokitesvara!*" Manifesting as the Zen master Tenkei, she went even further, asking, "Is the Buddha- Mind Seal something that can be transmitted or is it ungraspable? Grab your nose and find out." Her manifestations as these two old grandmothers were her best ones since she incarnated as Tozan and said, "He is you, but you are not him."

"The Emperor was regretful and wanted to send an envoy to bring Bodhidharma back." Although Master Chih cut the Emperor's meat into tiny little bites, he still choked on it.

Still, Master Chih tried to perform a Heimlich maneuver, telling the Emperor "Don't say you will send someone to bring him back. Even if everyone in China went after him, he would not return." Today we might say that he is closing the barn door after the cow has already escaped.

Nevertheless, why is it that Bodhidharma would not return? Once, Obaku, the teacher of Rinzai said, "Don't you know that in the whole Empire of China there are no teachers of Zen?"

The Verse

> The ultimate meaning of the holy truths, vast emptiness.
> What, then, is discerned with a single glance?
> "Who is facing me?"
> Like an echo, "I don't know."
> Continuously unfolding, in darkness, he silently crossed the river;
> Inevitably, entangling vines cover the ground.
> Even if everyone in China went after him, he would not return.
> Emperor Wu habitually rehashes the past.
> Cease uselessly conceptualizing over former times.
> The essential nature of reality is pure, clear, and luminous.
> Setcho looked around and said, "Is the Zen Ancestor here!"
> He answered himself, saying, "He is!"
> Setcho said, "Bring him here to wash my feet."

"The ultimate meaning of the holy truths, vast emptiness." There is no anguish, cause of anguish, cessation, or path.

"What then, is discerned with a single glance?" Practicing prajna paramita clearly discerned the five skandhas are empty, transforming anguish and distress.

"'Who is facing me?'" Form is exactly emptiness, emptiness exactly form.

"Like an echo, 'I don't know.'" In emptiness, there is no form, no sensation, no perception, no formulation, and no consciousness.

"Continuously unfolding, in darkness he silently crossed the river." Far beyond delusive thinking.

"Inevitably, entangling vines cover the ground." Right here is Nirvana.

"Even if everyone in China went after him, he would not return." Neither appearing nor disappearing, not stained, not pure, without gain, without loss.

"Emperor Wu habitually rehashes the past." There is no ignorance, and no ending of ignorance.

"Cease uselessly conceptualizing over former times!" There is no wisdom and no attainment; with nothing to attain, the bodhisattva lives by prajna paramita, with no hindrance in the mind, no hindrance, and therefore no fear.

"The essential nature of reality is clear, pure and luminous!" There is no old age and death, and no ending of old age and death.

"Setcho looked around and said, 'Is the Zen Ancestor here!'" All buddhas of past, present, and future depend on prajna paramita attaining anuttara-samyak-sambodhi.

"He answered himself, saying, 'He is!'" This is truth, not mere formality.

"Setcho said, 'Bring him here to wash my feet.'" Gate, gate, paragate, parasangate. Bodhi, svaha!

Part III
Sayings and Doings of Louie Wing
Arranged alphabetically by topic

Death: No Death

Unborn and undying

The vast, unnamable, fathomless void was never born and can never die. The myriad things only appear separate from the void when viewed through delusion. When you cease conceptualization, all things are unborn and undying.

I remember my teacher

While speaking with his students, Louie Wing said, "I remember my teacher said, 'Birth and death have no real inherent qualities. The one source, void and luminous, shines within each of you. Within the realm of nonduality, awaken the mind that perceives impartially and realize freedom from anguish. The vast, unnamable, fathomless void cannot be inflated or diminished. In the ten times it is entirely complete, perfect and seamless, through and through. Identify with the reality that you embody, which is the reality that embodies you. The myriad of things flow forth from, abide within, and return to the unnamable void. Old age, sickness, and death are like images in a dream. Eternal wisdom, void, yet luminescent, harmoniously accords with circumstances. Awakening to reality, you cut off the ten times and realize the dimensionless void. Wherever you are, knowing and known, perceiving and perceived, are one continuous occurrence. The one source of the myriad things constantly preaches, illuminating the void, and manifesting the forms, without a single objective particle.' How marvelous that this is no other than your own true self."

Turner asked, "What are the 'ten times'?"

Louie Wing said, "It is a Buddhist term for all time. That is, the past, present, and future of the past, present, and future, plus the whole of them together."

Turner said, "Umm…"

Louie Wing said, "Take the past, for instance, it has its own past, present, and future, making three times. The same is true of the present and the future, for a total of nine times. Then all of them together are considered as one more time, making ten. Understand?"

Turner said, "Yes, I do."

Louie Wing said, "Too bad."

Step back into the source of your own awareness

If you want to awaken you must step back into the source of your own awareness. No matter what arises in your experience, follow it back into the source of your fundamental awareness. When seeing, hearing, tasting, touching, smelling, feeling, and thinking arise, find their source in your mind. Do this continuously wherever you are and whatever you are doing.

If you keep this up you will eventually realize that the concept of your "self" is an illusion; like a person in a dream or a reflection in a mirror, it has no independent existence. Then you will awaken to the truth that you have never been born and can never die.

Liberation

After Louie Wing was finished teaching, Kilee asked, "What is liberation?"

Louie Wing said, "It is to move and act harmoniously in any environment, secular or religious, sacred or mundane. You move and act among the wealthy and the poor, the foolish and the wise, and you see that all of these states are but transitory manifestations, now arising from the vast, unnamable, fathomless void, now dissolving back into it.

You see your own appearance in the world, experience the vicissitudes of your life, and perceive your own future disappearance. Yet, when you look for your beginning or your end, you find that there is not a trace. You realize that, as your own birth and death have no true reality, so it is with all things and people, animals, plants, mountains, worlds, and stars. When you truly awaken to this reality, it is called liberation."

Your true identity

One day Jennifer asked, "What do you mean by 'ceasing conceptualization'? What do you mean by 'no birth and death'? What do you mean by 'liberation'?"

Louie Wing replied, "I was wondering if you were ever going to ask a question. The smoke has been pouring out of your ears for weeks. I see you were just saving them up!

"'Ceasing conceptualization' means that your mind does not get tangled up in views and notions of self and other while participating in the activities of the world. When you cease conceptualization, you discover that your true nature and the nature of all things are identical. Realizing your true identity, you discover that you have always been free from birth and death.

Being free from birth and death and not hindered by views of self and other is called liberation. It is a mistake to believe there is some kind of a special doctrine or esoteric teaching apart from awakening to your own true mind."

Death is no-death

Your own mind is reality,
Reality is your own mind.
When things are realized as no-things,
Death is realized as no-death.

Delusion: Reality Misperceived

Evil is delusion

After one of Louie Wing's youngest students died of leukemia, Jessica asked "What is evil?"

Louie Wing said, "Evil is delusion. If you awaken to reality, you realize that all the many things were never born, that the world is like a dream, there is not a single particle of evil anywhere. You realize that the whole universe is pure and immaculate, and this is reality. Delusion and awakening are simply two forms of perception, one distorted, one clear. Like two people gazing at the moon, one through dark glass and one without obstruction. Though each perceives it differently, the moon is the same.

Ultimately there is no awakening, no delusion, no past, no future, no now. There is no need to seek reality; you already are reality. Reality is not something that will happen at some particular time, it simply is. Spiritual practice does not create reality. In awakening nothing is added, in delusion nothing is taken away. In the past, present, and future there is nothing but this reality. If you think that there is a reality other than this, that thinking, too, is simply a partial view of reality itself."

The great truth of the sages

The great truth of all the sages is simple and straightforward. They have all directed you to your own mind, attempting to cause you to look deeply, see its true nature and realize liberation.

The essence of your mind is void and serene, clear and luminous, and free from all hindrances. However, you veil it with dualistic thinking, giving rise to delusion, and blocking yourself off from its pure, clear luminescence.

You turn away from the eternal source and chase after the temporal illusions that you create by your own conceptualization.

The wisdom is inherent in you

The wisdom of the sages is inherent in each one of you. It is only because of delusion, based on conceptual, dualistic thinking, that you fail to realize it. You should know that the reality of a sage and the reality of an ordinary person are the exact same reality. The only difference is that the sage realizes delusion, while an ordinary person is in delusion about realization.

Last words of a dying teacher

I remember when one teacher announced that she was going to die. Orville, a layman who had been a regular donor and loyal follower of hers, came and made a request.

He said, "Abbess, please, for the sake of us slow learners, give us some final clear instruction on how we may attain liberation? What is truth and what is delusion? What is a sage and what is an ordinary person? What is liberation and what is bondage?"

She replied, "In order to realize truth, just realize the nature of delusion. To seek liberation apart from delusion is like seeking the ocean apart from the nature of water. Delusion is simply one perception of true nature. An ordinary person that sees the true nature of delusion is a sage. A sage that sees true nature as delusion is an ordinary person. When the true nature of your own awareness is unhindered by conceptualization, and remains pure, clear, and luminous, that is liberation. When the true nature of your own awareness is veiled by conceptualization, and subjected to views, notions, and preferences, that is bondage. A single moment of conceptualization is a single moment of bondage; a single moment unhindered by conceptualization is a single moment of liberation."

Later that night, a monk that was meditating in the garden saw the abbess walking along a path that led into the woods. Nobody ever saw or heard from her again.

You lack nothing this very moment

Making heroic efforts in meditation and other forms of spiritual practice in order to manifest awakening is simply adding delusion to delusion. There is nothing to manifest. You lack nothing as you are at this very moment.

When you make efforts, thinking there is something to awaken to, you are positing a gap between what is awakened to, and the one that awakens. There is no gap between reality and your own mind. If you cling to the slightest notion that there is something to be gained, you are only entangling yourselves deeper in delusion. Your mind, right now, hearing this talk, is nothing other than the vast, unnamable, fathomless void.

Both delusion and awakening are illusory

Ceasing conceptualization and experiencing your own true nature, which is free from the concepts of both delusion and awakening, is true awakening. Awakening is only meaningful when contrasted with delusion. If delusion is illusory, how much more so is awakening! That is why the true sages of all the great traditions have urged you to cease clinging to any concepts.

Delusion of right vs. wrong

The vast, unnamable, fathomless void is truly inconceivable. It is "vast" because it reaches everywhere. It is "unnamable" because it is all-inclusive and names only apply to abstractions. It is "fathomless" because its depth can never be measured and it is beyond conceptualizing. It is "void" because there is no-thing in all of space and time.

The unnamable void of your own true mind has always been functioning perfectly. If you cease conceptualization and stop becoming entangled in dualistic thought, you will realize it directly. When you conceptually divide the void up with ideas of right and wrong and then set about trying to do what is right, while avoiding what is wrong, you are just adding delusion to delusion. Simply let go of all your notions and views and step back into the pure and clear, luminous awareness of your own mind. Only then can you truly do what is right and avoid what is wrong. Remember that right and wrong is the unnamable void, but the unnamable void is not right and wrong.

Adding delusion to delusion

When you grasp or reject anything you add delusion to delusion.

Big self, small self?

A visiting Zen monk asked, "You say that our own mind is the unnamable void; do you mean the mind of the big self or the small self?"

141

Louie Wing said, "Do your big self and your small self wear the same sized shoes?"

The monk said, "Many Zen teachers talk about a big self and a small self. Are you saying that the teachers of Zen are wrong?"

Louie Wing said, "According to Zen, *all* notions of self, big or small, are illusory. Grasping these illusions as reality only shields you from reality. You must simply cease all such conceptualizations and then you will realize the unnamable void and your own mind are not different."

The monk said, "What do you mean when you say, 'the unnamable void and your own mind are not different'?"

Louie Wing said, "It is simply your own effort to grasp them that causes you to make a distinction between them."

To hold any view is delusion

Ceasing conceptualization frees you from attachment to objects; illumination of wisdom frees you from attachment to no objects. To hold any view of objective reality is delusion based on conceptualization; to hold a view of no objective reality is delusion based on conceptualization.

The delusory nature of delusion

One afternoon, Charles asked, "If delusion blocks us off from our true mind, how does ceasing conceptualization stop delusion?"

Louie Wing said, "The arising of delusion and the stopping of delusion are both delusory conceptualizations. Delusion is merely a misperception of reality. If you just stop conceptualization, delusion cannot be found."

Ideas do not taint true practice

After a talk, Marilynn said, "Sometimes you say that spiritual practice is not necessary, and sometimes you say that we must cease conceptualization. I am confused."

Louie Wing said, "True spiritual practice is not tainted with the *idea* of spiritual practice. Ceasing conceptualization is not ceasing thought. Spiritual practice does not *create* reality; it directs you to what is already real. Ceasing conceptualization does not destroy delusion; it reveals its falsity."

Marilynn said, "But you have said that delusion is reality too."

Louie Wing said, "When you see the reality of delusion, it is no longer delusion or reality."

Awakening, delusion, and the unnamable void

When you awaken, the unnamable void is awake. When you are deluded, the unnamable void is deluded.

Everything pours forth from your own true mind

Cease grasping at illusions, cease running from phantoms. There is a Zen story about a man that painted a dragon. When he finished, he put down his brush, looked at the picture, and was afraid. All the myriad things are nothing but the one mind of each of you, why should you fear your own creations? Why should you chase after possessions, everything is already yours. Everything pours forth from your own true mind.

The sages of all the great spiritual traditions were not born as sages; they were no different than any one of you. Once they awakened to the true nature of their own awareness, greed and fear naturally fell away. What did they not already possess? Since there was nothing outside of their own minds, what was there to fear?

If you want to awaken, let go of everything. When conceptualization ceases, the myriad things cease, and all that remains is your own pure and clear awareness. It has never been hidden from you. Now is the time, here is the place.

The unnamable void is already complete

As soon as you indulge in conceptualization you screen yourself off from your own pure and clear awareness. The vast, unnamable, fathomless void is already completely established; if you try to cultivate it, you add delusion to delusion.

Do not establish a concept of non conceptualization

The vast, unnamable, fathomless void is beyond conceptualization, but do not establish a concept of non conceptualization. When you truly awaken to the unnamable void, you will not indulge concepts about the unnamable void.

Just cease all conceptualizing and you will awaken to that which is beyond description, definition, and conceivability. However, if you build up an idea about *not* conceptualizing and then set about trying to stop conceptualizing, you will just be adding delusion to delusion. A concept is an abstraction. A concept can never represent reality as it is because it is abstracted from the whole of what it is supposed to represent. A concept is an illusion. If you see concepts as things that can be stopped, you grant substance to illusions.

When you cease conceptualizing, you will experience the real essence behind the illusions. This does not mean that illusion is reality. People who cling to the idea that everything is reality just as it is, are also in delusion adding to delusion. When you awaken there is no one who awakens and nothing that is awakened to. You walk without "walking," see without "seeing," eat without "eating."

Doctrines: Temporary Expedients

Do not become mesmerized by teachings

The truth informing the teachings of all the great traditions is not contained within their words. The true nature of reality cannot be figured out or learned through study. In the Zen tradition, they sometimes say that the teachings are like fingers pointing to the moon or like a piece of broken tile used for knocking on a door. Do not become mesmerized by the finger and fail to see the moon, do not cling to the piece of tile once the door opens. If you actualize the truth that informs the teachings, you will discover that moons point at fingers, doors knock on broken tiles.

You must experience it directly

If you do not experience it directly, but simply cling to intellectual understanding, you will never achieve the peace of true liberation. You must let go of all ideas and notions about reality and spiritual practice, abandon all views of religion, awakening, void, mind, and the rest. As long as you continue to grasp conceptual understanding, you will remain in a tangle of views about self and other.

Remember, even if you memorized all the teachings of all the sages in the ten times, and even if you understood every single doctrine of every single tradition, if you do not experience it directly you will never be truly free. Then, even if you could lecture on all the scriptures, explain all of the doctrines, and speak with eloquence on the subtle esoteric teachings of all the great traditions, it would only amount to the ordinary understanding of human intellect, not that of an awakened human being.

144

Temporary expedients

It is impossible to talk about anything without making divisions where divisions do not really exist. When you ask about delusion, I talk about awakening; when you ask about the one, I talk about the many. When conceptualization is cut through, there is no division at all. All of the teachings about "this" against "that," "self" as opposed to "no self," "sacred" versus "mundane," and the like, are temporary expedients for guiding you to the experience of reality where all divisions will finally have been seen through.

No such thing as absolute truth

Only when you truly cease all forms of conceptualization will you finally achieve liberation. The various teachings of all the great spiritual traditions are temporary expedients. When you finally realize awakening all of the teachings will be seen through. In the meantime, it is important to avoid becoming attached to any particular teaching or method and regard it as some kind of absolute truth. There is no such thing as an absolute truth. All that is essential is that you cease conceptualization and step back into the clear awareness of your own mind.

True teachings, false teachings

The various teachings of the great spiritual traditions were all prescribed at different times and to different people. That is why they sometimes seem to say different things.

If a teaching leads you to awaken to your mind, then it is a true teaching, even if it comes from a fool. If a teaching does not lead you to awaken to your own mind, then it is a false teaching, even if it comes from a sage.

Truth becomes delusion when it is conceptualized. Delusion becomes truth when conceptualization ceases. Since delusion is illusory, all teachings to overcome delusion are also illusory.

Ceasing conceptualization is liberation

Ceasing conceptualization means not becoming fixated on anything at any time no matter where you are. When you are confronted with perceptions, feelings, and thoughts, do not allow yourself to become separated from your own fundamental awareness. When perceptions, feelings, and thoughts arise, simply observe them as they are without becoming caught up. If they require a response from you, respond; if they do not require a

145

response, simply allow them to arise, abide, or dissolve naturally in the unnamable void of your own mind. Ceasing conceptualization is liberation. Conceptualization is delusion. Even if you constantly ponder and contemplate the sacred doctrines of the great spiritual traditions, unless you have awakened, it is nothing but conceptualization. Only when you have ceased conceptualization and awakened to the reality of your own mind, will you be able to truly grasp the sacred doctrines.

The right path is not right or wrong

A visiting Tibetan monk asked, "How do I know which path is the right path?"

Louie Wing said, "To search for the right path is the wrong path. The right path is not right or wrong."

The monk asked, "Then how do I attain Buddhahood?"

Louie Wing said, "There is nothing to attain; just cease conceptualization. Buddhahood is your own original state; just cease screening it off by conceptualization."

The monk asked, "Can I achieve enlightenment just by that understanding?"

Louie Wing said, "You are originally not deluded, so there is nothing to achieve. The unnamable void transcends definitions, descriptions, and doctrines. Cease searching for it through conceptual constructs. It is beyond cause and effect and has nothing to do with the past, present, and future. The unnamable void is truly unnamable. Though void, it manifests all the myriad things, so what would you turn away from? What more would you search for?"

'Being here now' entangles you in the past and future

Henry asked, "There are teachers from traditions that talk about keeping your attention focused only on the present moment. They say that the past is gone, the future has not arrived, and only the present is real. What do you think about the practice of focusing on the present moment?"

Louie Wing said, "Trying to focus on the present moment will only cause you to become entangled with the past and the future."

Henry said, "But the whole idea of the practice is based on becoming free of the past and the future."

Louie Wing said, "Yes. The notion of a 'present moment' only has meaning in contradistinction of the notions of 'past' and 'future.' If the concept of the 'present' is posited, the concepts of 'past' and 'future' are automatically validated. This goes for all doctrines, formulas, rules, practices, and the like. If you continue to seek anything outside the reality of your own mind, you will simply revolve in continuous conceptualization. If you cease conceptualization and step back into your own pure awareness you will not discover any kind of an 'answer,' but your questions will certainly be resolved."

You exchange clarity for delusion

After a class, Alissa approached Louie Wing and asked, "If the only task is to cease conceptualization, why do all the great religions expound ethical codes and various forms of spiritual practice for overcoming hindrances and achieving liberation?"

Louie Wing said, "The ethical codes, precepts, commandments, perfections, and all the rest have no effect on the unnamable void. The void does not arise from them; they arise from the void. The unnamable void is the source and essence of all practices; how could it be altered by them? Just as waves do not alter the nature of water, ethical and spiritual practices do not alter the nature of your own fundamental awareness. When circumstances arise for particular practices to be performed, then perform them; when they do not, let them go. If you have not yet testified to the fact that the unnamable void is nothing other than your own fundamental nature, then all notions of 'right' practice or doing 'good' are still delusory. You will not know whether your actions are in accord with reality at all. There is a saying that goes something like this: 'Let me help you before you drown', said the monkey as he placed the fish up a tree.

"Your own essential awareness is the unnamable void, outside of which nothing exists. It is pure, clear, and luminous. When you attach yourself to any concept, even concepts about right and wrong conduct or good and bad practices, you exchange clarity for delusion. The vast, unnamable, fathomless void is not attained through steps, stages, or ranks. It is always functioning perfectly and completely; how could it be produced, attained, or activated through practices or deeds?"

Dream: Clues to Reality

Like a dream person

I arise from the void,
Like a dream person.

A dream person arises from me,
Like a void person.

Dreams in a dream

Ultimately, the teachings of all the sages should be seen through. Even the most sublime teachings of the buddhas and Zen masters are no more than dreams in a dream. You should know that everything that involves discrimination and conceptualization is a dream. True awakening is not awakening. True dreaming is not dreaming. Both enlightenment and delusion are conceptual constructs, dreams in a dream. Ultimately, there is neither one who awakens nor anything to awaken to. If you truly awaken, there is no awakening. Enlightenment is a conceptual description created by the human intellect. It is only valid in contradistinction to delusion. That is why I call it a dream. When dualistic thinking is abandoned, and there is no discrimination at all, there is neither delusion nor enlightenment. Remember, all conceptualization, whether of delusion or enlightenment, is a dream.

Illusions are false perceptions of reality

Shortly after Jim tested positive for AIDS, he asked "If all the myriad things are dreams and illusions, then our own minds must be illusory too. Like a dream person who can no longer exist when the dreamer awakens, when we die our minds can no longer exist. When our bodies have become dust and ashes, how could our minds still exist?"

Louie Wing said, "Illusions are false perceptions of reality; a dream person is composed of a dreamer's mind. When an illusion is seen through, the reality that was falsely perceived does not cease to exist. When a dreamer awakens, the mind that the dream person was composed of does not cease to be. Your body and mind consists of the vast, unnamable, fathomless void. When you die, the void, which is your true essence, does not cease to exist."

Delusion is like a person in a dream

Awakening to reality is awakening to your own true nature. If you try to discover reality outside your own mind, you are simply adding delusion to delusion. Delusion is like a person in a dream thinking they are separate from everything else in the dream. The dream person, the dream world, and all the things in the dream are nothing but the one mind of the dreamer. If the dream person realizes that he or she is actually dreaming, they instantly realize that everything they encounter in the dream is nothing other than their own mind.

Trying to find a telescope with a telescope

When you hear me talk about "awakening" and "ceasing conceptualization" do not imagine that there really are such things and then set about trying to find them. The mind that you are using to search with is the very mind you are looking for. How can you find mind with mind? How can you discover the unnamable void with the unnamable void? How can you become aware of awareness? All of this would be like looking at the sky through a telescope trying to find a telescope. It is a futile proposition.

Imagine that you are dreaming and you meet someone who tells you that this is just a dream. At first, you have some doubts and you go around pointing out how everything is so real. Then this person tells you to stop running around and step back into your own mind. When you do, you suddenly remember who you really are in waking life. You recall the fact that you are so and so, and that you work at such and such a place, and all the rest of the things that make up your waking identity. In such a case, you realize that you were never separate from your true self. You also realize that every thing around is no-thing. All is one; all is simply your own mind. Even the "person" who told you about the dream is not real. They are not a "person" at all. What has changed? Only your perspective has been corrected.

But suppose that, instead of stepping back and remembering who you really were, you continued to run around in the dream world trying to find the truth. You would never find it. No matter how far you searched, you would never find anything outside your own mind.

Similarly, if in your waking life you insist on wandering around looking for something to attain, you will never find it. Only by stepping back into the pure and clear awareness of your own mind will you be able to awaken to your identity with the vast, unnamable, fathomless void. Nothing will be lost or gained. Only your perspective will be corrected. You will simply be realizing what has been true all along. Where then, could you discover any "thing" at all?

A dream with no beginning and no ending

Doing good is a dream,
Committing evil is a dream.

Your body is a shadow; your mind is space,
You are a dream with no beginning and no ending.

Duality: One Side of Wholeness

When one awakens, all awaken

The unnamable void gives birth to the myriad things;
Looking deeply at any thing reveals the unnamable void.
Ceasing conceptualization, one awakens;
When one awakens, all awaken.

In clear and pure awareness there is no discrimination

One morning when Louie Wing and several students were enjoying some tea, Brady asked, "What do you mean when you say that with awakening there is no delusion or awakening?"

Louie Wing said, "When 'you' become aware of 'your' own fundamental awareness, you are still discriminating between your awareness and the one that is aware of it. When you truly awaken you simply become that awareness itself; in that clear and pure awareness there is no discrimination at all."

Brady asked, "What does it mean to have no discrimination at all?"

Louie Wing said, "It means that all the myriad things are illumined without the entanglements of attachment or aversion."

Abiding in the place where there is no right or wrong

Deana asked, "How can we avoid getting entangled in ideas of right and wrong?"

Louie Wing answered her, "By abiding in the place where there is no right or wrong."

Deana asked, "When you abide at that place, where are right and wrong?"

Louie Wing said, "When it is right, there is nothing but right in the whole universe; when it is wrong, there is nothing but wrong in the whole universe."

The second tree in the Garden of Eden

In the biblical creation stories, Adam and Eve lived in perfect unity with

God and nature. They did not even know they were different from each other. This is how infants are; they do not discriminate between themselves and their mothers or the environment.

When Adam and Eve ate the fruit of the knowledge of good and evil they suddenly began to discriminate. They knew they were different from each other, and were thus cast out of the garden. This is how it is for people as they mature; they sense a difference between themselves and everything else in the world. From this, grasping and aversion arise.

Now, in this tale, the gods–yes, "gods," for at this point the biblical God uses the plural "we," and "us"–even God becomes differentiated with the knowledge of good and evil, this and that, male and female. The gods fear that Adam and Eve may eat from another tree in the garden, the tree of life, and become immortal.

When people first hear about awakening to the vast, unnamable, fathomless void, it is like becoming aware of the second tree in the Garden of Eden. The unnamable void, like the tree of life, is guarded by two cherubs and a flaming sword. The two cherubs, like all dualities, must be transcended. Ceasing conceptualization cuts away the barrier of duality like a flaming sword.

Now, what happens when the fruit from the tree of immortal life is consumed? Again, we are back in the garden living in perfect unity with God and nature–but no longer as unconscious infants, but as conscious-ness itself. Here is the experience of the eye seeing the eye. Awareness is aware of itself.

This is the meaning of the sages when they say things like "seeing without seeing" and "hearing without hearing" and "speaking without speaking."

When each thing is all things, all things are no-thing

A sage does not hold views of self and other that is why a sage is called a sage. A sage realizes that each particular thing is at once all things, and when each thing is all things, all things are no-thing. Realizing that there is no-thing, where could fear or greed abide?

Zen without koans is like Christianity without Christ

A visiting Zen monk asked, "In the Rinzai School of Zen they intro-spect koans. In the Soto sect we are taught that introspecting koans in meditation only leads to intellectual understanding and diverts us from true, objectless meditation. Do you think that koans are even necessary in Zen?"

Louie Wing said, "Zen without koans would be like Christianity without Christ. The koan literature and practice methods are really the only major factor that distinguishes Zen from the other Mahayana Buddhist schools. If you are attracted to a path that does not utilize koans, fine, but why call it Zen?"

The monk said, "We don't disregard koans; we just don't use them for objects of meditation."

Louie Wing said, "If you distinguish meditation from no meditation then you turn meditation itself into an object."

The void and you are not two or even one

Awakening and delusion are like wakefulness and dreaming,
Awake or dreaming you are you.
Dreaming or awake you are not you,
The void and you are not two or even one.

Enlightenment: The Experience of Reality

Trust it and enjoy the ride

If you truly awaken, you will not be concerned with reality; you will not be enamored with enlightened masters or teachers; you will not be tangled up in ideas about the rewards of spiritual practice. You will transcend conceptualization, alone and free, you will work and play without being caught up in things and ideas. The entire universe could shatter, and you would not be afraid. All the treasures of the world could be offered to you, and your joy would not be increased. Do you want to know why? It is because you realize that all things are void. All things arise from the un-namable void and flow back into it. The entire universe is nothing but the unnamable void, which is your own true mind and body. The myriad things are manifestations of the one unnamable void. Since they are like dreams, shadows, or illusions, why would you try to grasp them and what could you possibly have to fear? Trust it and enjoy the ride.

Cross over, cross over!

If you see through the illusory nature of the myriad things, and awaken to the reality of your own mind—and even if you merge with the unnamable void–that is still nothing but a dream in a dream. Even if you transcend dualistic notions about awakening and delusion, and are free to come and go as you please, there is still something more to realize: crossing over, crossing over!

A sudden realization occurs

If you want to know what awakening is like, all I can say is that a sudden realization occurs when you cease becoming entangled in dualistic, conceptual discrimination.

What do you call this!

One morning Julie was at Louie Wing's place, going over her notes from the talk of the previous evening.

Louie Wing called out from his bedroom, "Who is here?"

Julie replied, "It is me, Julie."

Louie Wing said, "Will you go to the fridge and get me a beer."

Julie quietly said, "Why don't you get it yourself."

Louie Wing called back, "What? I didn't hear you."

Julie said, "Never mind," and looked in the refrigerator. Not finding any beer, she said, "Sorry, there is no beer."

Louie Wing came out of the bedroom and rummaged through the refrigerator. Inside, he discovered a can of beer. Turning around, he thrust the can in front of her face. In a voice like thunder, Louie Wing roared, "What do you call this?"

In an instant, everything fell away, and Julie merged with the vast, unnamable, fathomless void. A moment later, the whole universe erupted with laughter.

Louie Wing grabbed her by the collar of her shirt and demanded, "What did you see that makes you laugh?"

She broke free from his massive grip, snatched the can of beer from his hand, opened it, and guzzled it down.

Louie Wing smiled and said, "It is never apart from your immediate awareness. Realization is nothing other then awakening to the fact that you and the unnamable void are not two. When you realize that, you awaken from the dream and remember what you have forgotten. There is not a single objective particle in the entire universe; all that you perceive is nothing other than your own mind. Now you understand why all the sages have taught that after awakening you are the same as before awakening. Both self and objects are nothing but conceptual ideas based on dualistic thinking. Both ordinary people and enlightened sages are the same vast, unnamable, fathomless void. That which you have realized is the one essence, the one mind outside of which nothing exists. Have no further doubt about it.

"Now that you have seen the illusory nature of all dualistic notions, cherish your experience and nurture your realization. The Heart sutra says, 'There is no old age and death, and no ending of old age and death'."

With that, Louie Wing walked out of the room. For a whole week, Julie wandered around as if deaf, dumb, and blind.

I advise you not to eat lunch with people like that

One day, after reading a popular Zen book suggested by one of his students, Louie Wing seemed uncharacteristically agitated, he said, "Anyone who thinks they can practice objectless meditation without first realizing that their own mind is the unnamable void, is delusional. Such people dwell in a pernicious vacuum. They simply swap the delusion of the many for the delusion of the one. They say things like, 'True enlightenment is simply understanding that there is no enlightenment,' and 'Just sitting is the essential teaching of Buddhism.' What drivel! Others commit acts of evil, claiming that since everything is void evil is not wrong. Such fools cannot tell up from down, right from wrong, a hamburger from a clump of dirt. I advise you not to eat lunch with people like that.

"If you really want to practice objectless meditation, you had better awaken to the reality of your own true mind first. Awakening has nothing to do with putting an end to rational thought. Rational thought, like all the myriad things, arises from, and returns to, the vast unnamable void, which is nothing other than your own true mind."

Mike suddenly burst out laughing.

Louie Wing said, "What is so funny, Mike?"

Mike said, "A car just drove through my liver."

Louie Wing said, "Where did it come from?"

Mike said, "There is not a single thing outside."

Louie Wing said, "What will you eat?"

Mike said, "Sun, moon, and stars."

Louie Wing said, "You must be hungry!"

Mike said, "I have never eaten a single thing." Then he stood and began walking out of the room.

Louie Wing said, "Hey Mike, are you going to leave us alone?"

Mike burst into laughter and left the room.

After Mike was gone, Louie Wing said, "And so it goes, and so it goes."

Seeing through to the very bottom

A couple of weeks after Mike walked out, he entered the room in the middle of a talk that Louie Wing was giving, and sat down.

Louie Wing stopped his talk, looked at Mike, and said, "So, did you see through to the very bottom?"

Mike said, "I don't know what you're talking about, Louie Wing."

Louie Wing said, "When you see through to the very bottom, you are the same as a sage."

Mike said, "When you don't see through to the very bottom, you are the same as a sage."

Louie Wing resumed his talk.

I was hoping to get a cup of tea

Later that night after most of the students had gone, Louie Wing held out a cup of tea to Mike. Just as Mike reached for it, Louie Wing pulled it away saying, "What is this?"

Mike said, "That is your problem."

Louie Wing said, "If that is how you are, why did you come here to-night?"

Mike said, "You are right, of course, but I do enjoy the talks, and I was hoping to get a cup of tea."

Louie Wing gave him the cup of tea.

Even no-delusion and no-awakening cannot be attained

Ultimately, there is no delusion and no awakening. Even "no delusion" and "no awakening" cannot be attained. That is why the sages of all time tell you not to seek for anything outside your own mind.

When you truly awaken there is neither something that is awakened to, nor someone that is awakened.

Nothing gained, nothing lost

When you awaken to reality,

Neither awakening nor awakened subsist.

Clear and pure, luminous and aware,

Nothing gained, nothing lost.

When awakening is not awakening, that is awakening

Ashley asked, "What is awakening?"

Louie Wing said, "Awakening is participation in the world without views about 'participation' or 'awakening.' Awakening is the cessation of producing delusion when confronted by perception, feelings, and thoughts. When perceptions, feelings, and thoughts are not perceptions, feelings, and thoughts, that is awakening. When awakening is not awakening, that is awakening. When birth and death are not birth and death, that is awakening. When you no longer discriminate between delusion and awakening, that is awakening."

Heraclitus was right

When you cease conceptualization and awaken to your own true mind, you will be free to work and play in this world without being hindered by fear and doubt. Just step back into the pure and clear awareness of your mind and realize what has always been without shape or form. You have always been without beginning or end. When you step back and look for some distinctive thing called "you" there is not a trace, and yet the clear and pure, luminous awareness of your own mind illumines all things. Heraclitus was right; the way up is the way down.

Can awareness be aware of itself?

The vast, unnamable, fathomless void cannot be understood by intellect or imagination. Even the most knowledgeable people on earth remain in delusion if they do not awaken to their own true mind. This is because all knowledge has its source in the vast, unnamable, fathomless void. How could any manifestation comprehend its own source? Can the eye see itself? Can the nose smell itself? Can awareness be aware of itself? When you cease conceptualization and step back into your own luminous awareness both object and subject vanish. In the pure, clear, and luminous awareness of your own mind there is just pure, clear, luminous awareness, without any notions of "pure" or "clear" or "luminous" or "awareness."

There are people who immediately awaken when the sages point this out. Others awaken after a shorter or longer period of practice. Some never awaken.

Always have been, always will be

If you cease conceptualization and awaken to the vast, unnamable, fathomless void all the myriad things awaken. In awakening, you remember that all the myriad things are you. Always have been, always will be.

156

The sages were not at all different from you

Louie Wing said, "The sages of all the great traditions in the ten times were not at all different from you people sitting here today. They saw things and heard things with the same seeing and hearing that you are using right now. They did not stop thoughts and feelings from arising; they just did not attach themselves to them. The mind of a sage illumines the myriad things without becoming identified by them."

Martin asked, "After someone has awakened, is it still necessary to practice or not?"

Louie Wing said, "When you truly awaken, practicing and not practicing are both seen through as merely conceptual ideas. Nevertheless, what I am calling 'awakening' is not a state of being; awakening is a continuous process, an ongoing unfolding. Of course, these terms, too, miss the point. It is truly beyond the realm of conceptualization. Just step back into your own pure and clear, luminous awareness and resolve the issue directly."

Do you need to tell people when you move your bowels?

During a talk, Ted suddenly stood up and announced, "Awakening is not realized through spiritual practice, nor can it be realized through conceptualization. How about that?"

Louie Wing said, "Why are you rambling about awakening and realization? Do you need to tell people about it when you successfully move your bowels?"

Ted quietly sat back down.

One spontaneously accords with circumstances

The essence and function of a sage is the essence and function of a person who has merged with the unnamable void. The sage overcomes discrimination and is not controlled by desire and fear. Subject and object are seen through, attachment and aversion dissolve, and one spontaneously accords with circumstances as they arise.

Not one, not many

When you awaken to your own true mind,
Nothing is concealed or revealed.
Awakened or deluded, you are as you are,
Not one, not many.

Many: Manifestations of the One

Up in the sky you cannot hear Mozart

Lift up the sky and look underneath.
A ball on a stream, bobbing and rolling,
Who would not enjoy reading Mark Twain?
Up in the sky you cannot hear Mozart.

Lifting the void

One day Lee approached Louie Wing and said, "I have understood what you mean by the void."

Louie Wing said, "Can you lift it?"

Lee said, "Easily."

Louie Wing said, "Let me see you lift the void?"

Lee placed his cupped hand out and made a move as if lifting.

Louie Wing said, "That is not lifting the void."

Lee asked, "Then how would you lift it?"

Louie Wing jumped to his feet, spun Lee around, grasped him by the back of his pants and hoisted him into the air.

Lee cried out, "Put me down. Put me down!"

Louie Wing said, "Be grateful I did not show you how to toss the void through a wall." Then he set Lee down.

Even the memory of it quickens my pulse

One time, when Louie Wing was walking home from a play with several students, a prostitute accosted him. She said, "There is something about you that makes me think you would be an interesting client. I think that you would enjoy it, too. I will give you a special price, what do you say?"

Louie Wing said, "My lady, it would be an honor." Then he said goodnight to his students and wandered off with the woman.

When word of this spread among his students, many were astonished and Lee confronted him openly, saying, "We thought you were some kind of a wise sage. How could you indulge yourself in sexual pleasure with a hooker?"

Louie Wing said, "Ah! Even the memory of it quickens my pulse!"

The center of the unnamable void is everywhere
The myriad things are void things. The myriad things arise from, abide in, and fall back into the vast, unnamable, fathomless void. In the fundamental essence of mind, all things are equal. Every thing, at every place, in every time, is the whole unnamable void. If you look at this cushion deeply, it is the center of all time and space. It is the principal around which everything else revolves. If you look at the Space Needle in Seattle deeply, it is the center of all time and space. This cushion then becomes an aspect of the Space Needle. If you pick out a star and look deeply, that star becomes the center around which all things revolve. Your birth is then one aspect of that star. Everything in the universe is like that. No matter what you focus your attention on, it can be seen as the central phenomena around which all things revolve. The center of the vast, unnamable, fathomless void is everywhere, including the very place where you are sitting now.

All stand up when you stand up
The sun, moon, sky, and stars,
Mountains, rivers, plants, and animals,
Houses, streets, pots, and pans,
All stand up when you stand up.

Delusion, anguish, and affliction are true nature
The vast, unnamable, fathomless void is not apart from all the myriad things. Your pure and clear luminous awareness is not separate from your delusion, anguish, and afflictions.

Where could you possibly find anything mundane?
Louie Wing held up a burnt matchstick and said, "This matchstick is the vast, unnamable, fathomless void. All the universes in all the meta-verses are totally contained within it. Not only that, but each superstring in each subatomic particle, in each atom, in each molecule, also contain all of space and time, and each does so without interfering with any other superstring or particle. Every particular thing you perceive is the totality of space-time. All things are void; the void is all things. Look! The vast, unnamable, fathomless void is coming forth as a slice of bologna! Where could you possibly find anything mundane?"

Illumining the many without leaving the one
Your awareness spontaneously accords with the flow,
Continuously fresh, now this, now this.
In perfect stillness, you follow the stream,
Illumining the many without leaving the one.

Meditation: The Keystone of Zen

Ceasing conceptualization is best
Danielle asked, "Is there any practice that is best for awakening?"

Louie Wing said, "The practice of ceasing conceptualization is best. If you can simply cease from habitual discrimination, your own luminous awareness will shine through. Take a step back from your tangling, dualistic thoughts. Take a step back from ideas of self and other, right and wrong, gain and loss, joy and sorrow. When thoughts come, step back and observe them; are you those thoughts or are you the one that observes them? Do the same thing with all your notions, ideas, and views. If you persist in this practice, you may suddenly cease conceptualization and awaken to your true identity: the vast, unnamable, fathomless void."

Step back and abide in your own clear awareness
Louie Wing said, "If you want to know a way in, listen. Cease chasing thoughts around in your mind, cease defining things around you, take a step back and abide in your own clear awareness, which precludes all conceptualization. Suspend all your ideas about right and wrong, self and other; cease judging and evaluating things and events and simply perceive the fundamental awareness that precedes, underlies, and succeeds all discrimination. There you will discover the unnamable reality of your own true essence."

Fred asked, "Is there any secret teachings beyond that?"

Louie Wing said, "There have never been any secret teachings. When you cease conceptualization, step back, and abide in your own luminescent awareness; you will discover that it has never been hidden."

Easy to understand, difficult to do
The truth of awakening is simple and straightforward, however, it is not

easy. All of the great sages serve as models of perseverance and determination. There are no secret formulas or esoteric doctrines; just cease conceptualization and observe your own inherent awareness. Put your mind at ease and clarify the essence. It is easy to understand, but difficult to do. However, if you persevere, arousing your determination, your mind and your environment will begin to unify into a single wholeness. Do not let up, but continue to step back from your habitual discriminations, and suddenly the vast, unnamable void stands forth as your own mind.

Settle into your own fundamental awareness

In order to cease conceptualization and realize the fact that your own mind is the vast, unnamable, fathomless void, you must step back from your dualistic thoughts and settle into your own fundamental awareness. If you persevere in all your activities and non-activities, you will awaken to your own true nature. It may happen quickly or after a long time but, as long as your aspiration is genuine, you will eventually achieve certainty.

When dualistic thoughts arise, gently step back into your fundamental awareness. When you become restless, irritable, or discontent, let go of your agitation and step back into your own fundamental awareness. Simply be aware of the myriad things without judging them, naming them, or dividing them up into concepts of this and that, self and other. Let go of all your habitual discrimination and step back into the pure stillness of your own fundamental awareness. Through ceasing conceptualization, you will awaken to your own true nature: the vast, unnamable, fathomless void.

Not a difficult to understand, mystical technique

Ceasing conceptualization is not a difficult to understand, mystical technique. However, people turn it into a concept, too, causing confusion and misunderstanding. When the sages of all times saw people suffering due to their own habitual conceptualization, they tried to show them how to step back from delusion and realize their own pure and clear awareness. Later, people developed intellectual interpretations about the various methods preached by the sages. Without realizing the fundamental truth of ceasing conceptualization, they misapply the teachings and set about trying to cease thinking altogether! They sit still for hours and days, suppressing their thoughts and trying to make their minds blank. They call this "just sitting" and "objectless meditation." It would be laughable if it were not so sad.

Even the idea of 'abandonment' is abandoned

Horst asked, "What is 'saving all beings'?"

Louie Wing said, "'Saving all beings' is abandonment."

Horst said, "Abandonment of what?"

Louie Wing said, "Abandonment of duality."

Horst asked, "What does that mean?"

Louie Wing said, "It means complete abandonment of all dualistic notions, such as good and evil, being and nonbeing, delusion and awakening, void and no-void, spiritual practice and ordinary activity, sacred and mundane. When you truly abandon all such ideas you realize that all is the unnamable void. When you truly 'save all beings' there are no notions of saving, saved, or savior. Even the idea of 'abandonment' is abandoned. When you have truly abandoned dualistic conceptualization, you realize that there is not a single being to save, and nothing to save them from. Your true nature is the unnamable void. That which is void is the vast and fathomless realm of reality. If you realize total abandonment of duality, you truly save all beings."

Serene in the midst of thought and emotion

Do you want to know a way in? Listen! Let go of all your ideas and preconceived notions about right and wrong, ordinary and holy. When thoughts arise, let them arise, observing them from the perspective of your own fundamental awareness. When thoughts go, let them go without clinging to them; you are not your thoughts. Let them arise and fall as they are. Like birds flying past a window, let them come and go without attachment or judgment.

Step back and rest in your own fundamental awareness, your own true nature. Your true mind is not involved with understanding or meaning; it is free, immediate, pure, clear, and infinitely present. Cease creating definitions and discerning meanings and you will awaken to the vast, unnamable, fathomless void.

Simply cease indulging intellectual interpretations, and allow your notions of good and bad, this and that, mine and not mine, and all other dualistic ideas to fall away. Your own fundamental awareness is serene in the midst of the stream of thought and emotion, as well as the activities of the everyday world. It is never caught up or confused by thoughts, emotions or perceptions. It is vast, free, and charged with infinite potential, inconceivable, boundless, and beyond all definition and limitation.

Cease conceptualizing, step back, and rest in your fundamental awareness, which perfectly accords with the myriad things while never being hindered by anything. It is not thinking nor is it the absence of thought; it contains and transcends all thought and no thought.

Cease judgments about what is good and what is bad; lay aside your notions about what is right and what is wrong; stop your arguments of this against that, self against other. Do not cling to or reject anything whatsoever.

When your views of right and wrong, this and that, ordinary and holy, and the like, are finally abandoned and no longer hinder you, then you will be free and at ease wherever you may be.

The void does not wait for meditation to manifest

If you cease conceptualization, you will awaken to your own mind, which is the one true essence of all the myriad things. There is no other task than that. The true sages never had any secret doctrines or esoteric formulas beyond this. Both sitting and walking meditation are excellent ways to step back into your own fundamental awareness and I recommend them to everyone, especially beginners. However, no particular style of meditation is right for everyone. All that is important is to cease conceptualization.

I have known people who initially realized awakening while chanting, standing, lying down, swimming, copying sutras, and a host of other methods. I heard about one monk who, frustrated after years of practice, quit the monastery, visited a prostitute, and awakened during sexual intercourse. I personally met a woman that achieved realization while working on an assembly line putting circuit boards in TV sets. The vast, unnamable, fathomless void is ever present and does not wait around for people to do the right kind of meditation in order to manifest. The true nature of your own mind is not bound by rules. Just abide in your own fundamental awareness without chasing after awakening or trying to run away from delusion. That is all there is to say.

Stopping and seeing

Brooks asked, "The classic Buddhist texts often refer to two basic forms of meditation: 'stopping' and 'seeing'. It seems that your teaching about 'ceasing conceptualization' is the same as 'stopping'. However, you do not talk about the complementary practice of 'seeing'. Why not?"

Louie Wing said, "Ceasing conceptualization includes both, 'stopping' and 'seeing'. By 'stopping,' the texts you refer to mean 'stopping delusion', that is, to stop discriminating between this and that. 'Seeing' means 'seeing reality'; this is seeing the one essence of your own true nature and all the myriad things. In actual experience, 'stopping' and 'seeing' occur simultaneously, which is to say 'stopping' is 'seeing'. When you truly cease conceptualizing, you immediately realize the true nature of yourself and all of space and time.

Brooks said, "Are you saying that 'stopping' is enough, and we don't need to worry about 'seeing'? Then why do the texts even refer to 'seeing' at all?"

Louie Wing said, "You misunderstood what I just said. Ceasing conceptualization includes both 'stopping' and 'seeing.' Ultimately, all such terms are temporary expedients. The reason 'seeing' is expounded in contradistinction to 'stopping' is so that people do not become attached to the concept called 'stopping'. All such terms are conceptual constructs, created to guide students to the reality of their own minds. Ceasing conceptualization means to cease creating concepts, not to cease thinking, feeling, or perceiving."

Brooks said, "I think I understand, but how are the expedients of 'stopping' and 'seeing' supposed to help students?"

Louie Wing said, "The expedient method called 'stopping' guides the student to the realization that all the myriad things are void or empty, like things in a dream or illusions. This helps the student to release his or her stubborn tendencies of grasping and aversion. However, if this expedient is taken as some kind of absolute truth, that is, if it becomes conceptualized, then there is the risk that the student will fall under the false view of nihilism. The expedient method called 'seeing' teaches the student that all the myriad things are manifestations of the vast, unnamable, fathomless void. This helps the student to release his or her attachment to nothingness."

Let go of all views

Ceasing conceptualization means to cease creating and applying concepts to the things and events we perceive through our senses, as well as the feelings and thoughts that arise from within. It has nothing to do with shutting out the world around us or suppressing our feelings and thoughts.

When you create or apply concepts to your perceptions, feelings, and thoughts, you separate what you perceive, feel, and think from the whole of reality. When you cease creating and applying concepts to your perceptions, feelings, and thoughts you will experience them as they truly are.

At the same time, if you hear me say, "cease conceptualization," and you immediately try to force your mind into silence, you have only made a concept out of "ceasing conceptualization." All you need to do is let go of all views, ideas, and notions and step back into your own pure and clear awareness.

No matter where you are or what you meet, simply suspend your judgments, notions, and prejudice and allow the experience to unfold of itself. True meditation has nothing to do with sitting or walking. True meditation is developing the power to maintain a free and serene state of being in any circumstances whatsoever. True meditation is the ability to rest in the vast, unnamable, fathomless void of your own mind at all times and places without holding onto ideas about "meditation."

At a mountain retreat or a noisy mall

Just observe the fundamental awareness of your own minds. Keep stepping back and back, until you cannot step back any further and rest there, at the very source of your own awareness. Once you have discovered the root of your awareness, keep going back to it, over and over again, until you are always abiding within it. If you are at a quiet mountain retreat or at a noisy mall, abide in your own fundamental awareness. When you are able to step back and rest in the vast, unnamable, fathomless void of your own true nature, in whatever situations arise, difficult or easy, painful or pleasurable, you will be experiencing the same liberation as all the sages of the ten times.

Zazen and sitting meditation are not the same

A visiting Zen student asked, "My teacher says that sitting meditation is the only authentic practice. He says that zazen is the one true path to awakening. What do you say?"

Louie Wing said, "First of all, zazen and sitting meditation are not the same. True zazen has nothing to do with sitting, standing, walking, or lying down. 'Zazen' is the term that the sages of the Zen tradition used to indicate the practice that I call 'ceasing conceptualization.'

"Having said that, I have found that sitting is usually the easiest way for people to practice zazen, especially beginners. However, once you begin to develop the ability to step back into your own clear awareness, you should practice it in all your activities and non-activities. You should not become attached to the form of sitting, nor should you have aversion for it. When it is time to sit, practice zazen while sitting; when it is time to work, practice zazen while you work. Ultimately, there is no final rule or best way to practice. Any method will become a barrier if you become fixated on it. Just cease conceptualization and step back into the pure and clear, luminous awareness of your own mind."

There is nothing to search for

If you truly aspire to awakening you must abandon all your ideas about searching for it. Searching for anything can only be done from the level of discrimination and conceptualization. Because the vast, unnamable, fathomless void contains, and is contained by everything in all space and time, there is nothing to search for. From the beginningless beginning, you have never been apart from it. It is your own source, manifestation, and destination. By conceptualization you become deluded and imagine that you are somehow separate from it. If you simply cease conceptualization, the false perception of such a division will naturally dissolve and you will realize that you have never been bound by anything.

Awaken and everything will become perfectly clear. All the myriad things are nothing but the one vast and fathomless void of your own mind. Every single thing you encounter is nothing other than your own true self.

Just let go of all your ideas, give up your views, cease your habitual conceptualizing, and continuously step back into the pure and clear awareness of your own mind. Step back into the very source of your perceptions, feelings, and thoughts.

Awareness, awareness, awareness

The most essential thing you must do is cease conceptualization. Continuously step back into your own pure and clear awareness. Awareness, awareness, awareness, all the time. The moment you notice yourself being carried away by dualistic ideas, step back. When greed, anger, fear, and delusion arise, step back into the source of your own awareness.

Keep this up until it becomes automatic and seamless. You must be able to persevere at all times and places. Dwell in your own fundamental awareness right in the middle of the vicissitudes of the everyday activities of life. When you notice that you are confused, step back. When doubt or fear plagues your mind, step back. Cease conceptualizing and simply observe your perceptions, feelings, and thoughts as they arise and fall over the surface of your own clear and pure, luminous awareness.

Perceptions, feelings, and thoughts arise and fall, come and go, but your fundamental awareness remains unmoved and clear. That is why the sages of the ten times urge you to awaken to the fundamental awareness of your own mind. When sound arises you hear it without making any effort; when you meet forms you see them without trying. Your own hearing and seeing do not come from anyone else.

If you truly aspire to awakening, then wholeheartedly throw yourself into ceasing conceptualization. Keep stepping back into the fundamental awareness of your own mind, no matter what your circumstances. If you persevere, you will truly awaken and realize what you have forgotten.

Settle into your own pure and clear awareness

Dawson asked, "How do I cease conceptualization?"

Louie Wing said, "Let go of all your concerns and entanglements, step back from your thoughts and ideas about good and bad, spiritual and mundane. When perceptions, feelings, and thoughts arise, do not interfere with them, either by engaging them or trying to suppress them.

"Settle into your own pure and clear awareness where nothing comes or goes, where meanings, explanations, and knowledge do not abide. Rest in that fundamental awareness, allowing your mind to be like the sky, without form, yet containing all forms, without knowledge, yet containing all wisdom.

"Simply cease indulging yourself in entanglements of all kinds, and allow your desires and aversions to fade away. Your pure and clear, luminous awareness illumines all things while remaining unmoved by any. Dwelling there, you are not caught up and turned about by perceptions, feelings, and thoughts.

"When your practice becomes continuous and seamless, spiritual and mundane, desire and aversion, awakening and delusion, and all your other ideas, views, and opinions can no longer bind you. Then you will know true liberation wherever you are, and whatever you are doing."

Allow even the present to dissolve

Wayner asked, "If we do manage to cease conceptualization and dwell in pure and clear awareness, won't we then become attached to pure and clear awareness?"

Louie Wing said, "When you truly abide in pure and clear awareness, all conceptualization ceases, including the concept of 'pure and clear awareness.'"

Wayner asked, "What is pure and clear awareness?"

Louie Wing said, "If you really want to realize it, then I advise you to discover it directly. When you are sitting in meditation or doing walking meditation or whatever your own method involves, stay aware of your own fundamental awareness. When perceptions, feelings, or thoughts arise, avoid making any judgments and let them be as they are. Do not fall into discrimination by making evaluations of good or bad, pleasant or unpleasant, and similar notions."

Wayner said, "When I try to meditate, difficult memories keep coming up."

Louie Wing said, "Memories are memories. It is only due to conceptualization that you apply the term 'difficult' to them. When memories arise, let them arise without attaching judgments to them. Let go of anticipations and fears for tomorrow. Rest in the pure and clear awareness of your own mind, neither grasping nor rejecting anything at all, and allow even the present to dissolve."

Allow reality to be as it is

After a talk, Linda approached Louie Wing and asked, "How can we cease conceptualization and awaken to reality?"

Louie Wing said, "Not by suppressing thought, reciting mantras, studying, contemplation, or isolation. Simply step back into the pure and clear awareness of your own mind and allow reality to be as it is. In your own fundamental awareness there is nothing that is not reality."

Allow them, allow them

When perceptions, feelings, and thoughts arise, allow them. When perceptions, feelings, and thoughts dissolve, allow them.

Mindlessness is not different from mindfulness

Noah said, "I was taught that mindfulness was the way to awakening. But it seems to me that your teaching about ceasing conceptualization is more like mindlessness."

Louie Wing said, "When you are truly mindful you are not hindered by discrimination and conceptualization. Mindlessness is not different from mindfulness."

The efforts of awakening

Nils asked, "Don't we have to make some kind of effort to awaken?"

Louie Wing said, "Yes."

168

Nils said, "Do you still make effort?"
Louie Wing said, "Yes."
Nils asked, "What kind of effort do you make?"
Louie Wing said, "When the alarm clock rings, I get up and brush my teeth."
Nils said, "Everything seems to be in order here."

Your own awareness is functioning perfectly
A visiting Zen monk said, "My roshi teaches his students to sit in meditation as much as possible and make their minds like calm water. Is this the same as your teaching of ceasing conceptualization?"

Louie Wing said, "Not at all. True meditation has nothing to do with sitting, nor is it concerned with longer or shorter amounts of time. You cannot make your mind like calm water or anything else for that matter. Besides, your own pure and clear luminous awareness is already functioning perfectly, why try to alter it?"

Reality: The Homeland of the Self

Reality has never fluctuated
Reality has never fluctuated; things are as they are. How could they be different from what they are? Everything is as it is. Even if it were possible to understand reality through conceptualization, it would not change a thing.

Neither existent nor non-existent
Stu asked, "If the myriad things are void, does that mean they are non-existent?"

Louie Wing said, "'Non-existent' is as much a dream as its opposite. In reality, things are neither existent nor non-existent."

Immeasurable, indefinable
The vast, unnamable, fathomless void, the source, manifestation, and destination of reality, cannot be measured or defined. It is the greatest of the great, infinitely infinite. It transcends time and space, eternally eternal. It is so big it contains everything in the ten times. It is so small that its entirety fits into a single superstring—and still has room enough to do cartwheels; that is why I call it the vast, unnamable, fathomless void.

The unnamable void is not nonexistent, and the myriad things are not existent. The myriad things are not, in reality, the myriad things—they are just called the myriad things. The unnamable void is not, in reality, void—it is just called void. True awakening transcends the many and the one, the myriad things and the void. A truly awakened being acts without action, thinks without thinking, perceives without perceiving, attaches without attachment, fears without fear, rejoices without rejoice, grieves without grief. Within the vast, unnamable, fathomless void not a single thing is born, not a single thing dies. And even this is nothing but a dream in a dream.

A seamless realm

The sages in the ten times never relied on sacred texts or verbal teachings; they only directed you to your own true nature. When I say "your own true nature," I am talking about the pure, clear, luminous awareness that is inherent in each of you. The vast, unnamable void is the true nature of your own delusion. The true nature of reality is the same in you as it is in all the sages in the ten times. It is what I call the vast, unnamable, fathomless void, the true nature of reality, the pure, clear, awareness of your own mind. It is the source and destination of all space and time. It is the single seamless realm: alone, serene, and free.

Reality does not vary from one individual to another

Your own true mind is not the discriminating mind of conceptualization. Your true mind is clear and pure awareness, completely unaffected by dualistic notions of right and wrong, self and other, awakening and delusion. When you are able to cease conceptualizing, you will spontaneously awaken. However, if you continue to become entangled in dualistic thought, even if you endure tremendous efforts of meditation, sitting for hours and hours, you will never awaken.

Entangled in ideas about practices and doctrines of the various spiritual traditions, you will be unable to realize awakening. Still, in the temporal world of everyday activity, realization of the truth comes to different people after differing lengths of time. Some people hear the teaching and cease conceptualization in an instant. Others are only able to put a stop to dualistic thinking after applying themselves to certain spiritual practices for a short period, while still others finally awaken only after long years of intense struggle.

Whether you awaken quickly or after a long period, the realization is simply becoming aware of the truth of reality. Spiritual practice does not create it. When I tell you that there is nothing to attain, I am not speaking metaphorically; it is the truth. Accordingly, whether you awaken in a moment or after a long period, the realization is the same. Reality is reality and does not vary from one individual to another.

It is eternal, pure, and unchanging

In all the ten times, in perfect unanimity, the great sages and enlightened masters have experienced this one truth alone, fulfilling the great potential and capacity of all beings. Through the limitless power of compassion, they have demonstrated, expressed, and indicated the single most profound and most important truth, the one essence of all the myriad beings.

Bypass the delusions of steps, stages, and gates, cease conceptual thought, and you will suddenly awaken to the one true essence. In all the ten times, this essence, still and pure, comprises the source of all the myriad things. It pervades all time and space, and transcends all dualistic thought. It is beyond notions of good and evil and precludes all knowledge. It is eternal, pure, and unchanging. It is right here and right now, unmoving, clear, and luminescent. All the myriad beings, sentient and insentient, embody it completely.

That is why the sages never bothered with anything else, but repeatedly directed you to your own true mind. There is only one true task: awakening to the reality of your own mind.

It has never been absent

The very thing that you are all seeking is, at this very moment, right there where you are sitting, pure, clear, and luminously aware. It is your own fundamental nature, the essence of all things. I call it the vast, unnamable, fathomless void.

It is the same in deluded people and sages. It contains and pervades all of space and time. It is manifest as your own mind and is the source of your own body. It is the essence of seeing, hearing, tasting, smelling, feeling, thinking, emotion, and consciousness. It has never been sick, tired, or hungry, and it has never been absent.

The treasure has never been outside

Cease conceptualizing, step back and observe your own pure and clear awareness: vast and mysterious, fine and subtle, void and magnanimous, ultimately transcending description or definition. It is empty, yet full to the brim, utterly passive, yet charged with infinite creativity. It is dark, yet it is able to illuminate all things, silent, yet the source of all sounds.

It is the source and energy of your own body and mind–you see by means of it, hear with its energy, move and act through and within it.

When you cease dualistic thought, you awaken to your own mind; when you awaken to your own mind, you realize your identity with the vast, unnamable, fathomless void. Your own mind is the void; the void is your mind. If you want to awaken to it, cease conceptualization.

Let go of all your ideas and notions and perceive the very source of perception, which is your own luminous awareness. The vast, unnamable, fathomless void is not outside of this awareness; this awareness is not outside the unnamable void. Outside of the void, there is nothing at all.

Yet, do not cling even to the unnamable void, and immediately reduce its potential and capacity; it is unlimited and defies fixation. Once you truly awaken to it, you can spontaneously flow in harmony with the myriad things. The vast, unnamable, fathomless void is not existent or non-existent; it is causeless, yet it is the cause of the myriad things. The void is neither right nor wrong; yet, right and wrong are the void.

Awakening to the pure and clear awareness of your own mind, you will discover that the treasure has never been outside. The vast, unnamable, fathomless void precludes both being and non-being. When you awaken to it, you realize that it is the source, substance, and destination of the myriad things, yet it is without source, substance or destination, and transcends the myriad things.

The source, manifestation, and destination of all things
To cease conceptualizing anything is awakening. When you realize that, everything is awakening, including conceptualization. To awaken to the luminous nature of your own mind is awakening to the vast, unnamable, fathomless void. The unnamable void is the source, manifestation, and destination of all the myriad things.

Conceive by not conceiving
The vast, unnamable, fathomless void has no shape or form and can only be seen by not seeing. It has no sound and can only be heard by not hearing. It transcends knowing and can only be known by not knowing. It is inconceivable and can only be conceived by not conceiving.

When you see by seeing, some things are seen and some things are not seen. When you see by not seeing, everything is seen. When you know by knowing, some things are known and some are not known. When you know by not knowing, everything is known. When you conceive by conceiving, some things are conceived and some things are not conceived. When you conceive by not conceiving, everything is conceived.

If you see one thing by not seeing, you will know how to see all things with not seeing; the same goes for knowing and conceiving. If you see a fire truck by seeing, you only see a "fire truck." If you see a fire truck by not seeing, you see the vast, unnamable, fathomless void.

Is there such a thing as the Devil?

A visiting Christian clergyman asked, "Is there such a thing as the Devil?"

Louie Wing said, "There is not even such a thing as God."

Nothing is lost, nothing is gained

Looking deeply, you see that the entire past is the entire present and the entire present is the entire past. The entire future is the entire present; the entire present is the entire future. The entire past is the entire future; the entire future is the entire past. The myriad things may appear to arise, change, and vanish but nothing is lost, nothing is gained. You must experience it directly.

All of time and space is you, there is no other

If you are moved with aspiration to awaken, consider the wholeness of each moment. Each moment includes all of space and time. The beginningless past is centered here; the endless future is centered here. Nothing exists apart from this moment here and now, which includes you. The whole universe includes you; you include the whole universe. Who hears? Who sees? Still, saying it like this is just an expedient technique utilized to help you let go of fear and doubt and begin to trust the vast, unnamable, fathomless void. All of time and space is you, there is no other.

You cannot see anything else

One day Jordan approached Louie Wing at lunch and asked, "You talk about the unnamable void, but can you show it to me?"

Louie Wing said, "Can you show me something that is not the unnamable void?"

Jordan asked, "Is it big?"

Louie Wing said, "Vast."

Jordan asked, "Is it small?"

Louie Wing said, "Fathomless."

Jordan asked, "Can I see it?"

Louie Wing said, "You cannot see anything else."

I did not get much sleep last night

Once when Louie Wing was giving a talk, Libby came in late. When she started to sit down Louie Wing said, "You have already missed most of the talk."

Libby said, "If that is so, then you have already missed most of my listening."

Rusty, who was sitting at the back of the room burst into laughter when he heard that.

Louie Wing looked around at the group and asked, "Does anybody else agree?"

Julie raised her hand to indicate her agreement.

Louie Wing looked at her and said, "How is it you agree?"

Julie said, "I did not get much sleep last night and now I am feeling drowsy."

Louie Wing then resumed his talk.

Religion: Maps of the Unnamable

How could truth be superior or inferior

Once, before a talk, Charles asked, "Which spiritual tradition is the closest to the truth?"

Louie Wing said, "The spiritual guides and awakened teachers of all the great traditions did not preach and demonstrate the reality of awakening because they had something they could give you. They simply directed you to look deeply into your own mind and perceive its true nature. How could there be any difference of superiority or inferiority among the awakened teachers within the various styles? All that is important is to awaken to the one true reality of your own mind."

Free to come and to go, to take up and to let go

Christ, Buddha, Allah, God, Tao, Brahma, The Great Spirit, Bodhi,

Gnosis, and all such similar words are terms for your own luminous awareness. Perceiving, feeling, turning your head, smiling, opening and closing your hands, and shuffling your feet, are all due to your own luminous awareness. Your own mind is the vast, unnamable, fathomless void. The unnamable void is your own luminous awareness. While this awareness will always remain a mystery, no matter what term you apply, when you truly awaken to it you are free to come and to go, to take up and to let go.

The only requirement

Let me state it as clearly as I can: the only requirement is to clearly see your own mind. This is what all true religion is.

Nothing wrong with putting it in those terms

A visitor asked, "I am personally drawn to Christianity. What do you say about the idea that we come to God only through his son, Jesus Christ?"

Louie Wing said, "Nothing wrong with putting it in those terms."

Mark said, "But you always say that we only find it in our own mind."

Louie Wing said, "Nothing wrong with putting it in those terms."

The visitor said, "Then where would Jesus fit in?"

Louie Wing said, "Yes! Stay with that."

Do religions and spiritual traditions differ?

A student asked, "Do all the religions and spiritual traditions differ or are they the same?"

Louie Wing said, "From the perspective of the human intellect, they differ. From the perspective of the vast, unnamable, fathomless void, they are the same."

Reality existed before the establishment of any religion

The truth of reality existed long before the establishment of any religion or spiritual tradition. It is simply the truth of the oneness of the essence of the vast, unnamable, fathomless void and your own mind. Your own mind is nothing other than the realm of all space and time, the unnamable void. Awakening to this reality is the function and reason of all true religious practice. The word "religion" in Latin is "religio," (re-link) meaning: "to link back," that is, to link you back to your own source. When you awaken to your own source, wrong notions cease to exist, ideas and concepts can no longer bind you, the tangles and snares of the various religions are transcended. Awakening to reality is realizing your own identity with the unnamable void. This reality is the essence of all things; it is the seer of seeing, the hearer of hearing, and the perceiver of perceiving.

Senses: Gates of Reality

Listen!

It is not easy to meet with wisdom and awaken to reality. I will show you a way in, listen! In hearing, there is no hearing. Hearing does not depend on hearing. Hearing is not born and it can never die. When sound arises, hearing does not create it. When sound diminishes, it is not extinguished by hearing. Nor is the nature of hearing created by the arising or diminishing of sound. Just realize that hearing is unborn and undying. Hearing does not come and go. How can you realize the wisdom of this? Listen!

Look, listen, smell, taste, touch, and think!

Right here, right now, your mind and body are shining forth as the vast, unnamable void. Continuously it flows forth as seeing, hearing, smelling, tasting, feeling, and thinking. If you want to attain certainty, then look, listen, smell, taste, touch, and think!

Undifferentiated and able to differentiate

The vast, unnamable, fathomless void is imperceptible, formless, intangible, and unmoving; it was never born and can never die. Though it is not separate from the myriad things, the myriad things do not alter it; like a clear mirror, it adapts to all things while fundamentally remaining unchanged by them. Similarly, your own basic awareness is able to perfectly perceive all things, without becoming entangled with them. The unnamable true nature or your own mind is, at once, undifferentiated and able to differentiate all things. When the neighbor's dog barks unexpectedly, your clear awareness spontaneously comprehends it; when a spider walks along the back of your neck, your luminous mind registers it. Who hears the dog? Who feels the spider?

Listening without listening, hearing not hearing

In the void nature of your own mind, there is a person that listens continuously but never hears. In the void nature of your own mind, there is a person that never listens but always hears.

Your eye does not discriminate

Louie Wing held up his fist and said, "Do you decide to see me raise my fist?" He then clapped his hands together and said, "Can you choose not to hear my hands clap?"

After a pause, Louie Wing said, "The mind that sees and hears is the vast, unnamable, fathomless void, the source, manifestation, and destination of all things. Your eye does not choose what to see, your ear does not choose what to hear. The void sees, the void hears. When you eat your lunch, do you know how to digest your food and get the right nutrients to the various parts of your body? When you breathe, do you know how to extract and dispense the oxygen from your lungs? Of course not. So how does it happen? It is nothing other than the function of the unnamable void, which is the true nature of each one of you at this very moment.

When a flower sees a flower.

You see with the eyes of all time and space; your ears are the hearing organs of all time and space; all time and space speaks with your voice. When you take out the garbage, all time and space takes out the garbage; when you fall in love, all time and space falls in love. When you see a flower, all time and space sees a flower; a flower sees a flower, a flower sees you, and you see you.

Who is it that hears?

Louie Wing clapped his hands together and said, "Hearing occurs without your interference. You cannot decide to hear or not hear; therefore it is not you that hears, but something that functions within you. Who is it that hears?"

Perception, perceiver, and perceived

Perception, perceiving, and perceived are not three different things. Your eyes, ears, nose, tongue, body, and mind are united with forms, sounds, smells, tastes, tactile objects, thoughts, and feelings, are never apart from the seen, heard, smelled, tasted, touched, conceived, and felt. When you cease dividing them up through conceptualization, they are experienced as one pure and clear luminescence. Ear, sound, and hearing, for instance, when experienced without conceptualizing, are not separate from each other. The same is true of the others. In the clear and pure awareness of your own mind, all of these are one luminescent reality, none of which have any objective existence. This luminescent reality is the vast, unnamable, fathomless void.

This is easy to grasp and easy to understand. Nevertheless, as soon as you begin to conceptualize about "one luminescent reality," you have just traded delusion for delusion. Truly, you must simply let go of all conceptualizations and experience it directly.

You will know it when "you" and "I" disappear

Once, during a talk, Louie Wing said, "Do not fall into ideas that there is really a difference between delusion and awakening or between your ordinary mind and your true mind. No matter what you are doing or not doing, it all comes from the vast, unnamable, fathomless void. Who is able to see and hear? Is it your eyes and ears? If you pluck out your eye or cut off your ear, are they capable of seeing and hearing? Who is it that breathes and digests food? Is it you? Can you choose to stop breathing? Can you cause food to pass through your body without digesting it?

These processes are the functions of the unnamable void, your own true mind."

Henry asked, "How can I realize that these functions are my true mind?"

Louie Wing said, "Can you hear the sound of the traffic outside?"

Henry said, "I hear it."

Louie Wing said, "Now, without giving that sound a name like 'traffic' or anything else, let yourself rest at the very place where your awareness of that sound manifests and tell me what you hear."

After a few moments, Henry said, "The sound is clear, but I don't know what to tell you without giving it a name."

Louie Wing said, "Just continue to practice hearing in the pure and clear luminous awareness of your own mind and you will eventually awaken."

Henry asked, "How will I know, and how will I be able to tell you about it?"

Louie Wing said, "You will know and be able to indicate it when 'you' and 'I' both disappear."

Each one of you is the whole universe

I remember my teacher said:

"Each one of you is the whole universe. Your seeing, hearing, smelling, tasting, touching, and thinking is the seeing, hearing, smelling, tasting, touching, and thinking of the whole universe which was never born and will never die. There is only one essence in the whole universe."

Look, listen, smell, taste, touch, feel, think!

The unnamable void is your own awareness,
Your own awareness is the unnamable void.
Never apart from right here, right now,
Look, listen, smell, taste, touch, feel, think!

The sound of dogs barking

Donna asked, "What happens when someone awakens?"
Louie Wing said, "There is the *sound* of dogs barking."
Donna asked, "What about before someone awakens?"
Louie Wing said, "There is the sound of *dogs barking*."

Words: Masks That Conceal and Reveal

In reality, both terms are illusory

After returning from a Zen center, Julian asked, "What is objectless meditation?"

Louie Wing said, "It is meditation on an object."

Julian said, "Why do you say it is meditation on an object?"

Louie Wing said, "'Objectless' is a conceptual construct that is only valid in contradistinction to 'object'. Each term is dependent on the other. To posit one is to validate the other; to deny one is to deny the other. In reality, both terms are illusory. If you grasp for objects, you are clinging to the delusion of a separate self. If you grasp for the objectless, you are still clinging to the delusion of a separate self. Therefore, I say, grasp neither the notion of object nor the notion of objectless. Then you will be in accord with the true masters of all the spiritual traditions."

This is the best I can explain

One night after the regular meeting, Louie Wing quietly requested a few of the students to stay after.

179

When the rest of the students had gone, Louie Wing said, "I want to talk to you about something that has been coming up regularly in our one-on-one interviews. Rather than wade through this muck and slop with each one of you, I would like to get it over with at once.

"Often, when people first hear about the unnamable void, they imagine that when they awaken their feelings of love and heartache, of longing and sentiment will instantly vanish. They reason to themselves, thinking, 'all things are illusory and void; there is not one single thing that is truly real. How could I feel affection or sorrow for illusions?' On one level, this kind of reasoning is in perfect accord with reality. Nevertheless, you should not think that this is the truth. The true experience of awakening cannot be reasoned out or imagined ahead of time.

"Remember: the myriad things are the void and the void is the myriad things. Parents and their children are one in the void, yet a mother or father that did not feel a special joy concerning their own child would not be worth talking to. Moreover, what kind of a human being does not experience sadness when their families or friends suffer and die? Form is emptiness; emptiness is form. Love and sorrow are void; the void is love and sorrow.

"When thinking comes, think. When crying comes, cry. When laughter comes, laugh. If you forcibly try to avoid or suppress feelings of affection or sorrow, then you are simply in delusion adding to delusion. You are denying the reality that is flowing naturally from the unnamable void. You are turning away from your own true nature.

"At the very moment of experiencing love, it is not something other than you. The very sensations of your feelings of grief are none other than your own true self: the vast, unnamable, fathomless void. Do not suppose that the unnamable void is incapable of harboring joy and sorrow, love and grief. Do you think that Buddha did not feel sorrow for the many suffering beings? Have you not heard that when his friend, Lazarus, died, Jesus wept? Do you think that Mohammed felt nothing when his followers were tormented? Do you imagine that Lao-tzu and Chuang-tzu did not feel affection for their own mothers?

"The unnamable void is the source of all things; do not try to imagine what it is or is not capable of. Even the psychologists are beginning to realize that depression, morbidity, melancholy, anxiety, and the whole plethora of so-called pathologies might not simply be abnormalities to be rooted out and annihilated; but could actually be guardian angels with messages that should be experienced deeply.

"Delusion itself is not delusion. The true nature of delusion is the vast, unnamable, fathomless void. This is the truth. However, until you truly awaken and experience it directly, I am afraid you will not be able to really understand. Joy and sorrow, as you now experience them, will be extinguished when you awaken—you could not hold them if you tried—but then you will know true joy and sorrow, which is no-joy and no-sorrow. If you must ponder such things, this is the right way to think about them—it may be better to say that this precludes right and wrong ways of thinking about them. This is the best I can explain, other than not explaining at all, which might have been a better choice. All of you should be able to hear these words without allowing them to become a nest of tangling briars, but do not talk about this with people of little wisdom—or worse, people who are truly wise! Ha!"

One of the best names for the unnamable
Kenny asked, "When you call it 'the unnamable void,' aren't you giving it a name?"

Louie Wing said, "Yes, and at the same time, trying to indicate that, ultimately, the myriad names for it fall short of defining it."

Kenny said, "What do you mean, 'the myriad names for it'?"

Louie Wing said, "Sometimes it is called mind, sometimes it is called body, sometimes it is called awareness, sometimes perceiving, sometimes feeling, sometimes thinking, sometimes it is called a man, sometimes a woman, sometimes it is called Maurice, sometimes Loretta. The *Tao Te Ching* says, 'Names may be used, but are none of them absolute.' How about you, what would you call it?"

Kenny said, "I don't know."

Louie Wing said, "Ah, yes, that is one of the best names."

The term 'unnamable void' is like an antibiotic
Jade asked, "What is the best way to stop delusion?"

Louie Wing said, "You do not need to stop anything; delusion is simply a misperception of reality. Just step back into your own clear awareness and observe the true nature of delusion."

Jade said, "But doesn't delusion stop when we awaken to the unnamable void?"

Louie Wing said, "Even the 'unnamable void' does not exist in true awakening. If you create a concept called the 'unnamable void,' you become susceptible to trading one delusion for another. The term 'unnamable void' is like an antibiotic; if you continue to use antibiotics after an infection is healed, you will only develop another illness. Attachment to the pure, clear, unnamable void can be even more pernicious than attachment to the myriad things. When you truly awaken, the unnamable void will fall away along with delusion. Then you will be able to freely participate in the world, without being lost, confused, and afraid. It is like a puppet play; when you think you are the puppet, you feel constrained, but once you realize you are pulling the strings…oh what fun!"

It is neither a name nor the unnamable

The unnamable void is truly unnamable,
The name just points to what is unnamable.
Once you truly awaken,
It is neither a name nor the unnamable.

The stink of spiritual practice

Personally, I would like to obliterate the vast, unnamable, fathomless void and extinguish everything that stinks of spiritual practice. Pure and clear awareness is nothing but a booby trap, ceasing conceptualization is the blackest poison of all. Awakening and realization are two clumps of hazardous waste. All of these terms are like carrots dangled from the end of a stick; they can lead you in the right direction, but if you focus too closely on them, you will just become cross-eyed.

Because of names, you can order a hot fudge sundae

After a talk, Jenny asked, "Is the unnamable void the same thing as the true mind?"

Louie Wing said, "The 'unnamable void' and the 'true mind' are both provisional terms aimed at guiding you to the reality itself. A name is not the thing itself; let go of the name and realize the reality.

Jenny asked, "If all names are provisional, why not dispense with them altogether?"

Louie Wing said, "Because of names, you can go to an ice cream parlor, order a hot fudge sundae, and get the thing itself. However, once you have the hot fudge sundae you can forget about the name…mm."

First, get the dog out of the road

When you cease conceptualizing in all of your activities and non-activities you will awaken to the reality of your own true mind. If your aspiration is genuine, and you continue to persevere, even if you are unable to completely cease conceptualizing all at once, you will eventually achieve awakening. Awakening does not depend on being 'spiritual' or 'religious'.

Imagine that you see a stray dog out in the middle of a busy road. It is lost and confused. The first thing to do is to get the dog out of the road before it gets run over. So you offer it some treats in order to coax it off the road. Once the dog gets out of the road, the treats have served their purpose. The teachings of the sages are like offering the treats to the stray dog. Once you have awakened, the term "awakening" has served its purpose. That is why all the sages have said that there is nothing to attain.

Those who speak do not know

In the library one day, Keanna approached Louie Wing and said, "The *Tao Te Ching* says, 'Those who speak do not know; those who know, do not speak'. When some questions were addressed to Buddha, he remained silent. Don't these examples, as well as others, indicate the supremacy of silence over speaking?"

Louie Wing said, "Remaining silent and speaking are the same thing. Speaking is one way of expressing something, remaining silent is another way of expressing something. Either way is effective if something is communicated; both are ineffective if nothing is communicated. Even the words, 'Those who speak do not know...' must be spoken to be communicated."

Throw away 'delusion' and 'awakening'

The vast, unnamable, fathomless void transcends words, deeds, and thought. How could anyone teach it to you? How could it be discovered in a book? Let go of all your ideas and views; throw away "delusion" and "awakening," step back into the pure and clear, luminous awareness that does not discriminate, and realize it directly.

No things in the entire universe

After a long talk, David asked, "What do you mean by 'the pure and clear, luminous awareness that does not discriminate'?"

Louie Wing said, "When you entangle yourself with ideas, concepts, and views, the pure and clear, luminous awareness and its manifestations are misperceived as separate entities; that is discrimination. All of the myriad things in space and time are nothing but the one vast, unnamable, fathomless void; they have no independent, separate nature of their own. All the various phenomena are simply particular aspects of the unnamable void. A DVD player is the unnamable void. We call it a 'DVD player' to differentiate it from the rest of the void for the sake of convenience; but in reality, it is not separate and 'DVD player' is only a name. When you take a name for a real entity, you trade your own pure and clear awareness for delusion.

"There are no things in the entire universe. All particular things are nothing but the one true essence, the unnamable void. Stop trying to find something outside of your own mind."

First awaken, then discern the teachings

A visiting student said, "It seems to me that your teaching is sometimes contradictory. One time you say, 'There is nothing to seek.' Then, at other times you say, 'Arouse your determination to cease conceptualization.' I am confused."

Louie Wing said, "That is because you are looking for some definitive doctrine in my words. There are no definitive doctrines, no absolute truths. In fact, there is nothing to attain. You should not allow my words or anyone's, to come between you and your own fundamental awareness. The best you can hope for from any so-called teacher are clues and hints about which direction to turn.

"If you want some guidance, the best I can do is to tell you this: do not allow yourself to be caught up in perceptions, feelings, and thoughts. Stop indulging in making useless discriminations between this and that, self and other. Whenever you notice that you are caught up in discrimination, step back into your own fundamental awareness. Do not waste your time comparing differing ideas and notions about this teaching and that teaching. Cease all this futile conceptualization and step back into the clear and pure awareness of your own mind. Only after you have experienced it directly will you be able to accurately discern the teachings."

I and the father are one

A visiting Christian monk asked, "What is awakening?"

Louie Wing said, "When Shakyamuni Buddha saw the morning star and realized enlightenment, he said, 'How wonderful. All beings are the Tathagata.'"

The monk said, "I am a Christian."

Louie Wing said, "I and the father are one."

Even not ceasing ceases

Frank asked, "If we cease using our minds to conceptualize, how will we be able to solve everyday problems?"

Louie Wing said, "Ceasing conceptualization is awakening to the pure and clear luminous nature of your own mind. When you truly awaken, conceptualization is not conceptualization. In the same way, delusion is not delusion, awakening is not awakening, fear is not fear, joy is not joy, and death is not death. In ceasing conceptualization, ceasing is not ceasing, and even not ceasing ceases."

When God is, there is no God

A visiting Muslim cleric asked, "How do you understand, 'There is no God but God'?"

Louie Wing said, "When God is, there is no God."

The cleric asked, "What do you mean by that?"

Louie Wing said, "'God' is a term that is used in contradistinction to 'other than God'. The term is only valid when you distinguish God from something else. When 'there is no God but God', what is there to distinguish?"

Avoid walking into traffic

Lee asked, "If ceasing conceptualization is the way to awaken, does that mean we should abandon reading and study?"

Louie Wing said, "Anyone with true aspiration for awakening will only benefit from careful reading and intense study of the scriptures and treatises of the sages."

Lee asked, "But wouldn't that lead to conceptualization?"

Louie Wing said, "Hopefully, away from it! Listen, ceasing conceptualization is not putting a stop to rational thinking. Reading and study, like anything else, can be subjected to conceptualization, in which case it is not true reading and study but grasping for some definitive doctrine."

Lee said, "I don't see how anyone could read and study without getting caught up in conceptualizing."

Louie Wing said, "Reading and study are no more prone to conceptualization than any other perception, feeling or thought. Reading and study, like seeing and hearing, can be performed from the perspective of your own pure and clear, luminous awareness."

Lee said, "Still, I don't see the benefit. It would just be adding something else to cease conceptualizing about."

Louie Wing said, "If it really causes you so much concern, then leave it for now, but remember, reading and study, like seeing and hearing, might help you avoid walking into traffic."

Even no-awakening does not exist

Already awakening is conveyed.
When it is realized it is no-awakening.
Each of you must experience it directly.
In true awakening even no-awakening does not exist.

Worldly Activity: Enlightened Activity

All activities are 'objectless'

When I talk about the void, you should avoid developing a concept of nothingness. Many people have fallen into this subtle trap, believing that they have discovered some ultimate truth. Some of them become false teachers who urge their students to sit quietly with blank minds. There are such teachers active today, claiming that they are teaching "objectless meditation." Sitting for long periods trying to suppress thoughts is not objectless meditation; it is abiding in a state of useless impotence.

You should know that there is not an objective particle in the entire universe. Once you truly awaken, you realize that all activities are 'objectless'.

You are liberated even if you are a thief or a murderer

Corinne asked, "Do you think it is beneficial to join a particular spiritual tradition?"

Louie Wing said, "Anyone can awaken to their own mind; there is no need to join a particular tradition or spiritual community. If they do not awaken to their own mind, people who join traditions and spiritual communities are as deluded as anyone else."

Corinne said, "But don't you think that people within such an environment have a better opportunity to awaken than those that aren't?"

Louie Wing said, "No. Why would they?"

Corinne said, "Well, they could stay more focused on their practice. There would be less distractions and temptations."

Louie Wing said, "In all of the spiritual communities I have ever witnessed there have been as many distractions and temptations as anywhere else. Besides, distractions and temptations have no bearing at all on awakening."

Corinne said, "Are you saying that it is just as easy to attain realization for someone that is, say, indulging in sexual activity on a regular basis?"

Louie Wing said, "All of the sages have only talked about awakening to your own mind. What does sex have to do with awakening or not awakening? All things are the vast, unnamable, fathomless void, including sex. When sex is appropriate to the occasion, you enjoy sex; when sex is not appropriate, you let it go. There is nothing wrong with sex itself; like all things, sex is void, and essentially pure.

"If you can just cease conceptualization, you will be free from birth and death, even in the midst of birth and death. Distractions and temptations will no longer trouble you no matter where you are, and no matter what tradition you join or do not join. If you can only put a stop to dualistic thought, you will awaken at once, even if you are a thief or a murderer."

Corinne said, "Thieves and murderers cause evil and suffering in the world. How could they ever attain realization?"

Louie Wing said, "It makes no difference who you are or what you have done; every single being is, in reality, the one true nature, the unnamable void. Once you realize your own true nature, you are liberated, even if you are a thief or a murderer."

Worldly and spiritual are not two

All activities are the activities of the vast, unnamable, fathomless void. How could it exist only within spiritual practices? Unfortunately, some contemporary teachers insist that students exclusively cultivate sitting meditation. Some even urge students to avoid worldly activities and deliberately isolate themselves, as if meditation could not be carried out in the midst of the everyday world of work, family, and social activities.

Students hear this kind of nonsense and wrongly conclude that awakening cannot occur without giving up their families, jobs, and positions in society. Some of them actually do abandon their families and responsibilities, and others abandon the idea of spiritual practice altogether. Both of these outcomes result from false teaching and are truly causes for regret.

You should know that anyone with genuine aspiration can awaken in whatever circumstances his or her life situation is in. In all times and places, people from all lifestyles have been able to realize awakening. It makes no difference if you are a king or a prisoner, a monk or a prostitute; if you persevere with great determination you cannot fail to achieve liberation.

The records of all the great traditions testify to the fact that realization has always been attainable by anyone who truly aspires to it. Modern times are no exception to this truth. I have personally met scores of awakened people at all levels of society and in all ranges of livelihood. And why wouldn't it be so? All people in the ten times are nothing other than the vast, unnamable, fathomless void.

Delusion arises because of conceptualization, not because of worldly activity. Awakening occurs by ceasing conceptualization, not by ceasing worldly activity. All the myriad things are nothing but the one mind, the unnamable void. In the reality of the one mind, all things are pure and clear, without gain, without loss. Does being deluded in a quiet mountain monastery have some advantage to being deluded anywhere else? What would be the use of that? If you cease dualistic thinking, you will awaken. If you do not, then isolating yourself in a quiet setting and sitting for long periods is just adding delusion to delusion.

Contemporary teachers who proclaim some benefit in this kind of withdrawal from the world are usually the only beneficiaries. Before you pay your membership fees, compare their words to those of the ancient sages that have stood the test of time. Repeatedly, the sages have declared the truth that trying to run away from delusion only adds to delusion.

The Third Ancestor of Zen in China said, "Your effort to suppress activity is just more activity." It is delusory to discriminate between worldly and spiritual, secular and religious, lay and monastic, the marketplace and a retreat center. Trying to suppress the flow of thought by changing your environment is like trying to make something disappear by closing your eyes.

There has never been any real division

Nic asked, "How do we cease conceptualization and become one with the unnamable void?"

188

Louie Wing said, "First of all, you do not 'become one with the void'. You are the void. Awakening is just realizing the fact. The unnamable void is your own mind. When you conceptualize, you are abstracting partial aspects from the whole. That is, you are dividing the one true reality into this and that, self and other. This can be done skillfully only when you realize that in reality, there are no such divisions.

"When you cease conceptualizing, you realize that your own awareness is pure, clear, and luminescent, that it is the unnamable void. You then grasp the fact that all the myriad things are not separate from the void, but are in fact the void itself. All the myriad things are nothing other than your own miraculous awareness, which is infinitely vast and eternally present.

"Once you realize your own identity with the unnamable void, you realize that there has never been any real division between things and times, self and other-than-self. All such divisions are merely delusions based on conceptualization. Then, knowing your own unity with all things and events, you enter any environment and participate in any activity without ever leaving what Dogen called, 'the homeland of the self'."

Spiritual practice and ordinary activity

In the pure and clear, luminous awareness of your true mind, spiritual practice and ordinary activity are not separate. The vast and fathomless, unnamable void meets you wherever you are. When perceptions, feelings, and thoughts arise, you respond harmoniously without ever moving away from the pure and clear, luminous awareness of your own mind.

In the real world is where you must achieve it

Thoughts, distractions, temptations, emotions, desires, fears, and passions are all concomitant with being a human being; where could you ever escape them? It is while you are right in the middle of these that you should practice ceasing conceptualization. It is essential to engage in regular sitting or walking meditation, but it is in the real, human world, where you must learn to achieve it. If you cannot apply it there, what is the use?

How could reality depend on practicing meditation?

True meditation is abstaining from conceptualization while engaged in the activities of normal, everyday life. As long as you continue to discriminate between spiritual practice and the activities of everyday life, you are simply in delusion adding to delusion. All activities are the vast, unnamable, fathomless

189

void; the vast and fathomless, unnamable void is all activities. How could reality only abide while practicing a particular form of meditation?

Because some people are exceptionally dull, arrogant, unmotivated or plagued by other hindrances, the sages set down distinct, easy-to-follow instructions. These instructions were only devised as temporary expedients for those who, for whatever reason, could not practice meditation while maintaining normal activities.

Unless you are plagued by some special hindrance, with a little instruction and practice you should be able to keep your perspective from within your own fundamental awareness wherever you are, and whatever you are doing. If you discriminate between mundane activities and spiritual practice, it is because you are deluded by conceptualization. Cease conceptualization and you will realize that there is nothing outside of the void.

Awakening has nothing to do with outward appearances

Jordan asked, "Is it easier to realize awakening for a monk or a nun than it is for a lay person?"

Louie Wing said, "Awakening has nothing to do with outward actions or appearances. It is only achieved by ceasing conceptualization. There is no benefit in shaving your head, taking precepts, or wearing robes. Nor is there any disadvantage if you own a home, work in the secular world, and have a spouse and children. People in the secular world who cease conceptualization awaken. Monks and nuns in monastic communities who do not cease conceptualization remain in delusion."

Cease conceptualization amidst conceptualization

When I talk to you about the unnamable void and ceasing conceptualization, you should be careful about attaching to names and getting caught up conceptualizing about them. The unnamable void is not apart from the namable; ceasing conceptualization is not apart from the conceptualizing faculties of your own mind. Step back into your own luminous awareness and cease conceptualization right in the midst of conceptualization.

Joyfully participate in the world of suffering

Corinne asked, "Anyone who looks around this world cannot help but see that people are suffering on a grand scale. Shouldn't we be trying to help them?"

Louie Wing said, "The true sages joyfully participate in the world of suffering without falling into views of suffering or not suffering. They see that they and all beings are identical with the vast, unnamable, fathomless void. Therefore, they help suffering beings while realizing that ultimately there are no beings to save and no suffering to overcome."

Your True Self: The Unnamable Void

Spontaneous participation

Your own mind is identical with reality. The great teachers of all the spiritual traditions have directed you to the nature of your mind in order to lead you to liberation.

If you want to awaken, do not seek for anything outside your own mind. Outside of your own mind, there is nothing. Not grasping ideas about good and evil, not depending on notions of right and wrong, let go of all dualistic thinking and realize that your true self is the unnamable void.

You cannot find a separate, independent self because there is no such entity. Therefore, you realize that every particular thing in the universe is also just an illusion, a conceptual abstraction that only appears to exist independently from the void. The unnamable void is the one mind. When you see anything, you are just seeing the unnamable void. Nevertheless, even the void is not a separate, independent entity; its existence depends upon all the myriad things. Every thing you encounter is identical with the void; it is no-thing. When one realizes that all forms are identical with no-thing, then birth is identical with no-birth; death is identical with no-death. Awakening to the mystery of your own fundamental awareness, you spontaneously participate in the dance.

Everything the sages have said has flowed from the void

Everything the sages of the ten times have said and done, all of the sacred teachings and writings, all of the religions and spiritual practices, have flowed forth from the one vast, unnamable void, which is nothing other than your own mind.

No other mission besides knowing your own mind

There is no other mission besides knowing your own mind. That is realization; that is awakening. Then, at last, your spirit will be free and at ease. If you say that there is some particular doctrine or some right religious tradition, you will only be adding delusion to delusion. Just let go of conceptualization and look into your own body and mind—only there will you discover the vast, unfathomable, clear nature of the void; the very essence of your own awareness. If you can truly cease all dualistic thinking for a single moment you will spontaneously realize certainty. Only then will you be truly free to take up or let go.

They simply directed you to your own true mind

The wise sages in the ten times did not establish institutions or formulations, but only pointed to reality, urging you to awaken to the essence of mind and to achieve liberation. They simply directed you to your own true mind; there is no other path, way, religion, or practice. True guidance is only affected by teaching people to cease conceptualization and abandon dualistic thinking.

Not one sage ever attained anything

Travis asked, "If our own mind is the unnamable void, what is it that the enlightened teachers transmit to their students?"

Louie Wing said, "What all the enlightened teachers have transmitted is nothing other than the teaching that your own mind is reality. They have simply pointed to the fact that the mind of each of you has always been identical with ultimate reality and is in no way separate from the vast, unnamable void. When any one of you experiences a single instant of this truth you will transcend the whole, tangling mess of enlightened teachers, gurus, roshis, saints, priests, swamis, and all the rest of the names and titles that seem to divide the wise from the ordinary. You have always been identical with ultimate reality, so do not delude yourself into thinking there is anything you can attain by performing certain practices. Not one single enlightened sage ever attained anything whatsoever."

You have to see your own mind

To realize liberation, you have to see your own mind. Anyone who sees his mind is instantaneously liberated. If you do not see your mind, praying, meditation, reading scriptures, doing good deeds, and performing spiritual practices of all kinds is ultimately useless. Such activities and practices may bring physical benefits, they might increase your knowledge, boost your prestige, and bring material rewards—but they will not cause you to realize liberation.

Awakened or deluded awareness functions perfectly

Ultimately, there is not a trace of delusion to escape or any realization to be attained. Each one of you has always been, is now, and always will be the one true essence. Awakened or deluded, your clear, pure, luminous awareness functions perfectly.

All things express reality

Your own true mind contains everything in all space and time. Its operation is infinite and mysterious. It is both the function and essence of all the myriad things. When you awaken, you realize that all things express reality. Then you will know that whatever you do and wherever you go, you are never apart from your own true mind.

The void includes even foolishness and despair

Do not hear the teaching that all things are void, and immediately fall into views of nihilism or nothingness. The void includes even such things as foolishness, tragedy, and despair. If it did not, why would the sages have bothered uttering a word? It is impossible to see people suffering needlessly without spontaneously arousing a sense of compassion.

Not realizing that the liberation you seek is functioning perfectly in your own mind, you search far and wide, study various doctrines, and seek guidance from enlightened teachers. Even if your aspiration is genuine, if you do not look deeply into your own mind, how can you ever find it? You are like fish in the ocean seeking water. Just let go of your ideas and step back into the pure, clear awareness of your own mind. Then you will be able to discern all the subtle teachings of the various traditions. You will comprehend the truth of life and death. Each of you is endowed with perfect wisdom, but until you stop seeking outside yourself, you can never realize it.

Step back into your own pure and clear awareness

If you have aroused genuine aspiration for awakening to the vast, unnamable, fathomless void, then cease conceptualization and step back into your own pure and clear awareness. The undiscriminating, undifferentiating, clear luminescence of your own mind is, at this very moment, nothing other than the unnamable source of all things.

It is you

As long as you continue to indulge yourselves in conceptual pursuits discerning what is spiritual and what is mundane, you will continue to be controlled by delusion. No matter how great your learning and understanding are, you will never realize true liberation until you cease conceptualization. As soon as you truly let go of your habitual discrimination you will realize that you have never lacked a single thing. Do you want to know what the vast, unnamable, fathomless void is? It is you.

Using a flashlight to seek a flashlight

The vast, unnamable, fathomless void,
Is not apart from your own mind.
Using your mind to seek the void,
Is like using a flashlight to seek a flashlight.

No one who is aware and nothing to be aware of

All of the sages in the ten times have declared that ceasing conceptualization is awakening to reality. Ceasing conceptualization is sometimes called no-mind, nonthinking, mindlessness, pure awareness, mirroring cognition, wisdom of equality, dying to self, having no thought for the morrow, cessation meditation, mindfulness, as is-ness, and other similar terms. Though it has been referred to by many names, they are all references for the one true path to awakening. Awakening is ceasing conceptualization. The vast, unnamable, fathomless void has never been separate from your own mind; your own mind has never been separate from the vast, unnamable, fathomless void. Identifying yourself with the thoughts that arise from your mind is conceptualization. Ceasing conceptualization is awakening to the mind from which all things arise: the unnamable void.

Your mind has no beginning or end, the unnamable void transcends all definition and description. Ceasing conceptualization, you naturally awaken to this truth. When you continuously cease conceptualization, attachment and aversion fall away. The vast, unnamable, fathomless void is everywhere and everything, without a single objective particle. When you truly cease conceptualization, even 'ceasing conceptualization' falls away. This is awakening to reality. Awakening to reality is sometimes called enlightenment, realization, Buddhahood, reaching the other shore, union with the divine, final salvation, entering nirvana, resurrection, becoming one with the Tao, seeing your true nature, and other similar terms. Though it has been referred to by many names, they are all references for the one true awakening of the spiritual path. Let go of all your views and step back into your own clear awareness where there is no one who is aware and nothing to be aware of.

Your question just now came from your own mind

Louie Wing said, "All the myriad things are nothing other than your own mind. That is why all of the sages have simply tried to get you to look deeply into your own mind."

John said, "If we are deluded, how can we know what our own mind is?"

Louie Wing said, "Your question just now came from your own mind. If not your mind, then from where could it have come? No matter what you are doing, no matter where you are, that is your own mind. Outside of your mind, nothing exists."

There is not a single objective particle anywhere

Your own true mind is always functioning perfectly. When you are deluded, nothing is lost; when you are awakened, nothing is gained. It is the vast, unnamable, fathomless void. Ultimately, there is no delusion or awakening. All the myriad things and all time and space are nothing but the one unnamable void, your own true mind. There is not a single objective particle anywhere. The unnamable void of your own mind is without shape or form, without delusion or awakening, self or other-than-self. Step back into your own pure and clear, luminous awareness where there are no things at all and discover the treasure of your own true nature.

The kingdom of God is within you

Arouse great determination and persevere in all of your activities wherever you are. Ultimately, it is up to each one of you alone. If the sages could have done it for you then you would already have achieved certainty. Do not depend upon teachers; do not depend upon doctrines. The kingdom of God is within you; it is only there that you will find it.

It illumines all things, yet remains forever pure and clear

The fundamental awareness of your own mind is like a luminous mirror. When a blackbird appears, it illumines a blackbird. When the sound of a chainsaw enters, it illumines the sound of a chainsaw. When a cool breeze brushes you, it illumines the cool breeze. When you remember your lover, it illumines the memory of your lover. Though it illumines all things, it remains forever pure and clear.

It illumines all the myriad things as they are

The fundamental awareness of your own mind is like a clear, luminous mirror; it illumines all the myriad things as they are.

That awareness is your true mind

Jessica asked, "As I stand here facing you, my mind is creating ideas and worrying about looking foolish; where is my true mind now?"

Louie Wing said, "As you stand here worrying and creating ideas, your true mind is perfectly aware of the fact. That awareness is your true mind. Now, if you cease conceptualization, there will be no-thing to call ideas and worry. Then you would be standing here facing me in pure and clear, perfect awareness, and even 'standing' and 'facing' and 'you' and 'me' would cease to divide the unnamable void, which is your own true mind."

Step back into the source of your question

Kenny asked, "Before we awaken to reality, where is the true nature of our own minds?"

Louie Wing said, "That question itself can only arise because of the power of the true nature of your own mind. If you just let go of all your conceptualizing and step back into the source of your question you will discover your own pure and clear awareness."

It is you whether you awaken to your identity or not

That which sees and hears, moves and thinks, is nothing other than the vast, unnamable, fathomless void: your own true mind. It has no fixed form, yet accords with all forms; how could it be defined as round or square, large or small? Having no characteristics of round, square, large, or small, it transcends all categories, descriptions, and limitations. Denying all categories, descriptions, and limitations, it is not up or down, long or short, ordinary or sacred, inside or outside, good or bad, self or other. Even the ideas of existent and not existent do not apply.

Yet, in spite of all this, your own awareness shines forth, pure, clear, and luminous. It is this awareness that is sometimes referred to as God, Buddha, Tao, Allah, Brahma, and the whole array of names used to indicate the fundamental ground of reality. It is what I call the vast, unnamable, fathomless void.

When you awaken to it, you realize your own identity with it. Delusion is simply a case of misidentification. However, it is you whether you awaken to your identity or not.

Your own mind is the vast, unnamable, fathomless void

Your own mind is the vast, unnamable, fathomless void. Cessation of conceptualization is awakening to the fact.

All is the unnamable void of your own mind

When self and other are forgotten,
What is there to grasp for, what is there to fear?
When you realize your identity,
All is the unnamable void of your own mind.

Appendix A: Text of *Genjokoan*

Genjokoan
From the *Shobogenzo* by Eihei Dogen
Translated by Ted Biringer

When all things are seen as the buddha-dharma, then there is delusion and enlightenment, there is practice, there is life and there is death, there are buddhas and there are ordinary beings.

When all things are seen as empty of self, there is no delusion and no enlightenment, no buddhas and no ordinary beings, no life and no death.

Buddha's truth includes and transcends the many and the one, and so there is life and death, delusion and enlightenment, ordinary beings and buddhas.

And though it is like this, it is simply that flowers, while loved, fall, and weeds, while hated, flourish.

That people drive the self to actualize awareness of the many things is delusion. That the many things actualize awareness of the self is enlightenment.

Those who are enlightened about delusion are buddhas. Those who are deluded about enlightenment are ordinary beings.

There are people who continue to realize enlightenment based on enlightenment. There are people in the midst of delusion adding to delusion.

When buddhas are buddhas they do not know they are buddhas.

Nevertheless, buddhas are buddhas and continuously actualize Buddhahood. Mustering the whole body-and-mind to look at forms, and mustering the whole body-and-mind to listen to sounds, they perceive them directly, but it is not like an image reflected in a mirror, and not like the reflection of the moon on water. As one side is revealed, the other side is concealed.

To realize the buddha-dharma is to realize your self. To realize your self is to forget your self. To forget your self is to be actualized by the many things. To be actualized by the many things is to allow the body-and-mind of your self and the body-and-mind of other than your self to fall away. All traces of enlightenment fall away, and the falling away of all traces of enlightenment is continuous.

The first moment you seek the dharma you are far removed from the environs of dharma. The first moment of true dharma transmission, your originally true nature is realized.

A person sailing along in a boat looking at the shore might have the illusion that the shore is moving. However, if they look closely at the boat they realize the boat is moving. Similarly, when they try to understand the many things based on deluded notions about body-and-mind they might have the illusion that their minds or nature are stationary. However, if they step back into fundamental awareness they realize nothing has a fixed self.

Firewood becomes ash; it can never go back to being firewood. Nevertheless, you should not take the view that ash is its future and firewood is its past. Remember that firewood abides in the dharma position of firewood. It has a past and it has a future. Although it has a past and a future, the past and the future are cut off. Ash exists in the dharma position of ash. It has a past and it has a future. The firewood, after becoming ash, does not again become firewood.

Similarly, human beings, after death, do not become alive again. This being so, it is the established teaching of Buddhism to deny that life turns into death. This is why Buddhists speak of no appearance. In addition, it is the established teaching of Buddhism that death does not become life. This is why Buddhists speak of no disappearance. Life is an instantaneous situation, and death is an instantaneous situation. It is like winter and spring. You do not think that winter becomes spring, and you do not say that spring becomes summer.

A person experiencing enlightenment is like the moon being reflected in water: the moon does not get wet, and the water is not broken. Though its light is wide and great, the moon is reflected in a puddle of water an inch wide. The whole moon and the whole sky are reflected in a dewdrop on a blade of grass and are reflected in a single drop of water.

Enlightenment does not break a person, just as the moon does not pierce the water. A person does not constrict enlightenment, just as a dewdrop does not constrict the sky and moon. The depth of the drop is the height of the moon. Whether large or small, and whatever the length or shortness of its duration the whole sky and the whole moon are discerned in each body of water.

When the dharma has not yet filled the whole body-and-mind people feel already replete with dharma. When the dharma fills the body-and-mind people feel something is lacking.

For example, when a person sails out beyond the mountains into the ocean, and looks around in the four directions, the ocean appears only to be round; it does not appear to have any other characteristics at all. Nevertheless, this great ocean is not round, and it is not square. There are an infinite number or qualities to the ocean: to fish it is like a palace; to gods it is like a string of pearls. Nevertheless, as far as someone's eyes can see, it just appears to be round.

As it is for the ocean, so it is for the many things. There are a multitude of qualities in the world of form and the world of the void, but you see and understand only as far as your eyes of practice and realization are able to reach.

If someone wants to know how the many things really are, they should remember that besides appearing square or round, the qualities of the oceans and qualities of the mountains are infinitely numerous; there are worlds in the four directions. Not only the periphery is like this; remember, the immediate present, and a single drop of water are also like this.

When fish swim in the ocean, no matter how far they swim, there is no end to the water. When birds fly through the sky, no matter how far they fly, there is no end to the sky. While this is so, fish and birds have never left the water or the sky. Simply, when their ability is great, their usage is great, and when their ability is small, their usage is small. Thus, each realizes its full potential and each experiences its full realm. If a bird leaves the sky, it will die at once; and if a fish leaves the water, it will die at once. Therefore, you know that water is life and you know that sky is life. Birds are life, and fish are life. Hence, life is birds and life is fish. Beyond this, there may still be further progress. The existence of their practice and enlightenment, and the existence of their life, are like this.

This being so, a bird or fish that tried to move through the water or the sky only after getting to the bottom of the water or the sky, could never find its way or find its place in the water or the sky. When people find this place, this action is *itself*, the actualization of the fundamental point (genjokoan). When people find this way, this action is *itself* the actualization of the fundamental point (genjokoan). This way and this place are not great or small, not subjective or objective; they have not existed since the past nor do they arise in the present; they are simply as they are.

When a person is experiencing the practice and enlightenment of the buddha-dharma, each practice is complete practice, and meeting each thing is mastering it. Here, the place exists and the way unfolds, and therefore the area of enlightenment is not conspicuous. For this enlightenment and the buddha-dharma manifest simultaneously and are experienced simultaneously.

Do not assume that what is realized will be grasped by consciousness, or will be recognized by the intellect. Although the experience of the ultimate state is realized immediately, its mysterious existence is not a manifest realization. Realization of the inconceivable is the inconceivable itself.

> Zen Master Hotetsu of Mount Mayu is using a fan.
>
> A monk comes up and says, "The nature of air is ever-present, and there is no place it does not reach. Why then does the Master use a fan?"
>
> The Master says, "You understand that the nature of air is ever-present, but you do not understand the truth that there is no place it does not reach."
>
> The monk says, "What is the truth of there being no place it does not reach?"
>
> At this, the Master just continues to use the fan.
>
> The monk does prostrations.

The actualization of the buddha-dharma, the living way of authentic transmission, is like this. A person who says that because the nature of air is ever-present they don't need to use a fan, or that without using a fan they can know the ever-present nature of air, does not know ever-presence or the nature of air. Because the nature of air is ever-present, the air of Buddhism manifests the gold of the Earth and ripens the Long River into fragrant cream.

Written and presented to my (Dogen's) lay disciple, Koshu Yo, of Kyushu Island, in the mid-autumn of 1233. Revised in 1252.

Appendix B: Names

- **Bankei Eitaku** 1622-1693. Popular and charismatic Japanese Zen master. Known for his teaching on "the Unborn."
- **Baso, Doitsu** (Ma-tsu Tao-i) 709-788. Third most influential master in the history of Zen, after Bodhidharma and Eno. He had at least eighty, and maybe as many as one hundred thirty, enlightened successors, including Hyakujo Ekai and Nansen Fugan.
- **Bodhidharma** 470-543? The traditional founder of Zen in China. Said to have been a monk who traveled from India to China in order to transmit the Authentic Teaching of Buddhism. All Zen schools regard him as the First Ancestor of Zen in China.
- **Ch'eng kuan** 737-820. Fourth Ancestor of the Huayen (Japanese: Kegon, Sanskrit: Avatamsaka) school of Buddhism in China.
- **Chuang-tzu** 369-286 BC. Taoist master; author of the *Cuang-tzu*, the classic text of Taoism. He is revered as the co-founder of Taoism, with Lao-Tzu.
- **Daibai Hojo** (Ta-mei Fa-ch'ang (Hui-Hai)) 752-839. Great influential Chinese master. A successor of Baso.
- **Dogen.** See *Eihei Dogen*.
- **Eihei Dogen** 1200-1253. One of the greatest masters of Zen history. Probably the greatest Japanese Zen master ever. An early transmitter of Zen from China to Japan. Author of the *Shobogenzo* (Treasury of the True Dharma-Eye), the most important Buddhist text produced in Japan, and one of the most important Zen texts in all of Zen history.
- **Eka** (Hui-k'o) 487-593. The Second Ancestor of Zen in China.

Successor of Bodhidharma. Legend says he cut off his own arm to prove his sincerity to Bodhidharma.

- [ ] **Engo Kokugon** (Yuan-wu K'o-ch'in) 1063-1135. One of the most influential masters in the development of, and practice with, Zen koans. The editor of the classic Zen text, the *Blue Cliff Record*.
- [ ] **Eno** (Hui-neng) 638-713. Sixth Ancestor of Zen in China. Second in importance only to Bodhidharma. The author of the *Platform Sutra*, the only Chinese work given the status of "sutra" (scripture).
- [ ] **Gutei Chikan** (Chin-hua Chu-chih) 9th Century Chinese master known for his almost exclusive technique of raising a single finger in response to questions about Zen.
- [ ] **Hakuin Ekaku** 1689-1769. A renowned and highly revered Japanese Zen master sometimes referred to as the Father of modern Zen. His highly energetic and charismatic approach to Zen teaching had a major effect on revitalizing Zen in Japan. One of the two most influential Japanese Zen masters (the other being, Eihei Dogen).
- [ ] **Haryo Kokan** (Pa-ling Hao chien) 10th Century Chinese master. Successor of Ummon.
- [ ] **Heraclitus** 6th-5th Century BC. Greek philosopher known for his short, "Zen-like" utterances.
- [ ] **Hogen Bun'eki** (Fa-yen Wen-i) 885-958. Important and influential Chinese Zen master. He is said to have had sixty-three successors. He is revered as the founder of the Hogen School of Zen.
- [ ] **Hotetsu** (Baoche), No dates. Chinese Zen master; a student of Baso.
- [ ] **Hui-k'o.** See *Eka*.
- [ ] **Hui-neng.** See *Eno*.
- [ ] **Hyakujo Ekai** (Pai-chang Huai-hai) 720-814. One of the truly great Chinese masters. He was a student of Baso Doitsu. He is revered as the founder of the Zen monastic tradition of rules and guidelines in China. He had a number of important heirs, including Obaku Kiun.
- [ ] **Joshu Jushin** (Chao-chou) 778-897. One of the most important and highly revered masters in all of Zen history. Many of his sayings and doings are incorporated into the great koan collections of Zen. He was a student of Nansen (Nan-chuan).
- [ ] **Lao-tzu** 6th Century BC. "Old Teacher." Author of the Tao Te Ching. Founder of Taoism (or co-founder with Chuang-tzu).
- [ ] **Lin-chi I-hsuan.** See *Rinzai Gigen*.
- [ ] **Ma-tsu.** See *Baso*.

- **Mumon Ekai** (Wu-men Hui-k'ai) 1183-1260. Important and influential Chinese master. Compiler of the classic koan collection the *Mumonkan* (Gateless Barrier).
- **Nansen Fugan** (Nan-ch'uan) 748-835. Great Chinese master with many important successors, including Joshu Jushin. Famous (infamous?) for his role in the story about cutting a cat in two with a knife, which is included in a number of koan collections. He was a student of Baso Doitsu.
- **Obaku Kiun** (Huang-po His-yun) d. 850. One of the great Chinese masters. Student of Hyakujo Ekai. Teacher of Rinzai Gigen.
- **Rinzai Gigen** (Lin-chi I-hsuan) d. 866/67. Founder of the Rinzai school of Zen. One of the greatest, most influential Chinese masters in Zen history, known for his thunderous shouts and sudden blows. Student of Obaku Kiun.
- **Ryutan Soshin** (Lung-t'an Ch'ung-hsin) 9th Century. Chinese master. Teacher of Tokusan Senkan.
- **Setcho Ju-ken** (Hsueh-tou Ch'ung-hsien) 982-1052 Great Chinese master. Compiler of the one hundred koans (to which Yuanwu added comments) that constitute the classic Zen text, the *Blue Cliff Record.*
- **Shakyamuni** b. 566 BC? One name for the historical Buddha, which means: Sage of the Shakya Clan.
- **Sozan Honjaku** (Ts'ao-shan Pen-chi) 840-901. One of the Great Chinese masters, co-founder (with his teacher, Tozan Ryokai) of the Soto school of Zen. Responsible for deepening and refining Tozan's *Five Ranks.*
- **Sosan** (Seng-ts'an) d. 606? The traditional Third Ancestor of Zen in China. Credited as the author of the Zen classic *Hsin-hsin-ming.*
- **Tendo Nyojo** (T'ien-t'ung Ju-ching) 1163-1228. Chinese Zen master. Teacher of Eihei Dogen.
- **Tokusan Senkan** (Te-shan Hauan-chien) 781-867. Greatly revered Chinese master. Successor of Ryutan.
- **Tozan Ryokai** (Tung-shan Liang-chieh) 807-869. One of the greatest Chinese masters. The co-founder (with his student, Sozan Honjaku) of the Soto school of Zen. He is the creator of the *Five Ranks* doctrine of Zen.
- **Ungan Donjo** (Yun-yen T'an-sheng) 781-841. Chinese Zen master. Teacher of Tozan Ryokai.
- **Ummon Bun'en** (Yun-men Wen-yen) 864-949. One of the most

important and influential Chinese masters. It is said that he prohibited the recording of his sermons, but thankfully, some disobeyed, secretly writing his words on their paper robes. In the great koan collections, his words are cited more often than other masters.

Notes

[i] Pine, Red, *The Zen Teaching of Bodhidharma*, 29

[ii] Hakeda, Yoshito, S, *The Awakening of Faith, Attributed to Asvaghosha.* (Columbia University Press, 1967), 96

[iii] ibid., 100-101

[iv] ibid., 101-102

[v] Aitken, Robert, *The Gateless Barrier: The Wu-Men Kuan (Mumonkan)* (San Francisco: North Point Press, 1990), 7-9

[vi] Cleary, Thomas, *Classics of Buddhism and Zen, Volume Four, Unlocking The Zen Koan,* 244

[vii] This is here rendered in the form that was assigned to me when I worked through it. For a more scholarly translation see, Aitken, Robert, *The Gateless Barrier: The Wu-Men Kuan (Mumonkan)* (San Francisco: North Point Press, 1990), 94

[viii] Gudo Nishijima & Chodo Cross, *Master Dogen's Shobogenzo*, Book 1, 279

[ix] Powell, William, F., *The Record of Tung-shan*, 27-28

[x] Powell, William, F., *The Record of Tung-shan*, 61

[xi] Powell, William, F., *The Record of Tung-shan*, 61

[xii] Ogata, Sohaku, *The Transmission of the Lamp*, 255

[xiii] Green, James, *The Recorded Sayings of Zen Master Joshu*, 34

[xiv] Gudo Nishijima & Chodo Cross, *Master Dogen's Shobogenzo*, Book 1, 239

[xv] Cleary, J.C., *Zen Dawn*, 125

[xvi] Powell, William, F., *The Record of Tung-shan*, 61

Notes

[xvii] Hori, Victor Sogen, *Zen Sand, The Book of Capping Phrases for Koan Practice,* 12.24, 461

[xviii] Ogata, Sohaku, *The Transmission of the Lamp,* 70

[xix] Conze, Edward, *The Large Sutra of Perfect Wisdom,* 64

[xx] Powell, William, F., *The Record of Tung-shan,* 62

[xxi] ibid., 76

[xxii] Powell, William, F., *The Record of Tung-shan,* 31

[xxiii] Conze, Edward, *The Large Sutra of Perfect Wisdom,* 104

[xxiv] Powell, William, F., *The Record of Tung-shan,* 62

[xxv] Green, James, *The Recorded Sayings of Zen Master Joshu,* 11

[xxvi] ibid., 12

[xxvii] ibid., 99

[xxviii] Cleary, Thomas, *Classics of Buddhism and Zen, Volume Two, Zen Letters,* 189

[xxix] Gudo Nishijima & Chodo Cross, *Master Dogen's Shobogenzo, Kei-sei-Sanshiki,* Book 1, 91

[xxx] Ogata, Sohaku, *The Transmission of the Lamp,* 10

[xxxi] Leighton and Okumura, *Eihei Koroku,* 3:243, 241

[xxxii] Kim, Hee-Jin, *Eihei Dogen: Mystical Realist,* xxv

[xxxiii] Red Pine, *The Zen Teaching of Bodhidharma,* 9

[xxxiv] Price, A.F. & Mou-lam, Wong, *The Diamond Sutra & The Sutra of Hui-Neng,* 79

[xxxv] Bloefeld, John, *The Zen Teaching of Huang-Po,* 78

[xxxvi] Watson, Burton, *The Zen Teachings of Master Lin-chi,* 24

[xxxvii] Braverman, Arthur, *Mud and Water, A Collection of Talks by the Zen Master Bassui,* 28

[xxxviii] Gudo Nishijima & Chodo Cross, *Zen Master Dogen's Shobogenzo, Hossho,* Book 3, 126

[xxxix] Bloefeld, John, *The Zen Teaching of Huang-Po,* 116

[xl] Bloefeld, John, *The Zen Teaching of Instantaneous Awakening,* 22

[xli] Cleary, Thomas, *Secrets of The Blue Cliff Record,* 328

[xlii] ibid., 328

[xliii] Cleary, Thomas, *Zen Letters,* 45

[xliv] Gudo Nishijima & Chodo Cross, *Zen Master Dogen's Shobogenzo, Gyobutsu Yuigi,* Book 2, 44

[xlv] Tanahashi & Aitken, *Moon in a Dewdrop: Writings of Zen Master Dogen.* San Francisco, CA: North Point Press, 1985, *Shobogenzo, Uji,* 80

Ted Biringer

[xlvi] Gudo Nishijima & Chodo Cross, *Zen Master Dogen's Shobogenzo, Tsuki,* Book 3, 3

[xlvii] Tanahashi & Aitken, *Moon in a Dewdrop: Writings of Zen Master Dogen.* San Francisco, CA: North Point Press, 1985, *Shobogenzo, Uji,* 77

[xlviii] Gudo Nishijima & Chodo Cross, *Zen Master Dogen's Shobogenzo, Inmo,* Book 2, 120-121

[xlix] Leighton and Okumura, *Eihei Koroku,* 6:437, 394

[l] Cleary, Thomas, *Classics of Buddhism and Zen, Volume Two, Teachings of Zen,* 24

[li] Tanahashi & Aitken, *Moon in a Dewdrop: Writings of Zen Master Dogen.* San Francisco, CA: North Point Press, 1985, *Shobogenzo, Uji,* 77

[lii] Cleary, Thomas, *Classics of Buddhism and Zen, Volume Two, Shobogenzo, Zenki,* 289

[liii] Gudo Nishijima & Chodo Cross, *Zen Master Dogen's Shobogenzo, Hokke-ten-Hokke,* Book 1, 219-220

Glossary

Allah. God, especially in Islam.

Avalokitesvara (Sanskrit). Kuan-yin (Chinese). Kannon or Kanzeon (Japanese). Bodhisattva of compassion; said to have many hands and eyes (for seeing and helping beings); one of the most important bodhisattvas in Mahayana Buddhism. His or her name means, "One who hears the sounds of the (suffering) world."

Bodhi (Sanskrit). Enlightenment; the state or experience of reality; direct realization of the truth of the oneness of the essential nature of all things.

Bodhisattva (Sanskrit). An enlightened, or enlightening, being; bodhi; "enlightenment" sattva; "being"; one who has reached the threshold of nirvana but chooses not to enter until all other beings have entered; a being that acts from compassion and wisdom to deliver all beings from suffering.

Bodhi tree. Enlightenment tree; the tree under which Shakyamuni Buddha was sitting when he realized enlightenment.

Brahma. The Hindu god of creation.

Buddha. Awakened one; the historical Shakyamuni Buddha; an awakened human being; the true essence and function of reality. See *Buddhahood, Shakyamuni*.

Buddha-dharma. The essence of Buddhism; the authentic teaching, law or truth of Buddhism; universal truth; the Way; the Tao.

Buddha-eye. The (spiritual) eye of an enlightened being, which can discern the truth of scriptures, reality; true dharma-eye; observing prajna (wisdom).

Glossary

Buddhahood. The attainment of perfect enlightenment in Buddhism, the highest realization; in Zen, because all beings already are Buddha, Buddhahood is not attained, but realized.

Buddha-mind. Enlightened, or awakened (to truth), mind.

Buddha-nature. True, or essential, nature; the essence and function of reality; inherent enlightenment.

Capping verse (also, **capping phrase**). A verse or phrase that succinctly expresses a particular truth; such verses and phrases are often drawn from classic literature.

Cessation. See *cessation and observation, meditation*.

Cessation and observation. Stopping and seeing; samadhi and prajna; wisdom and compassion; tranquility and insight; the two primary modes of meditation in Buddhism, used in conjunction for balancing serenity and wisdom; "cessation" is the stopping of delusion, "observation" is the cognizance of truth or reality. See *nonthinking*.

Dharma (Sanskrit). Law, truth, reality, teaching; thing, or being, esp. when spelled with a small 'd' (dharma).

Dharmakaya (Sanskrit). The all-inclusive aspect of reality; dharma: law, truth, reality, teaching; kaya: body, form; one of the 'three bodies of Buddha'; the empty, equal, or void aspect of reality; all things, from the perspective of 'oneness.'

Emptiness. Sunyata (Sanskrit); the void nature of reality; the essence of all things; oneness; equality; the vast, unnamable, fathomless void.

Enlightened-eye. See *buddha-eye*.

Gatha. A short verse or poem, often a succinct formulation of wisdom.

Koan(s). Short stories or sayings unique to Zen Buddhism; the most distinctive characteristic distinguishing Zen from other schools of Mahayana Buddhism; expressions which contain, transmit, and evoke enlightened wisdom; direct expressions of specific wisdom; most koans come from the recorded sayings and doings of the classic Zen masters.

Koan-introspection. The assimilation of enlightened wisdom (bodhi prajna) through the illumination of koans within observation meditation; evoking the specific wisdom within particular koans; a method (unique to Zen) for the transmission of enlightened wisdom. See also *koan, transmission, prajna*.

Li and shih. Universal and particular; *li* represents the universal, absolute, all-inclusive, etc., *shih* represents the particular, relative, individual, etc.; in the Huayen (Japanese: Kegon) school of Buddhism, li and shih philosophically demonstrate the interdependence and non-obstruction of the universal and the particular, each particular and all particulars, and each particular and each particular.

Maha Prajna Paramita (Sanskrit). Great Perfection of Wisdom. See *prajna, prajna paramita, prajna paramita sutras.*

Mahayana (Sanskrit). 'Great vehicle' or 'big ferryboat' Buddhism, used in contrast to 'Hinayana' or 'small vehicle' Buddhism; Mahayana is distinguished by its universal teaching aimed at saving all beings, in contrast with Hinayana which aims at personal, rather than universal liberation.

Manjusri (Sanskrit). Monju (Japanese). The bodhisattva of wisdom; one of the most important bodhisattvas in Mahayana Buddhism, often depicted wielding a double-edged sword that kills and gives life in a single stroke (Kills delusion and/or confusion, gives life to wisdom and/or clarity).

Mind to mind transmission. See *transmission.*

Nirvana (Sanskrit). The goal of all Buddhist schools; the full and complete actualization of enlightenment; complimentary to 'samsara' (the cycle of birth and death); in Zen, nirvana is not separate from samsara. See *samsara.*

No-mind. See *nonthinking.*

Nonthinking. Cessation meditation; the state or condition that includes, yet transcends, both 'thinking' and 'not thinking'; balanced with observation meditation, it is the essential art and keystone of Zen practice and enlightenment; depending on the context, nonthinking is often used synonymously with 'zazen', 'shikantaza', 'cessation', 'samadhi', 'objectless meditation', 'mindfulness', 'mindlessness', 'no-mind', 'no-thought', and others.

Prajna (Sanskrit). Wisdom, knowledge, insight, enlightened wisdom.

Prajna paramita (Sanskrit). Perfection of wisdom; the wisdom which leads one from samsara (the cycle of birth and death) to nirvana (perfect enlightenment, or bodhi). See *prajna, samsara, nirvana, bodhi.*

Prajna paramita sutras (Sanskrit). The perfection of wisdom sutras (scriptures) expounding the teachings of prajna paramita; in Zen (and Mahayana generally), the most popular and influential of these are the Heart Sutra (Mahaprajnaparamita-hridaya-sutra) and the Diamond Cutter Sutra (Vajrachchedika). See *prajna, prajna paramita.*

Roshi. Venerable teacher; the honorary title of a Zen master (usually a veteran master); in the West, it is often misunderstood, and misrepresented as a title of rank or authority.

Samsara (Sanskrit). The cycle of birth and death: birth, abiding, death, and re-birth; the compliment of nirvana; a metaphor for life, especially for the difficult aspects of life; in Mahayana Buddhist teachings, samsara and nirvana are nondual.

Shastras (Sanskrit). Written treatises that analyze, interpret, and amplify the teachings of the Buddhist sutras (scriptures).

Shih and Li. See *Li and Shih*.

Shikantaza. Sole sitting; shikan: 'only', 'just', or 'sole'; taza: 'sitting'; 'objectless' meditation, in contradistinction to meditation focused on an object such as a koan or the breath.

Sunyata (or, **shunyata**) (Sanskrit). See *emptiness*.

Skillful means; **Upaya** (Sanskrit). Enlightened techniques, skills, or methods employed to deliver beings from suffering or delusion to liberation or enlightenment.

Stopping and seeing. See *cessation and observation*.

Sutra (Sanskrit). Scripture.

Tathagata (Sanskrit). The 'thus come' one; a name for the Buddha; an enlightened being. See *Buddha*.

Transmission. The transmission of wisdom (prajna); wisdom transmitted from the enlightened mind to the enlightened mind though personal contact with a teacher, through scriptures, written treatises, koans, and through awareness in the world; also associated with the tradition of a Zen master recognizing the enlightenment of a student, and thus 'certifying' the student's qualification to teach; often misunderstood as the transmission of esoteric or secret knowledge from teacher to student.

True nature. The essential nature of the universe; the essential nature of all things.

Upaya (Sanskrit). See *skillful means*.

Vast, unnamable, fathomless void. The inconceivable, all-inclusive source, manifestation, and destination of all beings and things in time and space; the true nature of all beings and things, each being and thing, and no-being and no-thing.

Zazen. Seated meditation, Za: sitting, zen (dyhana: Sanskrit) meditation; the keystone of Zen practice and enlightenment. See *cessation and observation, nonthinking, shikantaza*.

Zen. Zen Buddhism; seeing your true nature.

Bibliography

Abe, Masao. *A Study of Dogen: His Philosophy and Religion.* Albany, NY: State University of New York Press, 1992.

—. *Zen and Western Thought.* Honolulu, HI: University of Hawaii Press, 1985.

Aitken, Robert, trans. *The Gateless Barrier: The Wu-men kuan (Mumonkan).* San Francisco, CA: North Point Press, 1991.

—. *Original Dwelling Place: Zen Buddhist Essays.* Washington, DC: Counterpoint, 1997.

—. *The Practice of Perfection: The Paramitas from a Zen Buddhist Perspective.* Washington, DC: Counterpoint, 1997.

—. *Taking the Path of Zen.* San Francisco, CA: North Point Press, 1985.

App, Urs, *Master Yunmen: From the Record of the Chan Master "Gate of the Clouds,"* Kodansha, America, 1994

Barrett, William, ed. *Zen Buddhism: Selected Writings of D.T. Suzuki.* Garden City, NY: Doubleday Anchor, 1956.

Berg, Stephen. *Crow With No Mouth: Ikkyu, 15th Century Zen Master* Port Townsend, WA: Copper Canyon Press, 1989.

Besserman, Perle and Manfred Steger. *Crazy Clouds: Zen Radicals, Rebels and Reformers.* Boston, MA: Shambhala, 1991.

Bielefeldt, Carl. *Dogen's Manuals of Zen Meditation.* Berkeley, CA: University of California Press, 1988.

—. *Recarving the Dragon: History and Dogma in the Study of Dogen,* in *Dogen Studies,* Lafleur, William R. Lafleur, ed., Honolulu, HI: University of Hawaii Press, 1985.

Blofeld, John, *The Zen Teaching of Huang Po,* Grove Press, New York, 1958.

—. *The Zen Teaching of Instantaneous Awakening,* Buddhist Publishing Group Leicester, England, 1974.

Bohm, David, *Wholeness and the Implicate Order.* New York, Routledge & Keegan Paul, 1980.

Braverman, Arthur, trans. *Mud and Water: A Collection of Talks by the Zen Master Bassui.* San Francisco, CA: North Point Press, 1989.

Broughton, Jeffrey L. *The Bodhidharma Anthology: The Earliest Records of Zen.* Berkeley, CA: University of California Press, 1999.

Buswell, Robert. *The Korean Approach to Zen: The Collected Works of Chinul,* Honolulu, University of Hawaii Press, 1983.

Campbell, Joseph. *The Hero With a Thousand Faces.* Princeton, New Jersey, Princeton University Press; 2nd edition (1973)

—. *The Inner Reaches of Outer Space.* New York, NY: Harper Perennial (November 1988)

—. *The Masks of God.* New York, NY: Penguin Books (1976)

—. *The Mythic Image.* Princeton, New Jersey: Princeton University Press (November 1, 1981)

—. *The Power of Myth.* New York, NY:Anchor, June 1, 1991.

Chang Chung-yuan. *Original Teachings of Ch'an Buddhism.* New York: Grove Press, 1982.

Chang, Garma, C.C., *A Prologue to Hwa Yen, The Buddhist Teaching of Totality,* Pennsylvania State Univ., 1971.

Cleary, J.C., trans. *Swampland Flowers: The Letters and Lectures of Zen Master Ta Hui.* New York: Grove Press, 1977.

—. *Zen Dawn: Early Zen Texts from Tun Huang.* Boston, MA: Shambhala, 1986.

Cleary, Thomas and J.C. Cleary, trans. *The Blue Cliff Record,* Boston, MA: Shambhala, 1977.

Cleary, Thomas, *The Book of Serenity: One Hundred Zen Dialogues.* Hudson, NY: Lindisfarne Press, 1990.

—. *Classics of Buddhism and Zen, The Collected Translations of Thomas Cleary,* 5 volumes, Boston, MA: Shambhala, 2001-2002.

—. *The Original Face: An Anthology of Rinzai Zen.* New York: Grove Press, 1978.

—. *Sayings and Doings of Pai-Chang.* Los Angeles, Center publications, 1979.

—. *Sectrets of The Blue Cliff Record,* Boston, MA: Shambhala, 2000.

—. *Shobogenzo: Zen Essays by Dogen.* Honolulu, HI: University of Hawaii Press, 1986.

—. *Timeless Spring: A Soto Zen Anthology*. New York: Weatherhill, 1980.

Conze, Edward. *Buddhist Wisdom Books*. New York & San Francisco: Harper & Row, 1958.

Cook, Francis Dojun, trans. *The Record of Transmitting the Light*: Zen Master Keizan's Denkoroku. Boston, MA: Wisdom, 2004.

Dumoulin Heinrich. *Zen Buddhism: A History, Vol. 1-India and China*. New York: Macmillan, 1988.

—. *Zen Buddhism: A History, Vol. 2-Japan*. New York: Macmillan, 1990.

—. *Zen Enlightenment: Origins and Meaning*. New York and Tokyo: Weatherhill, 1979.

Foster, Nelson, and Shoemaker, Jack, *The Roaring Stream: A New Zen Reader*, New Jersey, The Ecco Press, 1996.

Green, James, *The Recorded Sayings of Zen Master Joshu*, Boston, MA: Shambhala, 1998.

Gregory, Peter G., *Sudden and Gradual: Approaches to Enlightenment in Chinese Thought*. Honolulu: University of Hawaii Press, 1987.

—. *Tsung-Mi and the Sinification of Buddhism*. Honolulu: University of Hawaii Press, 2002.

Griffiths, Paul J., *On Being Mindless: buddhist meditation and the mind-body problem*. Delhi, India: Sri Satguru Publications, 1986.

Gugich, David M. *The Unwilling: Poems of the Viet Nam War* Lopez Island, Washington: White Geese Enterprises, 1992.

Hakeda, Yoshito, S., *The Awakening of Faith,* New York, NY: Columbia University Press, 1974.

Heine, Steven and Dale S. Wright, eds. *The Koan: Texts and Contexts in Zen Buddhism*. Oxford, UK: Oxford University Press, 2000.

Heine, Steven. *Did Dogen Go to China? What He Wrote and When He Wrote It*. New York, NY: Oxford University Press, Inc., 2006.

—. *Dogen and the Koan Tradition*. Albany, NY: State University of New York Press, 1994.

—. *Zen Skin, Zen Marrow: Will the Real Zen Buddhism Please Stand up*. New York, NY: Oxford University Press, Inc., 2008.

Isshu, Miura and Ruth Fuller Sasaki. *The Zen Koan: Its History and Use in Rinzai Zen*. New York, NY: Harcourt, Brace & World, 1965.

Jha, Nirmala. *Law of Karma*. India: Capital Publishing House, 1985.

Kapleau, Roshi Philip. *The Three Pillars of Zen*. Garden City, NY: Anchor Press/Doubleday, revised ed., 1980.

Kim, Hee-Jin. *Dogen on Meditation and Thinking: A Reflection on His View of Zen*.

State University of New York Press, Albany, 2007.

—. *Eihei Dogen: Mystical Realist*, Revised, Third Edition. Wisdom Publications, March 25, 2004.

—. *Flowers of Emptiness, Selections from Dogen's Shobogenzo,* The Edwin Mellen Press, New York, 1985

Kodera, Takashi James. *Dogen's Formative Years in China.* Boulder, CO: Prajna Press, 1980.

Kraft, Kenneth. *Eloquent Zen: Daito and Early Japanese Zen.* Honolulu, HI: University of Hawaii Press, 1992.

—. *Zen: Traditions and Transition.* New York: Grove Press, 1992.

Lafleur, William R., ed. *Dogen Studies.* Honolulu, HI: University of Hawaii Press, 1985.

Leighton, Daniel and Yi Wu. *Cultivating the Empty Field: The Silent Illumination of Zen Master Hongzhi.* Rutland, VT: Charles E. Tuttle, 2001.

Leighton, Daniel, and Okumura, Shohaku, *Dogens Extensive Record: A Translation of the Eihei Koroku,* Wisdom Publications, 2004.

Luk, Charles (Lu K'uan Yü). *Ch'an and Zen Teaching,* 3 Vols. Boston, MA: Red Wheel/Weiser, 1993.

—. *Secrets of Chinese Meditation,*

McRae, John R. *The Northern School and the Formation of Early Ch'an Buddhism.* Honolulu, HI: University of Hawaii Press, 1986.

Murti, T.R.V. *The Central Philosophy of Buddhism: A Study of the Madhyamika System.* London, UK: Alden & Mowbray Ltd., 1955.

Nhat Hanh, Thich. *Being Peace.* Berkeley, CA: Parallax Press, 1988.

—. *The Diamond that Cuts through Illusion: Commentaries on the Prajñaparamita Diamond Sutra.* Berkeley, CA: Parallax Press, 1992.

—. *The Miracle of Mindfulness.* Boston, MA: Beacon Press, 1999.

—. *Peace is Every Step: The Path of Mindfulness in Everyday Life.* New York: Bantam Books, 1992.

—. *Zen Keys.* New York. Anchor Press, 1974.

Nishijima, Gudo, (Translator) and Cross, Chodo, (Translator), *Master Dogen's Shobogenzo,* Book 1, BookSurge, 2006.

—. *Master Dogen's Shobogenzo,* Book 2, BookSurge, 2005.

—. *Master Dogen's Shobogenzo,* Book 3, BookSurge, 2006.

—. *Master Dogen's Shobogenzo,* Book 4, BookSurge, 2006.

Nishijima, Gudo, *Shinji Shobogenzo,* Guildford, Surrey: Windbell, 2003.

Ogata, Sohaku, trans., *The Transmission of the Lamp: Early Masters.* Wolfeboro, NH: Longwood Academic, 1988.

Okubo Dosho, ed. *Dogen zenji zenshu.* 2 vols. Tokyo: Chikumu shobo, 1969, 1970.

Powell, William F. *The Record of Tung-shan.* Honolulu, HI: University of Hawaii Press, 1986.

Price, A. F., & Mou-lam, Wong, *The Diamond Sutra & The Sutra of Hui-Neng,* Boston, MA: Shambhala, 1990.

Red Pine, trans. *The Diamond Sutra: Text and Commentaries Translated from Sanskrit and Chinese.* Washington, DC: Counterpoint, 2001.

—. *Poems of the Masters: China's Classic Anthology of T'ang and Sung Dynasty Verse.* Port Townsend, Washington: Copper Canyon Press, 2003.

—.*The Zen Teaching of Bodhidharma.* San Francisco, CA: North Point Press, 1989.

Reps, Paul. *Zen Flesh, Zen Bones.* Harmondsworth London, England: Penguin Books, 1986.

Sasaki, Ruth Fuller. *The Recorded Sayings of Ch'an Master Lin-chi.* Kyoto, Japan: The Institute for Zen Studies, 1975.

Senzaki, Nyogen and Ruth Strout-McCandless. *Buddhism and Zen.* San Francisco, CA: North Point Press, 1987.

Shainberg, Lawrence. *Ambivalent Zen: A Memoir.* New York, NY: Pantheon, 1995.

Sheng-yen, Master, with Dan Stevenson. *Hoofprint of the Ox: Principles of the Chan Buddhist Path as Taught by a Modern Chinese Master.* Oxford, UK: Oxford University Press, 2001.

Stambaugh, Joan. *Impermanence is Buddha-Nature: Dōgen's Understanding of Temporality.* Honolulu, HI: University of Hawaii Press, 1990.

Stone, Jacqueline. *Original Enlightenment and the Transformation of Medieval Japanese Buddhism.* Honolulu, HI: University of Hawaii Press, 1999.

Suzuki, Daisetz T. *The Awakening of Zen.* Boulder, CO: Prajna Press, 1980.

—. *The Lankavatara Sutra.* Boulder, CO: Prajna Press, 1978.

—. *Studies in The Lankavatara Sutra.* Boulder, CO: Prajna Press, 1981.

—. *The Zen Doctrine of No-Mind.* London, UK: Rider, 1986.

Tanahashi, Kazuaki, ed. *Enlightenment Unfolds: The Essential Teachings of Zen Master Dogen,* Boston, MA: Shambhala, 1999.

—. *Moon in a Dewdrop: Writings of Zen Master Dogen.* San Francisco, CA: North Point Press, 1985.

Thurman, Robert A. F. *The Holy Teachings of Vimalakirti: A Mahayana Scripture.* University Park, Pennsylvania: Pennsylvania State University Press, 1976.

Waddell, Norman, and Abe, Masao, *The Heart of Dogen's Shobogenzo.* New

York, NY: State University of New York, 2002.

Waddell, Norman, trans. *The Essential Teachings of Zen Master Hakuin.* Boston, MA: Shambhala, 1994.

—. *The Unborn: Life and Teachings of Zen Master Bankei,* 1622-1693. San Francisco, CA: North Point Press, 1984.

—. *Zen Words for the Heart: Hakuin's Commentary on the Heart Sutra.* Boston, MA: Shambhala, 1996.

—. *Wild Ivy: The Spiritual Autobiography of Zen Master Hakuin.* Boston, MA: Shambhala, 2001.

Walker, Brian Browne. *The Tao Te Ching of Lao Tzu,* New York, NY: St. Martin's Griffin, 1995.

Watson, Burton, trans., *The Zen Teachings of Master Lin-Chi,* Boston, MA: Shambhala, 1993.

Wright, Dale S. *Philosophical Meditations on Zen Buddhism.* Cambridge, UK: Cambridge University Press, 2000.

Yampolsky, Philip, trans. *The Platform Sutra of the Sixth Patriarch.* New York, NY: Columbia University Press, 1967.

—. *The Zen Mater Hakuin: Selected Writings.* New York, NY: Columbia University Press, 1971.

Zenkai Shibayama. *A Flower Does Not Talk: Zen Essays.* Rutland, VT: Charles E. Tuttle, 1998.

—. *The Gateless Barrier: Zen Comments on the Mumonkan.* Boston, MA: Shambhala, 2000.

Index

Index

Acknowledgements

Like the verbal teachings of Zen, my words of thanks can only hint at the reality of the gratitude within my heart.

My deepest thanks to Nils Larsen for many years of guidance, encouragement, and friendship along the Ancient Way: Gassho brother! Special thanks to my good and great friend Stu Mclean for the crazy wisdom lessons of a lifetime. Thanks also to my dharma brothers and sisters Rae, Jim, Julian, Rusty, and Libby, for their living, enlightened examples.

I bow in gratitude to all the scholars and translators that have helped transmit the wisdom of Zen by making the literature of Zen and Buddhism accessible to English readers. Thank you Thomas Cleary! There are too many others to list, but I would like to single out a few that have been especially enlightening to me: Arthur Braverman, J.C. Cleary, Steven Heine, Victor Sogen Hori, William Powell, Mike Cross, D.T. Suzuki, Kazuaki Tanahashi, Taigen Dan Leighton, Peter G. Gregory, Robert E. Buswell Jr., Norman Waddell, and Philip Yampolsky. Deepest thanks to Hee-Jin Kim whose landmark book, *Eihei Dogen: Mystical Realist,* is by far the finest work available in English on Eihei Dogen and his teachings.

My heartfelt thanks to the Zen masters that pioneered the efforts to transmit the authentic practice and enlightenment of Zen to the West: Robert Aitken Roshi, Thich Nhat Hanh, Nyogen Senzaki, Shibayama Roshi, Shunryu Suzuki Roshi, Taizan Maezumi Roshi, Yamada Koun Roshi, and Hakuun Yasutani Roshi.

Thanks also to the teachers that have taken up the torch and continue to enlighten the Way for others. I am profoundly grateful to the two Zen masters that have so freely given more than I could ever repay. Eileen ('Een) Kierra, dharma teacher in the lineage of Thich Nhat Hanh, and master of "The Big Ferryboat" (Mahayana), who has serenely and skillfully demonstrated the art of delivering beings to the other shore. Nine full bows to Jack Duffy Roshi, Zen teacher and dharma heir of Robert Aitken Roshi. Thank you for helping me discover the three dimensional nature of vision.

I want to thank everyone at American Book Publishing for all their support, encouragement, and professional guidance. Thanks to Nathan Fitzgearl for his early advice and encouraging words.

I am especially grateful to my editor, Julie L. Jacokes, for her professional guidance—and her *infinite* patience. Wielding the sword of Manjusri, she knows how to both kill and give life with a single stroke. Thank you!

Thanks to my dearest friends, Fred and Donna Adams. Your love and support have guided me every step of the way.

Thanks to my mom, for instilling the love of reading, and to my dad, who always believed in me.

Thanks to James Patterson for helping to clear the path to Louie Wing's cabin. Thanks to Rune, Bill, and Bill's friends.

Special thanks to Ken Burtness for the cover photo.

Finally, to my wife Donna, this book is as much yours as it is mine. Without your encouragement, it would never have been published, and without your love, it could never have been written.

About the Author

Ted Biringer discovered his affinity with Zen at the early age of 21. A merchant marine from the age of 16, his lifestyle precluded regular participation in a community and other traditional activities of Zen training. Nevertheless, he developed a regular routine of study and practice based on the Zen records and supplemented by personal interviews and correspondence with Zen masters from various lineages.

His correspondence with one master led him to a friendship with a long time Zen practitioner. For a number of years, the two friends operated a "roaming" meditation group, providing space and encouragement for people from all lifestyles in the Skagit Valley area of Northwest Washington.

In 1994, Ted Biringer began working with an American Zen master trained in the Japanese traditions of both Soto and Rinzai Zen, as well as the Zen tradition of Vietnam. For thirteen years he participated in dokusan (formal, one-on-one student/teacher training) with his teacher. Although mostly following a traditional course of koan progression, dokusan was often augmented by forays into the teachings of Zen Master Dogen.

Ted Biringer studied writing for two years under the late David Smith, the Northwest-based investigative journalist and war correspondent.

He is licensed as a Master Merchant Marine Officer and First Class Pilot. He works in Puget Sound as a Captain for the Washington State Ferries.